TRANSFORMING POWER

FROM THE PERSONAL TO THE POLITICAL

JUDY REBICK

PENGUIN
CANADA

PENGUIN CANADA

Published by the Penguin Group

Penguin Group (Canada), 90 Eglinton Avenue East, Suite 700,
Toronto, Ontario, Canada M4P 2Y3 (a division of Pearson Canada Inc.)

Penguin Group (USA) Inc., 375 Hudson Street, New York, New York 10014, U.S.A.
Penguin Books Ltd, 80 Strand, London WC2R 0RL, England
Penguin Ireland, 25 St Stephen's Green, Dublin 2, Ireland (a division of Penguin Books Ltd)
Penguin Group (Australia), 250 Camberwell Road, Camberwell, Victoria 3124, Australia
(a division of Pearson Australia Group Pty Ltd)
Penguin Books India Pvt Ltd, 11 Community Centre, Panchsheel Park,
New Delhi – 110 017, India
Penguin Group (NZ), 67 Apollo Drive, Rosedale, North Shore 0632, New Zealand
(a division of Pearson New Zealand Ltd)
Penguin Books (South Africa) (Pty) Ltd, 24 Sturdee Avenue, Rosebank,
Johannesburg 2196, South Africa

Penguin Books Ltd, Registered Offices: 80 Strand, London WC2R 0RL, England

First published 2009

1 2 3 4 5 6 7 8 9 10 (WEB)

Copyright © Judy Rebick, 2009

Author representation: Westwood Creative Artists
94 Harbord Street, Toronto, Ontario M5S 1G6

Photo on p. i © DavidSmileyPhotographer.com

Manufactured in Canada.

Library and Archives Canada Cataloguing in Publication data available
upon request to the publisher.

ISBN: 978-0-14-316946-8

Visit the Penguin Group (Canada) website at **www.penguin.ca**

Special and corporate bulk purchase rates available; please see
www.penguin.ca/corporatesales or call 1-800-810-3104, ext. 477 or 474

For Rosie and Sophie,
that their world be a better place

If the world is upside down the way it is now, wouldn't we have to turn it over to get it to stand up straight?

—EDUARDO GALLEANO, *UPSIDE DOWN*

CONTENTS

INTRODUCTION

A Better World Is in the Making

THE GENESIS OF THIS BOOK took place in three places that were worlds apart. In May 2005 on Cortes Island, B.C., near the end of a tour to promote my last book, *Ten Thousand Roses: The Making of a Feminist Revolution*, I attended Media That Matters, a retreat for media activists at Hollyhock, a famed educational retreat centre among tall trees and magical forests. When Bill Weaver, the filmmaker who had invited me, wrote me in the winter explaining that this year's theme would be "Neither Left nor Right: Re-defining a Radical Centre," I wrote back: "I hope you know I will be a dissenter."

"What else is new?" he replied. "Perfect." Knowing I would be welcome, I went intending to play hooky for most of the event and just enjoy the island. Instead, I found a wonderful group of people who were not only intelligent and creative but also kind and caring— and a process that was deeply respectful and democratic. After a few years of intense activism, I had some time to think about what I was doing.

In the process of discussions, I faced the fact that I was at the end of my rope in terms of political activism. In the extraordinary year of 2001, I had initiated two major projects: www.rabble.ca, a successful left-wing news and discussion website; and the New Politics Initiative, an exciting but ultimately failed attempt to unite the Left in a new party. This was in addition to my involvement in the Toronto Social Forum, a gathering of a diverse group of fifteen hundred people at Ryerson University. At the beginning of a new century, with the spectacular emergence of the anti-globalization movement in Seattle and the extraordinary potential of innovative technologies to spread the ideas emerging from these movements, it seemed that anything was possible. Then September 11 happened, and the new movements seemed to disappear as quickly as they had arisen.

By the spring of 2005, I felt that the Left was at a dead end. I didn't have any more ideas about how to get out of the mess we were in, and I couldn't see anyone who did. It was at Media That Matters that I decided to step back from political activism and move into a more reflective stage of work that included going to Latin America to see for myself some of the ideas and practices emerging from the Left there.

In January 2006, I was in Caracas for the second time in a year because my earlier trip had been cut short by a violent bout of food poisoning. Before I got sick, though, I had heard Hugo Chavez speak to a relatively intimate group of three hundred people. In this speech, he talked about Jesus, about magic, about how much love he had for the people of the Middle East and how much he could see what they and the people of Venezuela had in common. Then he launched into a discussion of what we could learn from the conversation between Lenin and Trotsky about the impossibility of socialism in one country.

At first I thought he was a bit of a crackpot, but later I realized that one of Chavez's great strengths is that he takes ideas from everywhere, experimenting with whatever will help his people. Like other Latin American popular leaders I have seen, he speaks from his heart as well as from his considerable intellect.

When I returned for the World Social Forum, a massive meeting of the world's social movements, I saw on the streets of Caracas, next to the T-shirts with images of Che and Chavez, a T-shirt with a picture of Jesus and the line "Jesus was the first revolutionary." At Hollyhock, too, there were quite a few people who combined their activism with spirituality. One of them, Canadian filmmaker Velcrow Ripper, was just beginning a new project on spiritual activism. We hit it off and started a dialogue about spirituality and activism that helped shape this book and his new film, *Fierce Light: When Spirit Meets Action*. We became great friends and have been continuing the dialogue ever since. Hollyhock helped open my mind to a broader group of people working for change in the world, people who share the same values of equality, diversity, and sustainability but who don't identify with the political Left.

In 2006, the World Social Forum was held in three locations: Bamako, Mali, in Africa; Karachi, Pakistan; and Caracas, Venezuela. I went to the one in Caracas. As usual at this meeting of the world's social movements, the event began with a lively demonstration. As people were gathering, I met three young political science students from the university who began to talk to me about Hugo Chavez. They were excited that he was introducing the idea of socialism for the first time. "People are a little afraid," said one of them, "because when they think about socialism, they think about the Soviet Union. But that's not what Chavez is talking about. This is twenty-first-century socialism. It is socialism of the people. Democracy is at its centre."

Everyone I talked to, from academics to street vendors, was supportive of Chavez but also critical. It was the first place I have ever been where poor people told me that their lives were better because of the government, and the first time since the 1970s that I had heard anyone talk about socialism in such positive terms.

The next day I attended a workshop with leftist activists and academics from all over Latin America, from Brazil to Mexico. They were discussing the relationship between social movements and political parties, a preoccupation of mine for decades as an activist in both the women's movement and in the New Democratic Party. I was amazed by the diversity of opinion in the group, from a social democrat who argued that we just needed strong social movements to keep political parties honest to a Mexican academic who argued that political parties were irrelevant and we needed to get rid of them. But what surprised me most was that no one denounced anyone. Each person listened respectfully and considered the different issues under discussion. The common view was that left-wing political parties almost everywhere were being corrupted by electoralism and power, once they achieved it. The debate was about different strategies of what to do about it. The old sectarianism of the Left was replaced by a clear-eyed desire to find solutions rather than just to be right. They all agreed that Latin America was finally on the offensive against neo-liberalism, and their urgent task was to figure out strategies that could be successful.

On the way out of the meeting, Pierre Beaudet, who at the time was executive director of the Quebec-based development NGO Alternatives, said to me: "Judy, you should write a book on Latin America. You can do it without either cheerleading or denouncing." Beaudet knows more about international social movements and politics than anyone I know, so I was flattered, but more than that I got that feeling in my gut when I know something is right for me. It seemed ridiculous, though. I am not an expert on Latin America. This was only my fourth visit, not counting a tourist trip to Mexico, and I don't speak Spanish. And yet …

In 2007, I went to the U.S. Social Forum in Atlanta, Georgia, and realized that what was happening in Latin America was a more advanced form of what was happening in other places around the world. Twelve thousand people gathered in Atlanta under the slogan "Another World Is Possible. Another U.S. Is Necessary." It was an extraordinary coming together of local and regional activists who were re-creating politics in their own area but having very little weight at a national level, where movement politics had been captured by middle-class think-tanks and non-governmental organizations. This was the most diverse gathering I have ever attended, a veritable rainbow of activists uniting across previous divides of race, age, class, sexuality, and gender and promising the most powerful social movement the United States has ever seen. As I watched the plenaries and the workshops, I realized that a new kind of politics was emerging in the United States as well: a bottom-up, diverse, compassionate, collective approach to social change in which issues and communities were coming together and producing something new and powerful. This is when I realized that this book would be about the kind of change, most visible in Latin America but happening globally, spreading its roots around the world, growing a new kind of politics that is emerging in different ways, depending on the local conditions but with a similar grounding in values and ideas.

As I write, Wall Street is collapsing in on itself after a decades-long orgy of greed, beginning with U.S. president Ronald Reagan and British prime minister Margaret Thatcher. Suddenly the market fundamentalism of conservative economics is giving way to demands that the government step in with a massive rescue package of almost a trillion dollars to stop an economic collapse. Even before the collapse, Democratic presidential candidate Barack Obama broke from the elite consensus that market forces could solve everything. In his acceptance speech for the Democratic nomination, Obama said, "For over two decades, he's [McCain] subscribed to that old, discredited Republican philosophy: Give more and more to those with the most and hope that prosperity trickles down to everyone else." But the reality is that the Democrats have subscribed to the same economic policies. Indeed, almost all political parties, including most European social democratic parties, above all Tony Blair's Labour Party, have supported such policies. In Latin America and Europe, they call it neo-liberalism*; in North America, we call it corporate globalization or sometimes neo-conservatism, the latest stage of capitalism first brought to us by Thatcher and Reagan. The idea that

---

*Liberalism refers to the laissez-faire capitalism without state regulations, workers' rights, or social programs that existed at the birth of capitalism. Thus, the regime of cutbacks, privatization, deregulations, market fundamentalism, and tax cuts that has become so familiar today is known as neo-liberalism. Neo-conservatism usually refers more accurately to Bush and Co., who combine this neo-liberalism with social conservatism.

the state could play the role of helping to share the wealth was discredited among the elites. The role of the state was no longer to look out for the people but rather to facilitate the creation of private wealth. Privatization of almost everything became the order of the day. Not only the economy but our very lives have been restructured by these ideas of individualism, consumerism, reductions in social services, privatization, deregulation, and tax cuts. Looking out for number one has become a prized quality. Social solidarity is slowly disappearing, to be replaced by greed on the one hand and charity on the other. Instead of understanding that the market creates inequalities that the state has a responsibility to correct through income redistribution, social programs, and regulation, we have come to believe that people or countries are poor because of their own weaknesses. Instead of sharing wealth through redistributive programs such as Employment Insurance and social assistance, we have re-established a system of noblesse oblige, in which we celebrate the über-rich who give a tiny part of their money away in grand gestures but rarely question why it is they have been permitted to accumulate such gigantic sums when tens of millions of people are starving. Politics has become a professional's game, where protests are ignored by ideologically right-wing governments and the majority of people are excluded or exclude themselves from the very decisions that most affect their lives.

In mid-July 2007, a front-page piece in *The New York Times* trumpeted "A New Gilded Age" in which wealth is concentrated in the hands of the rich like it has not been since the age of Rockefeller and Carnegie. Today, the share of income for the top 0.01 percent of families is as high as it was in the 1920s, about 5 percent of the income of the United States. From the 1940s to 1980, it was a little more than 1 percent of income. What this means is that all the struggles of ordinary people, from the trade union battles of the 1930s to the civil rights movement of the 1960s and the women's movement of the 1970s, have been distorted if not reversed. Instead of workers, black people, and women getting a fairer share of the money and power, neo-liberalism has allowed some people of colour and women into the ranks of a somewhat larger elite and let the vast majority fall farther and farther behind. As I read that article, I wondered why they expressed no concern about the economic collapse of 1929, provoked by just such inequality. A year later, we are in the midst of a collapse just as severe, and suddenly the market fundamentalists are in essence nationalizing key banking institutions. Cowboy capitalism will have to be reined in by the very same state regulation so discredited by right-wing propaganda.

While I can't help but feel a certain delight in watching Wall Street, the symbol of the greed and destruction of this economic system, in chaos, two factors lead to a more sobering assessment. The first, as we learned in the Great Depression, is the certain knowledge that it is those at the bottom who will suffer most; and second is that, outside of Latin America, there is no political force that is proposing a real alternative to this failing system.

The promise of trickle-down prosperity has failed to deliver for the vast majority of people on the planet; yet none of the traditional political players are providing any alternatives. Walden Bello, a famed intellectual from the Philippines, told a meeting at York University a couple of years ago that the social movements in his country, famous for people's power, were getting discouraged by the fact that every time they mobilized to bring in another government, the new government was just as bad as the old one. Everyone knows what's wrong with the system, but the old ways of change just don't seem to be working any more, he explained. "Neo-liberalism is like the train conductor who gets shot in an old Western and dies with his hand on the accelerator. He's dead but speeding the passengers inexorably toward total disaster."

The disaster that has claimed Wall Street so dramatically has been creeping up on most people for decades. In Toronto, where I live, 50 percent of the population today is considered low income, compared to 19 percent in 1970. During the same period, the middle class has shrunk from 66 percent to 32 percent. Meanwhile, only the income of the very rich is growing. What's more, most of the poor both in Canada and the United States are people of colour. Racism has mostly gone underground, affecting the standard of living and quality of life of people of colour even as, on the surface, multiculturalism and tolerance of diversity is the prevailing myth.

At an international level, the crisis of inequality is even deeper. The imposition of the so-called Washington Consensus* on developing countries by the International Monetary Fund and the World Bank has deepened the misery of those already impoverished, provoking almost total economic collapse in some countries and deepening the obscene divisions between rich and poor already created by colonialism and earlier structural adjustment policies. As minimal social programs are cut, more and more money goes into security to protect elites against their own people. Through the Bush administration, neo-liberalism has been militarized, with a war without end continuing in the Middle East despite the opposition of the majority of people of the world—including those in the United States.

The other related disaster has been relentlessly progressing all my life but has finally caught up to us. The environmental crisis has reached such epic proportions that even the neo-conservatives, who used to see environmentalism as a left-wing plot, have been forced to recognize the crisis facing the globe if we do not change our destructive ways of living and producing. The next decade will see a critical battle for the survival of the planet.

The majority of people in North America still think we need a fairer and more environmentally sustainable world but also believe there is nothing they can do about it. Most people feel a deep and abiding sense of powerlessness, at least until the campaign of Barack Obama. What was most significant in Obama's nomination campaign (where voter turnout increased by 100 percent in many places) and in the election turnout (the highest in U.S. history) was the

---

*The Washington Consensus is a reform package for developing countries based on neo-liberal policies and imposed by the International Monetary Fund and the World Bank as a requirement for their funding.

mobilization of people who previously saw no point in voting. Up until now, there had been a precipitous decline in participation in elections, as politicians and journalists, the people most admired in my youth, fell to the bottom of the list of trusted vocations. In the 2008 Canadian election, voter turnout was the lowest in history. A young man I know said it well: "It's not that we are cynical. It's that the machine is so powerful, we just don't believe we can stop it."

But there are signs of hope for those who look. The combination of the economic and environmental crises can also produce an opportunity for profound and transformational change. Indeed, it is often out of times of crisis that the most profound change comes. The Russian Revolution emerged after the First World War, the New Deal after the Great Depression, the vast expansion of the welfare state and the emergence of the ideas and movements for human rights and equality after the horrors of the Second World War. Today, we face a crisis of even greater proportions, with the very survival of the planet at stake. This book is about the ideas, people, and practices that may provide the paths to change we need—not only to survive the changes ahead but to bring about the transformations that can lead to a better world.

I believe we are in a time that is of equal historic significance to the Industrial Revolution, the period that produced many of the ideas of the society in which we now live. The combination of the environmental crisis, globalization, and new technologies is producing profound new ideas about social and political change. And in response, more and more people working for progressive social change understand that the crisis is too great for differences of ego or ideology to divide us from others who share the goals of social justice, equality, and environmental sustainability.

In looking at many of the new efforts at progressive social change, particularly in Latin America, North America, and Europe, I have found that what has emerged for me is a new understanding of power. The Left has always seen power as residing in the state and in the corporations. Seizing state power or winning it in an election is the first step to transforming society. The women's movement posited a different approach, saying that power also resides in our relationships to one another. Men have power over women, and to change society we need to transform those relationships of power in the here and now as well as working to change the laws and structures of society. Anti-racist activists and theorists make a similar point about white supremacy and racial discrimination. In both cases, the change involves not only changing societal structures and oppressive relationships but also changing ourselves. Most members of a group that has faced marginalization and discrimination internalize feelings of inferiority, and members of the dominant group internalize a sense of entitlement. Consciousness-raising groups in the early days of the women's movement, the black power movement during the civil rights movement, and the queer pride movement and identity politics during the rise of anti-racist politics were all designed to transform oppression into pride and dignity.

What emerges from the new political directions around the world is that transforming power at every level is what is common and central to progressive social change in the twenty-first century.

Ideologies that place all the power in someone else's control lead on the one hand to a culture of complaint and blame and on the other to a sense of powerlessness. As Van Jones, a human-rights and environmental activist from Oakland, says, "Martin Luther King didn't become famous by saying, 'I have a complaint.'" The Left, in North America at least, has lost much of its vision, allowing the Right to frame the issues and spending all of our time fighting against their ideas instead of putting forward our own. We are the anti-globalization, anti-racist, anti-war movements, but what are we *for*? Many of the groups and individuals profiled in these pages are building new alternatives at the same time as protesting reactionary policies. Envisioning and creating a new world in the soil of the old is critical to building movements for change in a society where cynicism and fear are so widespread.

Another common element is the idea that change has to come from the bottom up, from the grassroots, from the people most affected by the change we need to make. The sense of entitlement among the middle classes of Europe and North America and the intense consumerism of our society makes it difficult for people of privilege to imagine a different kind of society, let alone fight for it. That is why many of these new ideas and practices are coming from the Global South and from marginalized groups such as indigenous peoples in the North. Those who have the least to lose have a world to imagine.

This is combined with an approach that is more about process than product, more about setting out on the right path than deciding on the destination. Central is the idea that change will not come from the right set of policies, the right program, or a better ideology. Rather, change will come from the process of building power from the bottom up. No one is trying to outline *the path* to change. In the diversity of our world, we realize there are many paths to change. "We make the path by walking"* is the famous phrase from the civil rights movement in the United States, which is now being put into practice by movements around the world.

Barack Obama is a symbol and a reflection of this new kind of politics. It is a positive sign of change when the politics of hope replace the politics of fear; when a desire for unity replaces a savage partisanship; when a black man represents the best hope of the electorate; when the entire world is rooting for someone to be elected president of the United States. But Obama's rise is just the tip of the iceberg; this book is about what lies beneath.

---

*From a poem by Spanish poet Antonio Machado: "There is no path—the path is made as we walk. As we walk, we make the path and then when we turn and glance back—we see the road that never again will be trod."

1

PEOPLE'S GLOBALIZATION

Ya Basta!

IN THE LATE 1990s, a young anti-globalization movement began to rebel against the increasing corporate control of the world through international agencies such as the World Trade Organization (WTO). The first visible example of this was the anti-WTO protest in Seattle in 1999. With its lack of leaders, use of affinity groups for making decisions, and odd alliances of environmentalists and teamsters, this was a new movement for a new century.

The same sort of group gathered in Quebec City in April 2001, in a rally against the Free Trade Area of the Americas (FTAA). "My generation doesn't believe that the traditional political institutions represent us," one demonstrator told me in trying to explain what happened. He and thousands of other young people suffered volley after volley of tear gas, and risked plastic bullets, arrest, and intense emotional confrontations with police time and time again. He hadn't participated in throwing stones at police, but he supported those who did.

In two locations, protesters battled riot police for hours in scenes that looked more like Northern Ireland than Quebec. Not more than one hundred participated in the front lines, throwing stones, but thousands supported them, pounding guardrails and posts with stones and placards in a deafening show of solidarity. Mostly, the police assaulted peaceful demonstrators who were simply blocking roads. Medics helping people clean their eyes of tear gas were among the most frequent targets of police.

And it had happened before.

In Chicago in 1968, the wild street demonstrations against the Democratic Convention became a turning point in a youth movement that had a profound and long-lasting impact on our culture.

The War Measures Act of 1970 produced a widespread movement for sovereignty in Quebec that, thirty years later, continues to struggle for its goals.

Oka also comes to mind, and the three-month standoff in 1990 between the Mohawk Warriors and the Army. A massive movement for Aboriginal self-government that could no longer be ignored emerged after Oka.

In the spring of 2001, I felt that Quebec City could be even more important. As youth battled police near the barriers around the Château Frontenac, where the FTAA meetings were being held, tens of thousands of demonstrators from unions, women's groups, environmental and international development groups, and student and cultural groups marched through the streets.

Before the violence began, the youth march had had a carnival-like atmosphere. The government had built an ugly wall (*la cloture*, as they called it in Quebec) around the Château to protect world leaders from the people opposing them. This wall became the target of the protest, and a group of hilarious activists, who called themselves the Deconstructionist Surrealists, thought of a teddy-bear-throwing catapult as a form of protest. When I told the idea to a wealthy dot.com friend who was a great fan of the original Surrealists, he agreed to finance it. So, as the wall went down before a wave of protestors, the catapult started hurling teddy bears at the astonished riot police. The playful catapult would have been on the front page of every newspaper in the world if it hadn't been for the massive tear-gas attack that lasted two days.

Organizers of the protest feared people would be frightened by the violence, but thousands more than expected arrived in hundreds of buses from all over Quebec and the rest of Canada. While some were indeed upset by the violence, others pledged to stand side by side with the youth the next time.*

All through the week before the demonstrations, twelve hundred delegates from across the Americas had developed a common platform and a common strategy against undemocratic trade deals. What was emerging was a mass and diverse movement for democracy and equality against corporate rule—and, for many, against capitalism—led by the youth. A flyer handed out at the bail hearings for the arrested demonstrators after the event said it all: "It didn't start in Seattle and it won't end in Quebec City." But things didn't turn out that way.

The events of September 11, 2001, and the U.S. government's reaction put a damper on the protests that had begun so brilliantly in Seattle and continued in Quebec. Even before September 11, the few stone-throwing demonstrators were the focus of attempts by media and government to discredit the protests, but afterwards the fear of terrorism was used to marginalize, criminalize, and vilify any kind of militant tactics. While the protests dwindled after September 11, their opposition to corporate globalization has had an impact on a number of levels. First, the brutal reality of global corporate capitalism has been exposed. The imposition of unfair trade rules, especially on the Global South, in the name of Free Trade has been revealed, and the FTAA, for example, is today for all intents and purposes dead. It wasn't killed by the protests, but political leaders in the Global South were given new strength in opposing trade rules that were unfair to their citizens. People who had been battling the harsh structural adjustment imposed by the International Monetary Fund (IMF) and the World Bank saw that they had allies in the North. And the impact was felt both ways.

---

*Following Quebec City and a much more violent incident in Genoa in July 2001, a major debate developed in the movement on the issue of how to deal with violence.

Many of the protesters were inspired by the Zapatistas (officially the Zapatista Army of National Liberation), an indigenous movement formed in Chiapas, Mexico. The first action of the Zapatistas against corporate globalization and for control of their own resources was to protest the North American Free Trade Agreement (NAFTA), so the group was well known to activists in the United States and Canada who were also protesting the agreement.

At the beginning of 1996, the Zapatistas reached out to sympathetic North Americans through the internet. The call of the savvy masked Zapatista leader, Subcomandante Marcos, reached tens of thousands of young people hungry for the vision of better world:

> On the one side is neo-liberalism with all its repressive power and all its machinery of death: on the other side is the human being. In any place in the world, anytime, any man or woman who rebels to the point of tearing off the clothes that resignation has woven for them and cynicism has dyed grey. Any man or woman of whatever colour in whatever tongue speaks and says to himself, to herself: Enough is enough!—*Ya Basta!* [Enough!]*

And Marcos defined a new kind of solidarity by identifying with every oppressed person everywhere. His challenge was no longer that people in the wealthy countries should support those in the poor countries, but rather that we should support one another:

> Who is Marcos? Marcos is a gay in San Francisco, a black person in South Africa, an Asian in Europe, a Palestinian in Israel, a Jew in Germany, an artist without a gallery or a portfolio, a woman alone in a metro station at 10 p.m. He is every minority who is now beginning to speak and every majority that must shut up

---

*Subcomandante Marcos, "Tomorrow Begins Today," at http://artactivism.gn.apc.org. All direct quotations from Subcomandante Marcos are not copyrighted.

and listen. He is every untolerated group searching for a way to speak, their way to speak. Everything that makes power and the good consciences of those in power uncomfortable—this is Marcos.

He spoke of organizing from below, decision-making based on dialogue and inclusion, and the connection among peoples struggling for justice. And he was pleased to see the anti-globalization movement learning these lessons. In a 2004 speech, Marcos said,

> We are pleased by this alter-globalization movement in the sense that it doesn't repeat the vertical model of top-down decision-making, and that helps it not have a central command, directives or something like that. And that the movement has known to respect the differences within it—the thoughts, the currents, the styles, the interests, and the form of decision-making.
>
> We think that this movement is translating not only into a critique of the model that the WTO and others represent but also, in many aspects, it's building alternatives not just on paper but in forms of grassroots organization in many places where you can say that there are the seeds of this other possible world.

At a time when the mainstream media was trumpeting the end of history and the end of alternatives, a visible movement appeared in the belly of the beast asking for something different. Who knows what would have developed if the attack on the Twin Towers had not taken place. As is, in North America, at least, there was a five-year hiatus in which what has come to call itself the global justice movement was invisible and mostly ineffective.

Nevertheless, these protests were just the beginning of a worldwide movement whose goal is to imagine and begin to create another world. And during that five-year period, much work has been going on.

In 2001, under the slogan "Another World Is Possible," a group of activists in Brazil established the World Social Forum (WSF) and put out a call to the social movements of the world to gather each year in Porto Alegre, Brazil. Originally it was meant to be a counter-conference to the World Economic Forum, where the masters of the universe (corporate, government, and media leaders) meet in Davos, Switzerland, to plan the coming year. But, as with most good ideas, the participants took it much further than the originators ever imagined. In 2001, 12,000 people attended; in 2002, 60,000; in 2003, 100,000. In 2004, the WSF moved to Mumbai, India, and grew to 150,000, and then in 2007 moved to Nairobi, Kenya, where the event was smaller but attracted an entirely new group of activists to the WSF movement.

In 2002, the World Social Forum put out a call for local and regional social forums. So, every year, in addition to the yearly events, tens of thousands of activists, scholars, workers, and students come together in different places in the world to network, share, and discuss the issues facing them in their regions. These gatherings have been ignored by the English mainstream media in the United States, Canada, and Britain, but have been well covered everywhere else in the world—and, of course, by the massive network of alternative media.

Karl Marx famously said that capitalism, by creating the industrial working class, gathered in factories, was in fact creating the seeds of its own destruction. Similarly, corporate globalization has created the seeds of its destruction by enabling an unparalleled connection among the peoples of the world, not only through technology but also through presenting them with issues that increasingly draw them together.

The World Social Forum has spawned unprecedented coordination and communication among the peoples of the world. So far the most remarkable event was the February 15, 2003, protest against the impending war in Iraq. The call for the demonstrations emerged from the European Social Forum and spread through the internet and then the World Social Forum in January 2003. It was the largest global demonstration in human history, and it was also the first time such a massive protest was intended to prevent a war. It was not only a rally against U.S. president George W. Bush and his ally British prime minister Tony Blair but also a cry from the hearts of the peoples of the world that we will never accept a war of civilizations provoked by our leaders. The millions that took to the streets on every continent, in so many cities and towns, were sending a message to both the government of the United States and Britain and to the peoples of the Middle East. There was no West versus East, no Christians and Jews versus Muslims: There was only a united protest against the government of George W. and what remained of his allies trying to dominate the world in order to benefit economically and politically. On every continent, in every language, with one booming global voice, we said, "No."

The large demonstrations in Europe and New York City were reported in the mainstream media. But that was not all. There were protests throughout Latin America and Asia as well; demonstrations in a large number of American cities; and even a rally of several thousand Israelis and Palestinians—together—in Tel Aviv. In every location, organizers were stunned by the size of the demonstrations.

At the time, the media reported that these were the largest demonstrations since the Vietnam War protests, but they were much larger outside the United States. In Canada, for example, there had never been a march of 150,000 in Montreal against the Vietnam War, or of 80,000 in Toronto. There had never been a march of two million in London, more than a million in Rome and Barcelona, and hundreds of thousands in France and Germany. The anti-Vietnam marchers were primarily students. The anti-war coalition members today are diverse in age, race, and culture, including immigrant communities in Europe and North America and the mainstream labour movement in the United States, which had not been involved in the anti-Vietnam protests.

The New York Times said that the protests marked the emergence of another superpower: "global public opinion." The size of the demonstrations showed that Bush's attempts to cloak American aggression by claiming it was instead a concern about terrorism and/or weapons of mass destruction had utterly failed. The demonstrations put the blame for war right where it belonged, on the shoulders of Bush and Blair. Writing about the action at the time, I was convinced that, should Bush attack Iraq anyway, opposition to the war would grow and grow, and indeed it has grown. In the United States today, 70 percent of the population opposes the war, and less than 30 percent supports Bush. Yet at the time I am writing, the United States is still at war in Iraq. So the difference between the anti-war protests of today and those of the 1960s is the state of democracy: Enormous protests and even massive public opinion now appear to have little impact.

AT THE WORLD SOCIAL FORUM in 2003, it became clear to me that the forum was really a process more than a product. The WSF has given us a new way of talking to one another, a new way of sharing our experience, and the impact is extraordinary. On so many levels, the spirit of the WSF has created multiple dialogues that may very well promote transformation.

The spirit of the WSF and indeed the global justice movement as a whole was probably best expressed in the extraordinary speech that year by famed Indian novelist Arundhati Roy. Speaking to a packed soccer stadium of thirty thousand attendees, she said,

> We may not have stopped it [the Empire] in its tracks but we have stripped it down. We have made it drop its mask. We have forced it into the open. It now stands before us on the world's stage in all its brutish, iniquitous nakedness. Empire may well go to war, but it's out in the open now—too ugly to behold its own reflection. Too ugly even to rally its own people.
>
> We can turn the war on Iraq into a fishbowl of the U.S. government's excesses. We can expose George Bush and Tony Blair and their allies for the cowardly baby killers, water poisoners, and pusillanimous long-distance bombers that they are.
>
> We can re-invent civil disobedience in a million different ways ... becoming a collective pain in the ass.

Our strategy should be not only to confront empire but to lay siege to it. To deprive it of oxygen. To shame it. To mock it. With our art, our music, our literature, our stubbornness, our joy, our brilliance, our sheer relentlessness.... The corporate revolution will collapse if we refuse to buy what they are selling—their ideas, their version of history, their wars, their weapons and their notion of inevitability.

Remember this. We be many and they be few. They need us more than we need them. Another world is not only possible, she is on her way. On a quiet day, I can hear her breathing.*

At that moment it felt to me as if the global movement was on the rise and would continue its rise. I still had the idea that a movement would emerge much like the movements of the 1960s, in which people's power would push governments to stop wars and implement more just policies, and where society would change because the majority of people in the world wanted it so. But a lot has happened since the 1960s to fundamentally alter that path to change.

When the WSF moved to Mumbai, India, in 2004 to further globalize, the nature of the gatherings, up until then dominated by Latin Americans and Europeans, changed. India is home to massive social movements. It is the world's largest democracy and has a vibrant and vital history of organizing. The WSF gave all those movements of poor people the chance to meet together for the first time and share strategies. So, instead of the large panel discussions that were so popular in Brazil, what drew the crowds in Mumbai were the locally organized workshops and movement gatherings.

Chico Whitaker, one of the founders of the World Social Forum, has said, "Each meeting under the banner of the WSF is an opportunity to cultivate a new political culture that replaces competition with co-operation." Whitaker believes that the WSF will leave its mark on the new century and that organizations such as the Organisation for

---

*Arundhati Roy, Porto Alegre, Brazil, January 27, 2003.

Economic Co-operation and Development (OECD) will have to begin listening to the networks the WSF has helped build.*

That the WSF started in Brazil is significant. Brazil is the home of one of the best-known proponents of popular education, famed educator Paolo Freire. Popular education is a system that starts from the knowledge of oppressed people and bases their education in that knowledge and in the need for action to resist their oppression. It is where education meets political action. Another factor is Brazil's Workers' Party (Partido dos Trabalhadores, [PT]), which is organized differently than other parties and includes all the currents of the Left in one democratically organized party. In addition, the PT created participatory budgets in cities where they were elected, and developed a method of including ordinary people in governing themselves.

As Moema Miranda, another founder of the WSF, who works with the Brazilian non-governmental organization IBASE, told me, it was the openness of the forum and its characteristic of giving people the freedom to connect with one another in the ways they wanted to connect that created its success.

> Neo-liberalism has all to do with fragmentation, with division, with individualistic perspective, in such a deep way that we did not even understand how much this was hurting ourselves. The WSF comes with this idea of open-space organizing and all the good feelings that were inside just come outside again. And at the same time, I think that it really offers possibilities to strengthen our struggles, and this is really about doing things against neo-liberalism.

This is the intangible thing about the World Social Forums—the way they make you feel as if another world is possible. Because so much of the problem in society is that sense of powerlessness, that

---

*Chico Whitaker, "The World Social Forum: What Is It Really About?" *OECD Observer* 248 (March 2005).

feeling that nothing we do makes any difference, gathering with others of like mind from all over the world and from different movements makes participants feel it is still possible to change the world. That's not enough, of course, but the forums also provide an opportunity for people working on global issues to come together regularly. There are new transnational coalitions forming around the issues of water, climate change, land reform, women's rights, and Aboriginal rights, and these have all emerged from, or built on, the worldwide and regional forums. In addition, the organizers have discovered that, by having an open structure and moving it around the world, the WSF is adapting organically to meet the needs of participants.

Even in the most difficult places on earth, the WSF finds hope. As Israeli prime minister Ariel Sharon consolidated his greatest electoral victory, Israeli and Palestinian peace activists met at the WSF in 2003 to develop a joint declaration for peace. It was read in English by both a Palestinian member of parliament and a Jewish doctor, to the same throng addressed later by Arundhati Roy and Noam Chomsky. It read, in part: "We Israeli and Palestinian peace activists are determined to pursue peace … an end to the occupation, the establishment of a Palestinian state, Jerusalem as an open city, and a just and fair solution of the Palestinian refugee problem." As the mayor of Porto Alegre, Brazil, read the statement in Portuguese, John Lennon's song "Imagine" was heard, first softly and then at full volume over the loudspeakers in the giant stadium. Spontaneously, thirty thousand people stood, held their hands high, and swayed and sang along. What was extraordinary was that the vast majority of participants were Spanish or Portuguese who spoke no English. Yet they knew these words. On the stage the Israelis and Palestinians too held hands, and then hugged and kissed one another. We were all dreamers and not the only ones.

I missed the Mumbai forum in 2004, but from all reports, there was an almost total transformation from the Brazil forums. In Brazil, WSP participants were primarily middle-class people; in Mumbai, there was a massive presence of Adivasi/indigenous peoples from Southeast Asia, especially India, and of Dalits (also known as Untouchables), who travelled from all over India to attend. For both groups, it was the first time they had been able to meet on a national and continental level, and later interviews with the Dalits at the Nairobi forum made it clear the WSF in Mumbai provided an opportunity for the transformation of their movement. In Mumbai, it was the workshops, marches, and cultural events that drew the huge numbers. Panels with big names debating grand ideas were not as attractive to these activists as the chance to share with people facing similar oppression and violence across the continent.

I DID ATTEND THE FORUM in Nairobi, Kenya, in January 2007, which mainly focused on the basic issues facing activists in Africa. I had never been to Africa before and thought it would be an amazing opportunity to get a sense of the social movements there. Media images of Africans as starving or sickly victims are so pervasive that even someone like me, who has worked a lifetime to rid myself of racist stereotypes, was stunned by the strength and power of most of the African activists I met there. I also convinced two friends with whom I had worked in the women's movement in Toronto to come with me. Akua Benjamin and Winnie Ng are respected leaders in the black and Chinese communities in Toronto and in the women's movement. It was a powerful experience for all of us.

One of the most moving moments was the forum to remember the Mau Mau Rebellion, the first anti-colonial uprising in Africa in the 1950s. Seeing that struggle through the eyes of Africans who credit it with much of the advances they have made since then was the kind of global consciousness-raising experience that happens at almost every WSF. One of the event interpreters started weeping as the Mau Mau survivors began to speak. He apologized in French to the people listening to his translation, saying, "I am sorry but you have to realize everything I am, everything I am able to do, I owe to these people."

The forum also reflected the problems facing progressive movements in Africa, such as their domination by Western-funded nongovernmental organizations (NGOs).

Ironically, poor people from around Nairobi protested that an entrance fee of five hundred Kenyan shillings, much beyond the means of a low-income person, meant their exclusion from the forum, or central gathering, held at a stadium outside of town. Even when activists among the poor gathered around the gates, they were excluded. So a group called the People's Parliament broke into the press conference to demand open access. Wangui Mbatia, the group's spokesperson, who emerged as a kind of movement superstar through her powerful, articulate presentations, spoke eloquently to the final meeting of social movements attended by more than a thousand people.

Mbatia talked about the importance of having the opportunity to meet good people from around the world, and then criticized the exclusion of the poor, but she ended with a series of recommendations from the poor people's social forum that was held in the slums. These recommendations were not only about ending poverty in Africa but also included expressions of solidarity with similar struggles around the world. She and others insisted that poor people's groups have to be involved from the beginning in planning forums. She and her group had had the opportunity to meet poor people's groups from India, South Africa, and Europe that they would never have met otherwise.

In an evening meeting organized by the Transnational Institute, a worldwide fellowship of scholar-activists led by my friend Hilary Wainwright, I met two astonishing men in their teens, Kevin Ovita and Stanley Kai, who were leading a political group called Wasani, which they said was Swahili for "artists in the hood." Wasani organizes among the youth in the slums surrounding Nairobi. Not only do they write hip-hop songs to educate about various forms of oppression, including violence against women, and use political graffiti to do the same, but they are also organizing young people to run for city council. They, too, got a chance to connect with the global social movements that, up to now, they have known only through their music.

There were thousands of Kenyans—and others from Uganda and Tanzania—who had their first contact with activists working on similar issues around the world. As one example, Council of Canadians chair Maude Barlow, the tireless Canadian activist who has been involved in the World Social Forum and other international organizations ever since the successful battle against the Multilateral Agreement on Investment (MAI) in the mid-1990s, was a featured speaker in Nairobi and helped to establish an African Right to Water coalition.

Last but not least, the Nairobi forum also put racism solidly on the agenda—and this came not so much from the Kenyans as from the black Brazilians. After four years of the WSF being held in Brazil, where almost half the population is black, it took the WSF in Nairobi for the issue of racism in Brazil to be discussed. A black Brazilian woman said it most eloquently: "I came to the Social Forum to make sure that the position of the forum includes the fight against racism. We can't fight for social justice without fighting against racism. A new world order has to repair the damage that has been done not only to black people in Africa but [to] people of African origin around the world."

Protests are nothing new at the WSF. In fact, they are the normal state of affairs. In 2002, in Porto Alegre, Brazil, women's issues had been practically absent from the agenda, especially abortion, a difficult topic for the Left in Catholic-dominated Brazil. Women with masks of big lips, saying "speak up against fundamentalisms," marched through the site, performed guerrilla theatre, and thoroughly enchanted delegates—and, one presumes, organizers, since women's issues and women made their way into the formal events of the WSF thereafter.

The big lips were still around in Nairobi, but this time they were celebrating in an awesome women's rally that combined dancing, short speeches, and solidarity across nations, races, and continents. There were probably more workshops on women's issues than any other, including one entitled "Denying Women's Reproductive Rights Is Genocide." Women were the lead speakers at the opening ceremonies and at every major event. I have no doubt that, after the protests of Nairobi, poor people will play a much larger role in organizing the next World Social Forum in 2009 in Belem, Brazil, than they ever have before.

Today, there is a lot of questioning about the World Social Forum. Because of the tremendous resources it takes to organize a forum, the International Committee (IC) agreed to change from yearly to biyearly events. In addition to controversies about how the IC is constituted, there is currently a major debate about how effective these forums are if they do not develop a global plan for action. There are several currents involved in debating and discussing the future of the WSF, but while the debates continue, people on the ground are using the tools of the WSF in ways that respond to their own realities.

Through the WSF and through online activism, people around the world are getting to know one another and sharing their experiences, knowledge, and wisdom. In earlier years, it was a small elite that was able to connect internationally; today's communication technology ensures it is a mass experience, and it is strengthening activism in myriad ways that will become apparent in the pages to come. What's more, the very notion of solidarity has changed. It is no longer just about those of us in the rich North helping those in the poor South. Instead, it has become clear that we have a lot to learn from one another. Nowhere has this been made clearer than at the first U.S. Social Forum.

IT WAS AT THE U.S. SOCIAL FORUM (USSF), which took place some six months after the Nairobi WSF, that the true potential of the open organizing of the forum manifested itself. Twelve thousand people— overwhelmingly poor and working class, about half people of colour, at least half women, and including a massive number of youth—gathered in Atlanta, Georgia, at the end of June. It was radical, it was militant, it was feminist, it was anti-capitalist and anti-imperialist, it was queer, it was loud and lively, and it was brimming with compassion, kindness, and a deep sense of solidarity. The slogan of the USSF was "Another World Is Possible. Another U.S. Is Necessary."

Marisa Franco from San Francisco's People Organized to Win Employment Rights (POWER) said at the opening of the June 29 session: "We're not talking about a platform or demands here. We're talking about how we can make things work better. We must connect with each other, walk vision as well as talk vision. No one else will do it for us. If another U.S. is necessary, another 'us' is necessary too."

Even though a good friend of mine was getting married that weekend, I decided I had to go to the first U.S. Social Forum. Although I had a feeling it was going to be very important, I was still stunned. Sitting in plenary after plenary, listening to speaker after speaker, most of whom were women and people of colour, almost none of whom I had ever heard of, and listening to the lively, warm, and intelligent responses from the audience, I felt that finally I was seeing what I had been fighting for my entire life. It was intoxicating.

And it was a major step forward for the World Social Forum movement. The idea of a U.S. Social Forum came from a couple of people who had gone to the 2001 WSF in Brazil and then took a few more with them to the next international forum in 2002. They formed a group called Grassroots Global Justice and began the process of organizing a U.S. Social Forum, firmly in the WSF spirit. One of them, Fred Azcarate—then with Jobs with Justice, an organization that helps to organize workers' struggles, and now with the American Federation of Labor and Congress of Industrial Organizations (AFL–CIO)—explained to the opening plenary that "It took this long because we wanted to do it right by building the necessary relationships among the grassroots organizations and ensuring the right outcomes." And the right outcomes were to create the conditions that would unite the disparate grassroots people's movements around the United States across race, age, issues, and region. They got the idea from the WSF, but they took it beyond the point anyone else has managed to reach, except perhaps in Mumbai. In Nairobi, poor people demanded a significant place in the WSF planning process, and, in Atlanta, they had one.

Hundreds of participants arrived via the "Freedom Caravan," which commemorated the civil rights Freedom Rides of 1961. Buses began in Albuquerque, New Mexico, and linked with others from the Gulf Coast and then from various places in the South that symbolize the civil rights struggle. In addition, a lot of fundraising was done to bring poor and low-income people to Atlanta. Instead of privileged middle-class people (often the majority of World Social Forums attendees), working class people, poor people, and students formed a large proportion of forum participants. It was also just about the most diverse and multiracial gathering I've ever seen.

According to veteran leftist journalist Steven Sherman, writing in *Monthly Review*:

> The remarkable accomplishment of the United States Social Forum was to bring together the largely white activists whose touchstone was the direct action at the WTO protests in Seattle with community and labor activists who mostly come from communities of color. This was all the more remarkable given the de facto racial segregation endemic on the U.S. left for the last thirty years. I think it's fair to say that, by the end of the forum, the confidence of both groups that they belong together and can work with each other had increased.

The National Planning Committee of the U.S. Social Forum represented what they call national and regional "base-building" groups, whose base was mostly poor and working-class people.

It seemed to me that the forum shifted the balance of power on the American Left from the middle class to the poor and oppressed. By this point, the burst of brilliance shown in the anti-WTO protests in Seattle in 1999 had settled into either a fairly mainstream Left, focused on improving the fortunes of the Democratic Party, or a highly marginalized and mostly white "anti-globalization movement."

Even the Seattle protests were highly problematic from this perspective. "Where was the colour in Seattle?" asked a famous article in the magazine *ColorLines*, by Latina activist Betitia Martinez. What at the time was called the *anti-globalization movement* appeared almost entirely white and focused on protesting corporate globalization. The visible Left in the United States is made up of mostly intellectuals and campaigners, many of them in Washington-based think-tanks and foundation-funded NGOs. The grassroots organizing that has been going on over the last number of years has been invisible to most of us outside of the country. The genius of the USSF organizers was to bring together all these local and grassroots groups in one place, using the Social Forum open process as a way to do it.

Every plenary focused on building alliances among myriad grassroots movements across the United States. Most of the emphasis was on a "black-brown" alliance to combat the racism that divides African Americans from their Latino and immigrant brothers and sisters. But there was also a lot of focus on student/labour alliances, and environmental discussions were completely linked to social justice issues. One of the remarkable things about the resurgence of the student movement in the United States in the twenty-first century is that it has been connected first to anti-globalization and then to workers' rights and environmentalism. Similar to other social forums, the connection among issues and communities was where the emphasis was placed. Support for gays, lesbians, and transgendered people who have been major targets of the Bush administration seemed universal.

The forum ended in a People's Movements Assembly, in which various campaigns and caucuses presented their resolutions. Several new national networks were formed, and the bonds of solidarity were forged among those who are usually divided. Domestic Workers United formed the National Domestic Workers Alliance. Taxi workers also formed a national alliance. Restaurant Opportunities Center (ROC) United, which had started with the employees from the restaurant in the Twin Towers, also formed a national ROC. In addition, a national Right to the City network was formed from a number of different community organizations working on housing and other urban issues. The problem of gentrification driving poor and working-class people out of the cities is a major new issue that was raised during the USSF. People left with a commitment to organize social forums in their regions, cities, and neighbourhoods. Over the course of the week, the Social Forum became a catalyst for creating a movement of movements everywhere.

"People are asking me when Atlanta has ever seen something like this," said Jerome Scott, founder of Project South and a veteran Atlanta activist, speaking at the opening march. "I've been reflecting on that, and my answer is Atlanta has never seen anything like this. The civil rights movement was mostly African American and last year's May 1 [immigration rights] demo was mostly Latinos, but this march was the most multi-national action I have ever seen. It was beautiful."

Another extraordinary feature of the forum was the role of indigenous peoples, who led the opening march and participated on several panels as well as their own plenary. Much of the vision came from them. Tom Goldtooth, who represents the Indigenous Environmental Network on the National Planning Committee, said, "We must talk from the heart and shake hands with one another. A prayer has taken place that this spirit is going to grow. No matter who we are, we must demand not reform of a broken system but transformation. We need to organize from the grassroots."

The plenary on Hurricane Katrina was stunning. Of course, I already knew that the true tragedy of Katrina was government neglect and inaction, not the hurricane itself, but what I didn't know is that, two years later, neglect had turned into what could only be called racial cleansing. The speeches from the stage and from the audience were powerful. Afterwards I felt that if the first American Revolution was started by a callous colonial power taxing what they thought was a compliant colony, the second one might be caused by a callous, racist, arrogant government thinking it could wipe out the hard-won place of African Americans in New Orleans after a storm provided it with the opportunity.

Another impressive feature of the forum was the handling of conflict. When the Palestinian contingent objected that they were the only group not permitted to speak for themselves in the anti-war plenary, the organizers read their letter of protest to the next plenary. When the report of the indigenous caucus was stopped at the end of their allotted time by the moderator of the People's Movement Assembly, who removed their microphone, they took grave offence and felt silenced. Within ten minutes, most of the indigenous peoples in the room were on the stage with the consent of the organizers. What could have been an explosive and divisive moment, causing a lot of anger and hurt, was handled with incredible skill by both sides, and the protest was permitted and interpreted in a way that created unity rather than division. I had the feeling that a new culture of solidarity was being born, one we had tried for in the feminist movement but never quite attained.

SIX MONTHS LATER, on January 3, 2008, the spirit of Atlanta showed itself in the surprising participation of young people in the Iowa primary to support Democratic presidential candidate Barack Obama. It's not that Obama's policies reflect the preoccupations of the activists at the USSF. It's that Obama himself is a symbol of the change that needs to take place in the United States. A mixed-race son of an immigrant, he represents the new America, just as the USSF showed the new America, no longer a nation polarized between black and white but a nation reflecting the globalization of the world through a multinational population. Obama speaks of hope instead of fear and of unity instead of hatred and polarization. He comes from the same experience of community organizing in poor urban communities as many of the U.S. Social Forum delegates do. During the primary campaign and on his website, Obama rarely says, "Vote for me, and I will do this or that." His appeal is about what "we" can do together. He makes it clear that problems can only be solved if all of us get active and involved. He taps into a longing for political and social engagement that I have seen in many places around the world and at home.

I have been exploring new approaches to political change for more than a decade now. The World Social Forum opened up more new worlds to me than I probably would have been able to discover in other ways. But my search started closer to home with a brush with participatory democracy in Canada in the early 1990s.

2

PARTICIPATORY DEMOCRACY
Power to the People

I FIRST STARTED TO QUESTION the elitism of my own politics during the No campaign against the Charlottetown Accord in 1992. This proposed amendment to the Canadian Constitution was supported by all the governmental elites and eventually defeated by a grassroots campaign.

Then prime minister Brian Mulroney was desperate to have Quebec sign the Canadian Constitution, which it had refused to sign when former prime minister Pierre Elliott Trudeau had repatriated it from England in 1982. Mulroney was committed, almost obsessed, with getting Quebec to sign. His first attempt—the Meech Lake Accord in 1987, which recognized Quebec as a distinct society—failed, despite support from almost all the premiers, because Aboriginal member of the Manitoba legislature Elijah Harper stopped its passage in that province by staging a dramatic filibuster in which he held an eagle feather and refused to sit down. Aboriginal peoples opposed Meech Lake because, while it recognized Quebec as a "distinct society," it provided no recognition of the rights of Aboriginal peoples.

English-Canadian women's groups also opposed Meech Lake because they believed it established a hierarchy of rights, in which language rights trumped women's rights. With the Charlottetown Accord, developed two years after Meech Lake, Mulroney thought he had answered the concerns of all of these groups but wanted to make sure by giving the people a voice. So Canada had its first national referendum in my lifetime.

The National Action Committee on the Status of Women (NAC) had been divided over the Meech Lake Accord because Quebec women supported it while English-Canadian women did not. When I was elected president of NAC in 1990, healing the split between Quebec and the rest of Canada was a priority. NAC started a process of discussions that included women from Quebec, First Nations, and English Canada. The discussions resulted in NAC taking the position that Canada was composed of three nations—English Canada, French Canada, and First Nations—each of which was multicultural and multiracial and each of which had the right to self-determination. This led us to argue for what the government called *asymmetrical federalism*, in which Quebec would have different powers than the other provinces and First Nations would have self-government. We participated in citizen conferences that were held on the government proposals for constitutional change and we also argued that the proposed elected Senate include an equal number of women and men.

We won a lot of our positions in the citizen conferences, but when the prime minister and the premiers disappeared behind closed doors, they dropped most of the proposals adopted at the conferences. They then called a referendum on their own proposals, which included Aboriginal self-government but had no equality protection for Aboriginal women.

After much discussion, NAC opposed the Charlottetown Accord because we believed it threatened women's, especially Aboriginal women's, rights. As NAC president, I had the extraordinary experience of criss-crossing the country and speaking to thousands of people in every imaginable setting, often debating cabinet ministers and other government representatives. At every meeting, people had their copy of the accord, which had been delivered in their mail, and pages of questions. Citizens took their opportunity to vote very seriously and participated to an extent rarely seen in politics.

The process started me thinking about the limitations of representative democracy. I realized that ordinary people had an extraordinary amount of wisdom, and—unlike almost every player in the political system, whether politicians, bureaucrats, corporations, unions, or even social movements such as the women's movement—they had no particular agenda. They were simply listening to the debate and deciding if they thought these changes were good for their communities. Furthermore, I realized, when people believed their vote would mean something, they voted in large numbers. The turnout for the vote on the Charlottetown Accord was 71.8 percent of eligible voters.

At that time, I believed that the conflict of ideas through the battling out of these various interests was working pretty well. After all, the women's movement had managed to accomplish major changes to the laws, reflecting our demands for women's equality. We rarely got exactly what we wanted, but that was how the game was played, and while I might have been on the outer fringe of the game, I had been in it for more than a decade by then. The debate and referendum on the Charlottetown Accord was a genuine process of democracy with a level playing field and a grassroots campaign, and it managed to defeat the plans of the elite. That night, sitting in the CBC-TV studios, I should have felt elation at the tremendous victory we had achieved. Instead, as I listened to premier after premier, I realized that they would proceed with their plans despite the referendum defeat and that nothing positive would come of the victory. Instead, the media and the politicians so rejected the exercise that they barely spoke of it again. On the tenth anniversary of Meech Lake, the media was filled with discussion. On the tenth anniversary of Charlottetown, it was as if it had never happened. The lesson drawn by the elites was never again to allow an excess of democracy or to give a voice to marginal groups such as feminists and Aboriginal peoples.

A FEW YEARS AFTER CHARLOTTETOWN, the rules changed. In 1995, Mike Harris was elected premier of Ontario. Much to the shock and dismay of progressive people, Ontario elected a hard right-wing ideologue with a clear agenda called the Common Sense Revolution with the intention not only to turn back the gains of the previous New Democratic Party (NDP) government but also the gains that social movements had made over decades.

Six months after the Harris election, labour unions, in alliance with social justice community groups, began a series of one-day rolling general strikes (called Days of Action) that shut down eleven cities and mobilized hundreds of thousands of people across the province. The labour movement organized coalitions in every city, ensuring that each organizing committee for the Days of Action included both a labour and a community chair. It was an extraordinary grassroots effort: 20,000 people hit the streets in London; 120,000 in Hamilton; and 250,000 in Toronto. In all cases, these were the largest demonstrations those cities had ever seen. In Toronto, the Day of Action was a Friday and the city was deserted except for the protesters and the police. Many workers participated actively in the strike using tactics such as secondary pickets, so that no one would be penalized for striking. It was hard to tell whether people were afraid to go to work that day because of media hysteria or stayed home because they passively supported the strike.

I was working at the CBC at the time, so I wasn't involved in the organizing, but I did act as emcee at the rally. Seeing the masses of people marching up University Avenue from Queen Street to the legislature and filling up both sides of the eight-lane-wide avenue chanting and singing was a powerful and inspiring experience.

The combination of one of the largest demonstrations in the province's history and the broadest coalitions ever built with a grass-roots educational effort should have yielded tremendous results. But Harris ignored it.

A new generation of activists had been brought into action. They would go on to organize the anti-globalization marches of a few years later, but the goal of the Days of Action—to force Harris out of office or, at least, to force him to back down on some of his policies—had no success. The failure to have an impact was devastating.

Instead of realizing that this was going to be a much longer struggle and building on the new partnerships that had formed between community and labour, the union leadership, with a couple of local exceptions, decided the effort had been a failure and retreated to a more usual strategy of trying to re-elect the NDP. There had already been serious differences within the labour movement in reaction to some of the policies of Bob Rae's NDP government, and these deepened by the next election. The Canadian Autoworkers and the Teachers' Unions called for strategic voting (voting for Liberals where they were strong and the NDP where they were strong) to get the Harris government out of power. Others, called the Pink Paper Unions, which included most of the private sector unions, supported the NDP in their usual manner.

The Harris Tories were re-elected.

As I REALIZED that the old tactics of protest and lobbying weren't working any more, I started looking for other models of change. The more I looked at the experiences around the world, the more I realized that Canada had resisted this right-turn, this neo-liberal restructuring, longer than almost anywhere on earth. Our battles against the Free Trade Agreement with the United States had raised public awareness of the dangers of the corporate agenda to such an extent that it had significantly slowed down the process at the federal level. So, while Margaret Thatcher and Ronald Reagan were assaulting their respective trade union movements and privatizing and cutting back public services, in Canada, for the most part, we were holding our ground against Brian Mulroney's attempts to do the same.

Even earlier, neo-liberalism had hit Latin America with the force of a tsunami. The dictatorships of the Southern Cone, which with the help of the United States and Cold War ideology had brutally defeated left-of-centre governments and movements in their regions during the 1970s, were able to impose the neo-liberal model almost instantly, because they had already viciously repressed any potential opposition. Democracy, it turns out, is the biggest enemy of neo-liberalism, for a system that redistributes wealth from the poor to the rich by definition cannot be a democratic system. In the Global North, right-wing governments had to overcome resistance from unions and other social forces. In the undemocratic areas of South America, however, they had already destroyed potential opposition through assassinations, kidnappings, torture, prison, and exile. The blood of thousands stained the triumph of capital in these regions.

Around the same time as the Days of Action were taking place in Ontario, Lula da Silva, then leader of the Brazil Workers' Party, now president of Brazil, spoke at a meeting in Toronto and talked about a new direction for the Left. He acknowledged the failure of the Left in South America and around the world and said that we needed new strategies—with the democratic participation of the people at the centre of those strategies. For the first of many times, I found someone from the other side of the world thinking the same things that I was thinking.

As mentioned earlier, in Brazil, partly because of the emergence of a new democracy after the failure of Communism and the move to the right of many European social democratic parties, the Workers' Party (known as the PT, the initials of its Portuguese name) had stepped into the emerging democracy looking for alternative strategies. I had heard about Lula, the charismatic steelworker who had run for presidency in Brazil in 1989, but it hadn't prepared me for meeting him. The Steelworkers Union in Toronto asked me to chair a meeting at which he would speak in November 1997, but when I walked into the break-fast planned for him that morning, I barely noticed the short, roundish man standing in a corner carefully watching everyone. It wasn't until he smiled that I got some sense of why his speeches in Brazil attracted tens of thousands and the adoration of millions. Later that day, he explained that the people of the world needed a new vision for a fairer society and that the democratic participation of the people had to be at the centre of that vision. "Do we have democracy only to have the right to cry out in hunger?" he asked.

He explained that when the PT was elected in Porto Alegre, in southern Brazil, they went to the community groups to ask what their priorities should be. People were suspicious, but they told the municipal government that child care should be the priority, not the public transit issue the party had featured in its campaign. The PT, being socialists, believed in state-run child care, but they couldn't afford it. Community groups stepped forward and offered to house the child-care centres for a fraction of the price it would have cost in the public sector. The party accepted that child care was more of a priority than transit and agreed that community groups, rather than the government, could provide the service. This compromise began to build trust.

People told the PT about where there was corruption and how it could be stopped, thus money was found for needed services and infrastructure improvement. So the PT mayor decided to formalize the process of citizen decision-making in the running of the city's business. A participatory budget was established in 1989, giving citizens the responsibility to decide on how to spend new monies in the city budget.

This participatory budget has been one of the most successful experiments in expanding democracy in the world, copied by hundreds of cities in Latin America and Europe and even a couple in Canada. The key feature of the participatory budget is that citizens decide on priorities. It is not just a consultative process. In Porto Alegre, the mayor's office provides the training and resources necessary to allow delegates, who are elected at a neighbourhood level, to read and consider a budget. The impact has been extraordinary, involving those who are marginalized by representative democracy, cutting down corruption, and showing people that by working with their neighbours, they can solve problems together.

One of the most interesting aspects of the process is that it promotes social solidarity. In Porto Alegre, budget delegates were so persuaded that all the money should go to the alleviation of conditions in the poorer neighbourhoods that the mayor had to add sectors such as arts and culture and education to the geographic sectors of the budget process, to make sure these areas also got some of the spending. A teacher I interviewed in Porto Alegre told me: "Our school needed a new gymnasium, but when we heard that there were still neighbourhoods that didn't have a proper sewage system, we thought, 'That's more important than our gymnasium.'"

Pepe Vargas is a PT deputy and was the mayor of Caxias do Sul, one of the towns in Brazil that implemented the participatory budget. He says that the budget process helps to train people out of the neo-liberal way of thinking as well. In an interview, he told me:

> Neo-liberalism isn't just an economic policy. It's also a vision of the world. It's an individualist culture of competition between the countries, among companies, and among people. So that's why people say that neo-liberalism creates an individualist culture and a competitive culture. It is very important for us to overcome this kind of culture. There's no way to build a new society based on that kind of mentality.
>
> Through the participatory budget process, people have to decide where to channel public funds. There also can be a kind of competitive process established. To avoid that kind of competition, we created the mechanism of a tour of delegates of the participatory budget process. On this tour, they get to know the reality of the other neighbourhoods. In that way, they see that there are some people living through a much more difficult situation than others, and that really helps to create bonds of solidarity between people. It's not unknown to have cases where a certain community may abrogate their own rights, give up their own claims in the interests in another community [as with the Porto Alegre examples]. That's a way of creating a culture of solidarity in practice, and not only at a level of rhetoric.

The story of Porto Alegre inspired me to take the idea of participatory budgeting and try to apply the principles to politics in Canada. The result was my book *Imagine Democracy*. And I wasn't the only one who saw the potential.

WITH 164,000 TENANTS and 1,542 employees, the Toronto Community Housing Corporation (TCHC) is one of the largest housing providers in North America. Its tenants are among the poorest people in the city. After it was decided to increase tenant involvement, TCHC looked to Porto Alegre's participatory budget and introduced a system by which tenants decide how to spend $10 million a year in capital funds. While the community housing manager has the final say, he or she almost always accepts the recommendations of the twenty-seven elected tenant representatives who serve as a tenant council. Each of the TCHC units makes proposals through their delegates, who bring the proposals to the council. When the things they want aren't funded through this method, the tenants may submit proposals of up to $1.8 million to be decided by an all-day meeting of tenants who gather yearly and hear presentations from every community housing unit.

According to Evelyn Murialdo, the staff person responsible for tenant participation: "They make incredible presentations. They have become very creative; they come with props. When it's for youth, young people do it; when it's for children, then the children play a role." Murialdo says that the impact on the tenants is incredible. "They have a lot invested in the changes for people. Fixing the local playground or the fixing of the sidewalk means a lot. They feel ownership. Poor people don't often get to experience that."

Derek Ballantyne, the chief executive officer of TCHC, would like to see the whole system move toward self-management. In addition, Murialdo wants to use these participatory methods to organize assemblies on a variety of issues to help tenants become more involved in their community, city, and province.

In 2007, a delegation of tenants and staff from TCHC attended the World Social Forum in Nairobi. Most of them were youth who had never travelled before. At a report-back meeting, one of the young women described what it was like to look out her hotel room window onto a slum that had no running water or electricity and realize that as poor as she was in the context of Canada, there were people in other places of the world whose poverty was far worse.

What I have noticed most over the years since TCHC started their participatory process is the involvement of tenants not only in planning for housing but in their community. When I was asked to chair a meeting on the Brazil participatory process at a large meeting in Toronto, I figured it would be cancelled when the mayor of Porto Alegre couldn't attend due to an election loss. Who would want to listen to bureaucrats talk?

The place was packed. The audience listened attentively through translation to some of what I thought were the most boring presentations I have ever heard. When discussion started, the lineups at the microphones were amazing. Young men in hip-hop outfits and single moms with babies on their hips asked detailed questions focused on how best to represent their buildings. It was clear how much participation in the budget had energized and engaged these people.

Murialdo recalls what happened the next day:

> Mayor David Miller was hosting a budget consultation with Torontonians. I got a really panicky phone call from a senior official at the City because there were hundreds of tenants registering, and this was going to create an embarrassment. Two thousand people attended the consultations and four hundred from Toronto Housing wanted to register. City officials felt that was too big a proportion, so they restricted our tenants to two hundred. At every table there were two tenants, and their voices were strong. Poor people don't usually participate in things like that.

As in Porto Alegre, the tenants engaged in the participatory budget at TCHC became interested in getting more engaged as citizens in their communities. Now Murialdo is working to get tenants involved in local community centres and in the upcoming provincial consultation on poverty reduction. There is very little money for this kind of work, even though the positive impact on tenants is recognized at every level of the organization. Murialdo points out: "TCHC [was] successful in coming up with $75 million for capital campaigns, but we don't have a penny funded by anyone to do the work we do. The elections are bigger than in Prince Edward Island. We work with Elections Ontario, using their method of secret ballots. It's a massive undertaking to elect four hundred delegates every three years, and we have very little money for it."

During the Canadian election in the fall of 2008, this tenant engagement translated into election involvement too. Says Murialdo: "Toronto Housing tenants are mobilized across the entire city now with amazing ability to communicate among themselves. I attended one all-party forum organized by tenant leaders. All political parties were invited, but the Conservatives didn't show. One hundred youth and one hundred and fifty tenants, the majority working with interpreters, attended the meeting and asked questions of the candidates. We've never seen this level of lobbying and presence in public forums before. It's quite humbling."

Quite a few cities in Europe, especially in Italy and Spain, have adopted the participatory budget. In a new edition of her book *Reclaim the State*, British socialist feminist Hilary Wainwright writes about a participatory budget in Seville in Spain:

> In Seville, an attentive visitor will find notice boards by many of the city's construction sites announcing "This park (or whatever it is) is designed by your neighbours." This means that it is the product of a budget making process in which Sevillians have come together with others to make investment proposals which are then debated and argued over in the neighbourhood and city

wide before becoming part of a citizens budget—accounting for 25% of the municipality's annual new spending—which is supported by the mayor and the municipal council and implemented by public servants working closely with the public (acting for once, literally as public servants).

The four-year-old participatory experiment in Seville was inspired in very direct and practical ways by the example of Porto Alegre in Brazil. The city is divided into 21 assemblies. 9,000 people attended the assemblies in 2006.

A striking feature of the Seville experience is the emphasis on the autonomy, the "self-regulation" of the process. Javier Navescues, an advisor to the process from the left think-tank FIM, explains their thinking: "It is important for the people to be able to deal with the state on an equal ground." He adds that the process is changing people: "people do not remain the same." I ask him about the fear that popular participation will strengthen reactionary and selfish views. It was a fear he shared but, in their experience, "people's reactionary side is not reinforced. In fact the opposite" and he gives an interesting example of a Gay, Lesbian, Transsexual and Bisexual Group with a project that had to be debated in a neighbourhood assembly dominated by gypsies with strong machista [macho] traditions.

The LGBT group put their proposals to the neighbourhood assembly. There was a strong argument, but it was agreed by the assembly. "The LGBT group told me that they would never normally have talked to these people. As a result of the PB process, they reached more people than ever before. The result of the process has been overwhelming support, and now far more of the project is being put into practice than they ever thought."

In Seville, participatory budgeting has led to the construction of a network of bicycle lanes across the city, as well as several swimming pools and sports grounds. Urban renewal programs, such as the construction of new drains and pavements, have also been undertaken in poorer neighbourhoods, and priorities have been agreed on for repairing schools. A community radio station is due to start broadcasting later this year.

In Toronto, a group of us tried to persuade then-new mayor David Miller, previously a member of the social democratic New Democratic Party, of the need for participatory budgeting. We even introduced Hilary Wainwright to some of his key bureaucrats. The result was a Listening to Toronto consultation that the mayor attended. In a speech he gave in March 2004, Miller was delighted with the results:

> In January, over 1,100 residents came out and participated in the City's Listening to Toronto budget consultations. We did a radical thing this year—we took the budget out to the people before the Budget Advisory Committee commenced its ongoing work.
>
> What did this mean? It meant that the residents of Toronto had a chance to tell us what things make our city great, what things pose a challenge for us, and what advice they would give us as we approach this year's budget. In a year when we must find a way to close a $344 million shortfall, Toronto's residents got to sit with their neighbours and chew over budget priorities.
>
> For me, it was an immensely rewarding experience—listening to people who came out on weekends and evenings to participate in the budget exercise.

But the experience was never repeated. The top-down nature of a large city government took over, and little is left of the ideas of participatory democracy in the City of Toronto. A big part of the problem is the continuing belief of the Left that policy is what matters and process is of little consequence. I thought participatory democracy, when combined with electoral reform such as proportional representation, was a way of reforming our political system to include the voices of ordinary people and to cut across the stale partisanship and self-interest that passes for politics by rooting it in the needs of communities. I underestimated the barriers to change in the system and the need for transformation, not reform. Our political system has become more and more centralized, less and less responsive to the needs of ordinary people—or even to the pressure of organized movements—and seemingly unable to deal with the fundamental issues of our time, except through smoke and mirrors. Even when the future of humanity is at stake, all that seems to matter is the next poll.

Even with all his power and money, Venezuela's Hugo Chavez understands very well the importance of popular participation to any transformation of society.

In Venezuela, some observers believe the emphasis that the Bolivarian Constitution (introduced in 1999) places on participatory democracy at every level is a major reason that Chavez has moved from a vision of a more humane form of capitalism to socialism for the twenty-first century. Writing in *Monthly Review*,* Michael A. Lebowitz points out that the constitution not only "declares that participation by people is 'the necessary way of achieving the involvement to ensure their complete development, both individual and collective'" but that it specifically focuses on democratic planning and participatory budgeting at all levels of society. It also stresses the importance of "self-management, co-management, cooperatives in all forms." According to Lebowitz, the constitution contains the seeds of socialism for the twenty-first century.

ON A VISIT TO A BARRIO in Caracas, Venezuela, in 2006, I got some idea of what they mean by this kind of democratic planning. Walking to the barrio on a tour organized by the WSF that year was a sobering experience. Overcrowded tin shacks and open sewers showed that despite the reports from poor people around Caracas that their lives

---

*Michael A. Lebowitz, "Venezuela: A Good Example," *Monthly Review* 59:3 (July–August 2007).

had improved since Chavez's election, there was a long way to go.

"We mobilize the people to identify the needs in the community," a young organizer from the community told us. "The government supports the solutions that we decide upon." This community, which had started organizing in this way before Chavez came to power, is more advanced than most, but it is a good example of what is happening. There is a food co-op, a health clinic, and a communications centre, also run co-operatively. The community decides what they want, the government provides the resources, and the community plans and carries out the project. These community organizations are called *missions* in Venezuela. They are a decentralized, democratic model for the delivery of social, health, and other community services, and they are highly successful.

A more recent form of participatory democracy in Venezuela is the emergence of communal councils. Created by law in 2006, they have expanded dramatically since Chavez's landslide re-election in December of that year. The communal councils are a basic unit of democracy based on two hundred to four hundred families in existing urban neighbourhoods and twenty to fifty in the rural areas. The councils are meant to be the basic units of democratic participation and planning, "responding to the needs and aspirations of communities in the construction of a society of equity and social justice," according to the law.

Moreover, these councils are meant to have economic independence, with Chavez announcing that 50 percent of the massive profits of the state-owned oil company will be redirected to the community councils. In addition, the councils have the power of oversight of projects at the national and municipal levels of government. Unlike the Brazilian participatory budget, which has been studied for a couple of decades, the communal councils are a new form of participatory democracy. Some critics are concerned that there is too much ambiguity about what government oversight will mean and what the relationship between the communal councils and municipal government will be. It remains to be seen how well they work in integrating citizen participation at every level of government, but the experiment is an incredibly exciting one and well worth watching.

ANOTHER FORM OF PARTICIPATORY DEMOCRACY based on economic necessity emerged in Argentina at the turn of the twenty-first century. In December 2001, neo-liberal restructuring of the economy—de-industrialization, privatization, a massive influx of foreign capital and cheap offshore imports, reforms of the function of the state that cut deeply into social programs, and a massive increase in the informal economy—led directly to an economic collapse. In 1975, industry represented 30 percent of the total gross domestic product (GDP). By the late 1990s, it was about 16 percent. These changes were accompanied by a deterioration of the job market. Between 1991 and 1994, the domestic economy grew by almost 23 percent, while the unemployment rate doubled and underemployment grew by more than 30 percent. The percentage of those holding formal jobs declined to only 40 percent of the workforce. The majority worked in precarious employment or in the informal economy. Wages fell too. In 1975, wages had been 43 percent of GDP; currently that figure is 20 percent.

The reaction to the crisis created by these changes was seen first among workers, who formed a new kind of union to organize employed and unemployed, in both the formal and informal sectors. The *piqueteros*, as they became known, used street blockades to demand subsidies for the unemployed. These protests were organized by the people on the blockades themselves, breaking with the tradition of the corporatist top-down labour movement created under Peronism,* in which labour leaders played a major role in government. Here, people ran their own show, often negotiating from the

---

*Peronism is a political movement in Argentina based on the idea of former president Juan Peron and his wife, Eva. It was a populist, nationalist movement that defied definition of Right or Left, but one of its characteristics was integration of the union movement into the state apparatus.

blockade itself, instead of choosing, or letting government choose, spokespeople.*

But it wasn't until the middle classes, quite large in Argentina at the time, were affected by the economic crisis and bank closures that a total political crisis led to a change in the system. Suddenly penniless and no longer believing in the myth that the growing wealth would trickle down to them, millions took to the streets on December 19 and 20, 2001, and forced the government to resign.

Most amazing was that it was a rebellion without leaders or hierarchies. The activists called it *horizontalidad* because of its flat structure. The desperation of the situation created new modes of social organization. At first, people just gathered in their neighbourhoods to support one another and find out the news, but then these gatherings became local assemblies that made decisions about participation in various protests and also created a barter economy, community gardens, collective kitchens, and other solutions to the problems they faced. Since the election of social democratic president Néstor Kirchner's government in 2003, these popular assemblies have declined, but the new methods of organizing by consensus and the participation of people in solving their own problems are now deeply valued.

Workers, too, took matters into their own hands. Instead of just accepting factory closures, they took over their factories and ran them themselves, not only producing goods but also often providing services to the surrounding communities. These workers were called *recuperados*. Unlike the top-down corporatist trade unions that had existed during the Peronist era, these organizations were bottom up, with strong participation from everyone and close to a consensus model of governance.†

---

*Isabel Rauber, "The Globalization of Capital and Its Impact on the World of Formal and Informal Work: Challenges for and Responses from Argentine Unions," in *Labour and the Challenges of Globalization*, ed. Andreas Bieler et al. (London: Pluto Press 2008).

†For an in-depth look at one of these factories, see the film *The Take* (2004) by Avi Lewis and Naomi Klein.

It is remarkable that in a country governed by a charismatic populist who ran a top-down corporatist regime and then by a brutal dictatorship that governed through fear, causing the disappearance of thirty thousand people, such powerful participatory and creative democratic solutions would come to the fore.

AT THE WORLD SOCIAL FORUM IN 2003, I participated in a debate about whether the participatory-democracy strategy of the PT or the self-organizing of Argentine workers was more important in the path to change. Socialists were more interested in Brazil, anarchists in Argentina, each ideology concentrating on the struggle that would justify its beliefs. The reality is that both strategies have their strengths and weaknesses. We can learn from both experiences and both have their limitations.

Whatever the limits of participatory budgeting as a strategy for fundamental change, it gives us an important model of how democracy can be transformed to work for people by including their voices in a central way. The pressures of the existing system on people in power are so great that even when they are committed to such a truly democratic process, as was Lula da Silva, it is difficult to implement it at a national level. The debate about how to do this continues in Brazil. The experiences of the people in Argentina show the power of horizontal organizing, in which strategies come from the people on the ground instead of from someone's theories of change, but the grassroots democracy was unable to translate into a national system for change and declined once a sympathetic government was in power.

Neither participatory budgets nor horizontal organizing within communities are sufficient to make fundamental changes, but both are essential elements that are needed to prevent the bureaucratization and corruption that has been the sabotage of so many struggles for social justice and equality around the world. They are also necessary to engage the creativity of thousands of people, many of whom have been the most marginal and excluded people in society, and to draw them into democratic processes.

What I have found, wherever I have looked, is that ordinary people, when they are given, or when they take, the opportunity, are quite capable of making good decisions—in many ways more capable than those who have the official positions of decision-makers. Nowhere is this more apparent than in Bolivia, where an indigenous majority took power under the leadership of indigenous coca farmer Evo Morales in 2006.

3

BOLIVIA

Hoping This One Will Be Different

DURING THE SUMMER OF 2006, I spent five weeks in Bolivia observing one of the most extraordinary revolutions in the history of humanity. Even though by then I had been attending World Social Forums in Brazil and Venezuela for several years, it was on the other side of the world, in Jordan, that I had decided to make Bolivia a major focus of my political rethinking.

That spring, Susan Harvie, a long-time activist with international unions and social organizations who was working for the NGO Alternatives at the time, had asked if I wanted to conduct a workshop on feminist organizing for Iraqi social movements. The workshop would be in Jordan. The idea of meeting Iraqis who, even in the midst of war and occupation, were working for women's equality was an offer I could not refuse. Meeting those women and men was deeply inspiring and moving. Here were people who had lived almost all their lives under the most terrible repression, who had experienced unbearable suffering and loss under Saddam Hussein, and now under U.S. occupation, and yet they continued to work for change not only with great courage and commitment but also with tremendous warmth and spirit.

After the workshop, Susan and I visited one of the greatest wonders of the world, Petra, the magnificent red stone city in the desert that was the site of the film *Indiana Jones and the Last Crusade*. On the four-hour drive from Amman, she spoke about Bolivia, where she had lived for nine years. She told me of a highly politicized society where 70 percent of the population was indigenous and where workers and peasants organized in unions and indigenous groups had mobilized over the last decade to bring down three governments in a row. In 1992, they decided they needed to elect their own government. She told me about Evo Morales, an indigenous coca farmer with no education who rose to lead the MAS (the Spanish name translates as Movement Towards Socialism), which was more a coalition of indigenous peasant organizations than it was a party, and of the powerful social organizations that made Bolivia one of the most politically active places on earth. By the time we arrived in Petra, I knew that Bolivia would be an important destination in my exploration of new politics.

As I was planning to work on a book in part about Latin America, I decided to continue my study of Spanish through intensive learning in a Spanish-speaking country. Why not Bolivia? What is happening in Bolivia is without precedent in modern history. It is a profoundly democratic revolution in which an oppressed and marginalized majority is taking charge. There are similarities with the victory of the African National Congress (ANC) in South Africa.

A deeply racist society, Bolivia had just elected an indigenous-led government, which was attempting, with some success so far, to implement policies based on indigenous practices and values. Little attention had been given to Bolivia—not only in the global media but even within the writings of the Left. When I started to look for information in 2006, the only written material I could find about Bolivia was decades old.

For the first two weeks I was there, I attended a Spanish-language school in Cochabamba. I was amazed at how political all my teachers were and how interested they were in discussing the Morales government and the hope they felt at its election. The other amazing thing about Bolivia is how untouched it seems to be by Western corporations and culture. In Cochabamba there wasn't a single McDonald's or KFC. Perhaps it's the isolation of the mountainous country or its turbulent political history or its poverty, but, with the exception of the largest city, Santa Cruz, going to Bolivia is like stepping back in time—but to a time I never knew existed. The walls at the language school were posted with stories of Quechua and Aymara (the major indigenous nations in Bolivia) heroes and heroines. The streets are full of indigenous women wearing bowler hats and native garb. Each of the thirty-four different indigenous communities in Bolivia wears distinctive clothing and hats. I never got an explanation for the bowler hats or how the women keep them on their heads in the windy climate, but it is a striking sight, especially on the head of a tiny woman wearing a very wide typical skirt and colourful shirt and jacket.

Two weeks later, Susan Harvie arrived to be my guide and interpreter and to facilitate my meetings in La Paz with Evo Morales and many of his ministers. My trip to La Paz was a revelation.

One of the most amazing signs of change is the number of campesinos (peasants) who have travelled in open trucks from their villages to La Paz to meet with their ministers. As I was waiting for someone outside the office of a government minister, I started a conversation with a young man who asked why I was interested in Bolivia. "I am interested in democracy," I responded, "and I think this is a very important experiment in democracy."

"Yes, we know a lot about democracy here in Bolivia," he said. "The problem is that our governments haven't understood it. We are hoping this one will be different." So far, it looks like this one is very different.

Rooted in centuries-old traditions of communitarian socialism, reciprocity, and a oneness with the earth, and combined with decades of radical and militant trade union and indigenous struggles, the Movement Towards Socialism (MAS) came to power in December 2005. Evo, as everyone here calls him, is not only the second indigenous leader in the Americas in more than five hundred years, but he is also a campesino and leader of the *cocaleros* (coca growers), one of the most militant trade unions in the country. Morales explained to me that the Bolivian indigenous organizations made a commitment at the Continental Indigenous Summit, held in November 1992 to mark the quincentennial of Christopher Columbus's voyage, to move from resistance to the taking of power. The MAS led by Morales is not a political party in the classical sense. It is what people here call a political instrument of the social organizations. All the indigenous campesino organizations came together and formed a political organization that could contest elections. While these organizations started the MAS, they were joined by most of the trade unions and neighbourhood organizations as well as various elements of the middle class, including intellectuals and elements of the urban Left.

Nonetheless, Morales's power is in the tremendous support he has from an amazingly well-organized and mobilized indigenous campesino movement. In the few weeks I was there, I attended two major demonstrations at which Evo spoke to thousands of peasants. The first one was a response to the Senate (which the MAS does not control*), which was holding up their agrarian reform. The other was the opening of the Constituent Assembly in Sucre, the ancient capital of Bolivia. At the nationally televised ceremony installing the Constituent Assembly on Bolivian Independence Day, August 6, Evo told the *Assembleistas* that they held ultimate power in the country, "more power than Evo Morales, more power than Parliament," and that they had a great responsibility to continue the progress created by the social movements. Of course, not everyone in the assembly supports the MAS, and the right wing, which has become much stronger and better organized in the last year, has successfully used the assembly to hold up various important changes sought by the MAS.

The assembly is not only symbolic of a refounding of the country with the indigenous majority finally in government but it promises to take some fundamental measures to change the economy as well as the

---

*Like most South American countries, Bolivia is structured like the United States, with a congress and an elected senate, an independent judiciary, and a president, with a separation of powers.

structure of the state. Since my visit, the often racist opposition has done everything possible to block these changes. From thugs to procedural wrangling to referendums on autonomy for the regions, the Right in Bolivia, supported by the United States, has thrown every roadblock short of a coup into the path of the peaceful revolution begun with Evo's election. At the time of this writing, they have not yet succeeded.

When right-wing thugs started attacking MAS Constituent Assembly members in the fall of 2007, instead of sending in the army, Evo called on the social organizations to mobilize, and they responded in their masses, backing off the violent opposition through their greater numbers. This is a peaceful revolution, the likes of which we have never really seen before. So far they have resisted violence themselves, even though they control the instruments of state violence, the army and the police. Understanding that there will be extreme opposition to this deep a transformation, the leadership of the MAS relies on the strength of an organized populace rather than the armed might of the state. On the other hand, they reject the idea that change can be gradual, and employ the same instruments used by the neo-liberal state.

Thus, like Hugo Chavez, they reject both the old revolutionary strategy of armed revolution, best represented in the person of Che Guevara, who was killed in Bolivia, and the social democratic strategy of change from within. For Morales, taking government does not mean taking power. Power, for those who have never had it, must be built from the bottom up, non-violently but not naively. There will be confrontation, but large numbers of people can resist it and turn it around.

A series of referendums on autonomy in the wealthier eastern provinces has been one way the Right has attempted to stall progress on Evo's reforms. Santa Cruz, the centre of opposition to the MAS— and the richest province—won its referendum for autonomy but the autonomy referendums lost in other provinces. To try to overcome the standoff with the right-wing prefects (as Bolivian governors or premiers are known), Evo accepted a referendum on his leadership. In July 2008, he won by 67 percent, including a much higher vote in Santa Cruz than he got during his election—but so did some of the right-wing prefects. At the time of writing, he has successfully negotiated an agreement with them to hold a referendum on a new constitution, developed by the assembly. Evo is using the instruments of democracy to stand up to the powerful forces that seek to prevent the changes that he seeks.

DESPITE HIS VILIFICATION in the mainstream media, Hugo Chavez is also using the instruments of democracy to back off opposition to his twenty-first-century socialism. When right-wing forces attempted a coup against him in 2002, going so far as to take over the palace and place him in custody, the people responded. One million strong, they surrounded the palace and demanded the return of their democratically elected leader. The palace guard, always loyal to Chavez, took back the palace once they saw the popular support. When Chavez came back to the palace, he asked for calm and no reprisals.* It was an extraordinary show of a kind of leadership that seeks a transformation of society rather than a complete destruction of the old to make way for the new.

While Chavez and Morales are great allies, they are not the same as leaders, sharing some strategies but differing on others. Both rely on the mobilization of the poor to maintain their power. Both are using the idea of new constitutions to create a new kind of society. Evo refers to it as refounding a non-colonial, non-neo-liberal state and is trying to use a constituent assembly as an instrument for change. Moreover, in Bolivia, it is the social organizations, not the individual leaders, who have the real power. As one Bolivian activist told me: "To

---

*For an in-depth look at this failed coup, see the Irish documentary *The Revolution Will Not Be Televised*.

us, power is a responsibility, not a privilege." It is a very different model than we are used to.

Despite well-organized and sometimes violent opposition, both Chavez and Morales have maintained and deepened democratic processes to make the changes they seek. When Chavez became impatient and proposed amendments to the constitution to give him more power as president, the people who so strongly supported him against the coup—and in his project of twenty-first-century social-ism—abstained.

Hilary Wainwright observed the vote. In her diary, she wrote:

> In the bus we listened to Chavez, humble and confident at the same time. The "people have spoken," he said, noting the way the result strengthened the legitimacy of Venezuela's democratic institutions. The constitutional proposals were defeated, he accepted. "Por ahora," he added, echoing a resonant phrase, "for now," that he'd used at an earlier moment of defeat that was also a precursor of victory: in a broadcast following the failed military coup he had led in 1992 against the reactionary oligarchs of the corrupt Venezuelan state.

Ironically, the defeat of the referendum illustrated in the strongest possible way the depth of the democracy that Chavez is building, contrary to the attacks against him. Some of the most important intel-lectuals in Venezuela, while supportive of most of Chavez's policies and process of reform, were, according to Wainwright, "critical of the degree to which the reforms centralized power in the hands of the president and treat popular power as part of the state rather than a source of autonomous power over the state." Chavez lost the referen-dum and, one hopes, drew the lessons.

AN IMPORTANT DIFFERENCE between Morales and Chavez is style. Chavez is an old-style *cadillo* (strong man) leader. Morales, on the other hand, is soft-spoken and often admits his lack of knowledge about things. In every speech I've heard him give, he tells about how he learned something—always with a twinkle in his eye. To me, he said, "I have learned that you cannot change a country in six months." It is an interesting difference from previous generations of left-wing leaders that as much as Chavez and Morales are deeply allied, they disagree on some fundamental questions. For example, Chavez calls his ideas "a Bolivarian revolution," or "Bolivarian socialism," referring to the great South American independence fighter Simon Bolivar. Introducing Chavez to a rally in Cochabamba, Morales said with a wry smile that Bolivar was a great man, but he didn't do much for the indigenous peoples. This ability to work closely together and be allies but disagree fundamentally on certain issues is another feature of the new politics. The sectarianism of much of the Left of my generation seems to be withering away.

But Hugo Chavez, and Evo Morales also, surprisingly, share something with Barack Obama. All three give their people a tremendous amount of hope. Giving people hope is an essential qualification for being a progressive leader in the twenty-first century. All three are also important symbols for their people, especially Morales.

During my first visit to Bolivia, we stopped on the road from La Paz to Cochabamba at the point of highest elevation, and three little children came to greet us. The older brother was about eight, his sisters, six and three. They were beautiful, and, like all tourists, I wanted a photo. "No photo," the brother said firmly. Susan Harvie, who was travelling with me as interpreter and friend, thought he wanted money, so she offered some. "No photo," he insisted.

"What would you like, then?" she asked him.

"A notebook," he replied.

Here we were, gringo tourists asking this peasant child what he would like from us, and what he wanted was a notebook so he could go to school. Everyone in Bolivia to whom we told that story, from cabinet ministers to union leaders, responded with tears. Even the poorest peasant children living on a mountaintop now believe that they can do whatever they want. "Evo gives us hope," one young teacher in Cochabamba told me. "We have never had hope before."

Could it be that the ancient Andean philosophies and values could provide us with some of that hope by providing a framework that could save the earth and save humanity? Evo thinks so.

> The indigenous communities have historically lived in community, in collectivity, in harmony not only with each other as human beings but with mother earth and nature, and we have to recover that. If we think about life as equality and justice, if we think of humanity, the model of the West, industrialization and neo-liberalism is destroying the planet earth, which for me is the great Pachamama [Mother Earth]. The model that concentrates capital in the hands of the few, this neo-liberal model, this capitalist model, is destroying the planet earth. And it's heading towards destroying humanity. And from Bolivia we can make a modest contribution to defend life, to save humanity. That's our responsibility.

Though inspiring hope is the first step to change, hope alone is not enough. What is extraordinary about Bolivia is that it is combining indigenous ideas and a decades-long tradition of democratic and disciplined social organization and struggle with the best of modern political ideas. Many of the thinkers cited in this book believe that what we need in this crisis is a combination of the best of ancient and modern knowledge.

Legendary Peruvian indigenous leader Hugo Blanco put it this way in a speech he gave in Toronto in 2007:

> European religion believes in a superior spirit who created nature to be in service of man. Our culture is completely different. For our culture, we are children of that nature. It's not that nature was created for us in our service, but we're children of nature and we have to live in harmony in her bosom. And in her

bosom we live in harmony with the plants that do us the favour of feeding us, with other plants as well that may not feed us but indicate to us whether the harvest will be good or bad, other plants that do us the favour of healing us, and in this way, the solidarity extends to all of nature. There is worshipping towards water, towards the sun, towards the river. The other characteristic of our culture is collectivity.

Filemon Escobar, a former leader of the Bolivia's miners, explains,

The happiness of Aymara or Quechua members of the community depends on everybody having [what they need]. Then there is happiness in the community.... In Western society, to "have" means that you can command everybody, like Bill Gates. In communitarian societies the "to be" has more importance than the "to have." As long as the members of the community, the people who live with you, have enough to eat, then you are fine. It's the human being who has value. So that the economy of reciprocity is first of all an economy of solidarity and it has an internal mechanism, which is extraordinary and which returns you to human values. And what do these human values consist of? Reciprocity and redistribution. And what does this consist of? In giving, receiving, and returning. So the economy of reciprocity is not an economy of accumulation. The economy of reciprocity benefits all the members of the community. And in that sense this economy recovers the human values that have been lost by the Western economy.

To symbolize these values, Evo cut his own salary and the salaries of all elected officials and government managers by 50 percent, from 10,000 Boliviano a month to 5000. He explained that, when he was a campesino, he had lived on 1000 Boliviano (US$125) a month, so he didn't know why he and other government officials couldn't live on 5000. The money saved hired three thousand new teachers. There were other initiatives early in his mandate. In his first six months he increased the minimum wage by 50 percent, launched a massive literacy campaign (with Cuba's help), and broadened free health care. He also: opposed the Free Trade Area of the Americas and started negotiations to join ALBA (the Spanish acronym for the Bolivarian Alternative for the People of Our America), an alternative trade agreement signed by Cuba and Venezuela; began the mechanized agricultural reform, which included providing hundreds of tractors to farm communities that did not have them; made changes to laws so that women could own land; and effected a redistribution of non-productive land to landless peasants. Perhaps most importantly, he announced that Bolivia would be nationalizing foreign gas and oil holdings in the country. On May 1, 2006, Evo announced that foreign companies would have six months to renegotiate their contracts or leave the country. In the true spirit of Andean reciprocity, the older wells are being taxed at 82 percent, exactly the same percentage the companies took for so many years and are now being forced to return. All the companies accepted the deal, and, for the first time in history, and as the MAS promised in the election, the Bolivian people are actually benefiting from the riches that lie under their land. Before the nationalization, the Bolivian people, through their government, received $3 million a year from hydrocarbons. Today, the figure is $2 billion, permitting important improvements to the national economy.

Political ideas emanating from Andean indigenous philosophy present a polar opposite to the ideas of neo-liberalism, but they are also quite different from many of the ideas of the traditional Left. The focus of most of these indigenous movements is on pluralism and a multi-ethnic or multinational state. This idea, it is interesting to note, is also reflected in global movements around the world in which not just a respect for differences, but a real celebration of them, is part of the movement.

In Bolivia, they are trying to create a country without any one group or culture dominating. This is complex work and involves questions of autonomy and decentralization in a country with thirty-four indigenous groups claiming cultural—and in some cases land—rights. David Choquehuanca, the foreign minister, explained to me:

> In [representative] democracy, you have the concept of submission of the minority to the majority. But submission is not to live well. And that's why we make our decisions by consensus and not by democracy. And to arrive at consensus, we have a process that includes up to five stages to arrive at equilibrium that does not exclude anybody. And for that reason we [the indigenous peoples] use the *Wiphala* [flag], made out of little squares. The little squares say that all of us are the same size. That nobody is either superior or inferior. And more than that, it says that all of us have to participate. A *Wiphala* cannot be without even one little square. And in addition, it's square. That means that we are looking for a society that's balanced and equal.

Here it is very difficult to understand how such principles can work in the modern world, but Escobar thinks that it is the only way things can work. He points to the Middle East as an example of what happens when you polarize instead of respecting that opposites can co-exist in balance. No one should be permitted to exploit, he says, but capitalism can co-exist with Andean reciprocity and communitarianism.

When it comes to relations with the United States, however, the strategy sounds very naive. David Choquehuanca said,

> We want to get along well with all countries. We want to construct a brotherhood of nations with other neighbours and beyond that. There's an Aymara word, *Latama*, that signifies the great family. All human beings belong to the great family. And there's another principle, which is the *Tumpa*. *Tumpa* signifies

the social control that must exist between all of us. Now the social control that must exist between all of us doesn't exist. It doesn't exist.

They've divided us with anthems and flags. The great family is dispersed, we're divided, we're fighting. We can't go on like this. We must have good relations. We need positive relations. We need constructive relations with the United States. We're in a process of change. We want them to understand us.

When I asked if they had had a response yet from the United States, he answered, "It's only recently that we've started. It's been five hundred years of disorder. So we're not going to recover that fast.... It's only been six months. I think the world will understand. And we need in this first stage the cooperation of the world."

The reality of relations with the United States is quite different, and in the face of right-wing violence after the referendums of 2008, Evo expelled the U.S. ambassador for supporting what he called an attempted coup. Speaking to the United Nations in September 2008, Evo said, "Why did we expel the U.S. embassy? Latin America rejected this civil coup, but the government of the U.S. did not denounce this terrorism. In Bolivia, right-wing groups are setting fire to gas, but the government of the U.S. does not condemn these acts of terrorism. I would like to hear the representatives of the U.S. denounce these acts of terrorism, but they know they are their allies, so why would they condemn them?"

The challenges are formidable, but so are the commitment, determination, and spirit of the people. For more than five hundred years they have waited for this moment, and now it is theirs.

While Evo Morales talks about the coming to power of the indigenous majority as a five-hundred-year struggle, he explains the key moments in the process took place only over the last twenty years. "After they imposed the neo-liberal model, the battle was the campesino indigenous movement against this neo-liberal model. And the fight can be summed up in two ways: for power and territory. We needed to gain political power in order to recover the territory, including all natural resources."

And there have been massive and successful struggles against various aspects of neo-liberalism since the early 1990s: from the famous water wars against the privatization of water in Cochabamba in 1992, to the fight, led by Morales, to protect the traditional growing of coca against the United States' attempts to eradicate it, to the brutal gas wars of 2003, where people in the El Alto just outside La Paz fought the government of the time to stop the sell-off of natural gas and won—at the cost of more than seventy dead and two hundred wounded.

While Bolivia is unique, the Andean ideas of society and change and their tradition of social organization seem to me to have a strong resonance in creating the paths that we need to follow today to achieve greater equality and justice—as well as ensure the survival of the planet. Moreover, the rise of the MAS is the most visible of the uprisings of many groups of indigenous peoples across Latin America, from the Zapatistas in Mexico to the Mapuche in Chile.

ANIBAL QUIJANO, a highly respected Peruvian intellectual, says that the "indigenous problem became the knot not yet untied that has bound and restrained the historical development of Latin America" because of how central the marginalization and oppression of indigenous peoples on the one hand, and their assimilation on the other, have been to the continent. In his view, the "the current 'indigenous movement' is the clearest sign that the coloniality of power is in the most serious of its crises since its establishment five hundred years ago."*

My Aboriginal friends in Canada have been talking for a long time about decolonization being central to any strategy for social justice

---

*Anibal Quijano, "The Challenge of the 'Indigenous Movement' in Latin America," *Socialism and Democracy* 19:3 (November 2005).

and equality, but it took my trip to Bolivia to really understand what they mean. As the descendants of settlers on this land, especially because most of us descend from immigrants who did not directly participate in that colonization, it is difficult to appreciate the centrality of colonialism to our societies. As the young U.S. Aboriginal leader Evon Peter points out, it is only when we start to understand its impact in excluding the knowledge and contributions of those whom it excluded, and begin to reverse it in our own minds, as well as in our governing structures, that we will find a path to equality and social justice.

4

UBUNTU

We Are People through Other People

ONE OF THE MOST IMPRESSIVE THINGS about Bolivia is the sense of community. I was often told that the deepest-held value among indigenous people in Bolivia is "I cannot be happy unless everyone in my community has what they need." The individual's happiness is completely tied to the community's well-being. We can find this idea in all cultures, from ancient Greece to modern South Africa. It is what the South Africans call *Ubuntu*: "We are people through other people."

Nelson Mandela says that what connects us as people is greater than what divides us. By working together we can achieve more than by dividing ourselves from one another through differences, whether political or cultural. This powerful notion exists in its strongest form among the most marginalized people on earth, such as the Dalits of India or among many indigenous nations of the Americas.

That we can learn from the experiences of these impoverished communities is an important element of the new movements. Paying heed to old ways of thinking and being may be central to re-establishing equilibrium with Mother Earth. It's not that we will all move back to living on the land in log cabins or teepees, but rather that we practise a way of being that is not based on dominating nature or one another, a notion of living well, as the Bolivians call it, rather than living better.

One of the most destructive elements of neo-liberalism is the way that sense of community is being destroyed, especially in large urban centres. Margaret Thatcher said, "There is no society, only individuals and families." We are encouraged to believe that we have to take care of ourselves and our families first and foremost, and not worry about our neighbours, friends, and co-workers. Individualism, not community, is what is valued in Western culture. So one of the ways every single person reading this book can help to create a better world is to contribute to building a sense of community in their neighbourhood and in their city or town.

The astonishing popularity of Barack Obama is due in part to his ability to give the people of the United States a sense of community again. Tens of thousands gathered during the primaries and the election campaign not only to hear him speak but also to feel their connection to others. Obama has what the greatest of movement leaders have: an ability to give people a sense of their collective power.

When Martin Luther King said, "I have a dream," it was the dream of the millions of African Americans who heard his words. Obama has the same ability to inspire through giving people a sense that they can do better together. In one of the most important speeches of the campaign, he said,

> Unity is the great need of the hour—the great need of this hour. Not because it sounds pleasant or because it makes us feel good, but because it's the only way we can overcome the essential deficit that exists in this country.
>
> I'm not talking about a budget deficit. I'm not talking about a trade deficit. I'm not talking about a deficit of good ideas or new plans. I'm talking about a moral deficit. I'm talking about an empathy deficit. I'm talking about an inability to recognize ourselves in one another; to understand that we are our brother's

keeper; we are our sister's keeper; that, in the words of Dr. King, we are all tied together in a single garment of destiny.

To recognize ourselves in one another is the key idea here. George W. Bush, Stephen Harper, and their ilk encourage us to see danger in others. Obama is encouraging us to see ourselves. This is also the core idea of Buddhism and, as Obama points out, of Christianity. In his book *The Left Hand of God: Taking Our Country Back from the Religious Right*, Rabbi Michael Lerner points out that most of the Bible talks about a loving, compassionate God. It is only a small part of the Old Testament that features the angry, vengeful God that is called up by the religious right.

Of course, we know that hatred and the inability to see ourselves in one another is not confined to religions, and that tens of millions of people were killed in the twentieth century by wars between national states with imperialist agendas. But at the moment, some of the most terrible acts on earth are being carried out in the name of religion, from the Israeli occupation of Palestine to the terrorist acts of desperate fighters for liberation from these occupations. In parts of the Middle East and in the United States, a fundamentalist form of religion offers a sense of belonging based on fury at the Other. This is the most visible form of religion in the world, from the Christian fundamentalism of George W. Bush to the Jewish fundamentalism of Israeli settlers in Palestinian lands to the Muslim fundamentalism of the Taliban and Al Qaeda. And some of the worst atrocities in history were executed in the name of religion, such as the Crusades and the stealing of children from Aboriginal communities to indoctrinate (and often abuse) them in church-run residential schools in Canada.

Yet there is a side to most ancient religious teachings that encourages us to find common cause and common interest with other humans and, in the case of Buddhism and indigenous spirituality, with all creatures on the earth and Mother Earth herself. And, despite the contradictions, this side of religion has allowed many oppressed peoples to find refuge in the church, the synagogue, or the mosque.

I first noticed Rabbi Lerner's group, Tikkun, because of their consistent criticism of Israeli treatment of the Palestinians. It is so rare to see practising Jews step outside the closed circle of the Jewish community when it comes to blind support for Israel's policies. Then I heard that Lerner had initiated a group called the Network of Spiritual Progressives in an attempt to take back religion from the Right. So, when he wrote his book, I invited him to Toronto to speak about it. At the time—the spring of 2006—he identified his priorities as challenging the religious Right and the secularist Left. When I caught up to him two years later, I asked how he was doing on those two fronts. He told me:

> We have been quite successful in spreading an understanding that religion cannot be reduced to fundamentalist or right-wing interpretation and that fundamentalists do not speak for the majority of religious people.
>
> There is a growing understanding in the Western world that there is a huge difference in approaches to interpretation of holy texts. On some readings, those texts are understood as justifying or commanding violence and demonizing people who don't agree with your religion. But there is another tradition of interpretation, often equally pervasive in the same religious communities, which interprets the texts in ways that lead the members of that religious community to join or even to lead the fight for social justice, equality, and ecological sanity. This latter approach sees God as a force for healing and transformation of the world (in Hebrew, we call it "tikkun," which is why I named my interfaith magazine *TIKKUN*) and as a voice for love and even for radical redistribution of wealth. And this way of hearing God's voice, which I call "the left hand of God," is growing in strength. We are seeing this more love-oriented approach grow in power and influence in the past few years, in Islam, Judaism, and Christianity. We've made lots of progress on that front.

We've been less successful in challenging the secularist fundamentalism and their deep religio-phobia and certainty that anyone who believes in God must either be psychologically damaged or stupid. This hyper-empiricism is itself a religious view, without any greater foundation than any other religious view. It is no excuse to say, "Well, that's only our guiding principle or our definition of rationality" because there is no reason to put that on a higher level of rationality than the views that say, "Well, belief in God is our guiding principle or definition of rationality." Yet the secularists are so arrogantly certain they are right and anyone who disagrees with them deranged that they are unwilling to be either compassionate or tolerant. They still retain the view that anyone who is spiritual or religious is a flake or psychologically underdeveloped.

Of course, I understand it to the extent that they identify religion with the racism and sexism and homophobia that exists in some corners of the Evangelical and fundamentalist worlds. But to make that identification, secular progressives have to intentionally shut out those of us who are progressive and spiritual, to ignore the powerful role played by religious progressives like Martin Luther King and Mahatma Gandhi.*

American prison and environmental activist Van Jones explains the different approaches to religion that fall on race lines:

One of the big problems that we have in the United States is that there are two kinds of progressives: there are the progressives who fled stifling, awful, patriarchal, abusive religious institutions to the freedom of sex, drugs, and rock-and-roll. And then you have those who fled the horror of drugs and the horrible things that are going on in certain communities, to the safety and the solace of houses of worship. As an African-American

---

*You can read more at www.spiritualprogressives.org.

man, the one place I know I can go where I'll be welcome, where I'll be respected, where I'll feel safe, where I'll feel at home, is a black church. It's the wall outside the church, the community outside the church, that is threatening, that is dangerous. That's where my peril lies. And so when you have people who have had the opposite experience, and their main experience with houses of worship has been authoritarian, oppressive, sexist, homophobic, their internal triggers are very finely tuned to be rabidly secular. I think that our opportunity is to find a way back into some harmony together. Those of us who are people of faith need to be very respectful and understanding that these institutionalized religions have been abusive, have hurt people, have created excuses for war and genocide.*

There is probably more discussion about religion and politics in the Muslim communities around the world than anywhere else. Abdul-Rehman Malik is a Muslim activist whom I first met when we were both speaking at the anti-Iraq War demonstration in Toronto in February 2003. He now works in London and is actively defining a new kind of Muslim political activism. In an interview, he explains,

> Most radical politics within a Muslim Islamic frame have been connected to political Islam, that is, a movement in varying degrees that believes the best way to encapsulate the politics that comes out of the religious message of Islam is the establishment of some sort of Islamic state. In varying degrees, this is what all political Islamic movements share.
>
> I am thinking of a radical politics that does indeed come out of our faith. Maybe it's a Muslim liberation theology, I'm not entirely sure. I believe our religion has a very radical social agenda—the alleviation of poverty, of taking care of those who

---

*In an interview with director Velcrow Ripper for his film *Fierce Light: When Spirit Meets Action* (2008).

are oppressed, of social justice in the most broad and profound-est way—I believe that is what Islam calls us to.

And I believe that, in a way, what we need now is a politics away from political Islam. A radical politics that comes from Islam as its inspiration, but does not lead us to an Islamic state. That instead becomes a tool, a vehicle rather, a religious discourse that inspires social action, very, very profound action.

I GAVE UP ON THE JEWISH RELIGION when I was about sixteen. It was much too patriarchal, and I didn't see the point in fighting that losing battle. Caught up in the secular soul force* of the 1960s, I never felt a need for another kind of spirituality. Then, when I became a Marxist, I bought the idea that "religion is the opiate of the people." It is this idea that created what Lerner calls a *fundamentalist secularism* among the Left. But in today's consumer-obsessed world, where old ways are being shredded by technology and fear of terror and there is no sense of meaning beyond the next paycheque, many are turning to spirituality for some sense of meaning and belonging. It is consumerism that is the opiate of the people in the Global North.

Spirituality, from yoga to forms of Buddhism, has been gaining ground in the Global North since the 1960s, when the Beatles looked for their gurus in India. At the time, I rejected that form of spiritual-ity as self-absorbed and romantic. The idea that changing the consciousness of every person, one at a time, will change the world seemed like wishful thinking that permitted too many people to accept injustice. Such forms of New Age spirituality continue to be popular, spread by figures such as Oprah Winfrey and distorted in a neo-liberal direction through fads such as the book and film *The Secret*.

What has changed since the 1960s is that a significant number of people who have turned to spirituality for meaning are realizing they

---

*Soul force was the name of Ghandi's rules for non-violent resistance, which were followed by the U.S. civil rights movement.

must act in the world to make it a better place. Not the least of this action is to take on the fundamentalists of every stripe who have turned religion into a weapon against the Other.

It must be said that while religion has historically played an aggressive and dominating role in society, there has always been the progressive side, such as the civil rights movement in the United States and liberation theology in South America. A progressive interpretation of religion never requires everyone to believe, and we should be as liberal in secular activism as well. I may not believe, but that doesn't prevent me from making common cause with those who do and recognizing their contribution to this massive project to save humanity and the planet from the scourge of greed, exploitation, and domination.

I have noticed that spiritual activists, from Quakers to Buddhists, understand a lot about changing human behaviour, working co-operatively, and maintaining their activism. Certainly the Quakers of the women's movement, such as Professor Ursula Franklin of the University of Toronto, have been some of the wisest, bravest, and most committed feminists I know.

Another person who bases her activism in her spirituality is a wonderful woman who calls herself Starhawk. Legendary in the anti-globalization movement, Starhawk participated in the front lines of every summit protest from Seattle to Genoa, organizing direct action and dance rituals and writing some of the most interesting descriptions and analyses of anti-globalization protests. I was very impressed with her book *Webs of Power: Notes from the Global Uprising*, so I attended a spirituality conference in Toronto a couple of years ago because she was a speaker. On the first day, I noticed her wandering around during the break. Since no one was talking to her, I introduced myself. She knew who I was as well, and we became instant friends. I asked her about the relationship between activism and spirituality:

> My politics have always been linked to my spirituality to the understanding that the Earth is alive and sacred and we're all a

part of that. So there's a way in which that lends itself more to organizing things like demonstrations and protests than just sitting in policy meetings.

But for me part of it is also about empowerment, it's about everyone finding that inner power and their own ability to act, but also putting it together with other people.... So there's a process of personal empowerment and healing that goes with what many people think of as spirituality. And I think it's clearly very important, but it doesn't stop there.

It's also about having a strategic understanding of power and understanding that oppressive power always rests on certain supports. One support is the willingness of people to comply with it. One support might be the resources it can commandeer. One support might be the level of violence it can bring to bear against people. And then you look at those supports and say, Okay, where do we have power in this? How can we withdraw our consent, how can we not comply with this system? And when enough people do that, it's like you pull one leg out from under the table, and the table falls.

I challenged this view, saying that one of my criticisms of this approach is that enough people never do it. It's always a minority that is conscious enough to withdraw consent or withdraw support. She had an answer:

I would say, sometimes enough people do it. The Soviet Union, I think that was the reason it fell, ultimately. But the other part of it is withdrawing consent in a way that directly interferes with the operation of the systems, that raises its costs of operating—its economic costs, its political costs, its social costs—that de-legitimizes it in the eyes of a larger public, even beyond that little minority. That minority can do things, you know, can create crises—like in Seattle or other places—that have larger reverberations.

In earlier years, when I defined my politics in narrower ways, I would have discounted Starhawk's approach as unrealistic and unworkable, but now I realize there are many paths to change, and pulling the legs out one at a time or building an alternative one leg at time are certainly important ones. Today, when change is difficult at a national or international level, community-based change is sometimes the most effective way to go.

Starhawk pointed to another strength of people who root their activism in spirituality:

> The other way is my sense of having a deep connection with what, for me, is the great underlying force of creativity in the universe—what I call the Goddess—and having a kind of practice that helps me keep an open channel to that. And having a practice that also helps me when I need healing or when I need renewal, or just need to restore my own energy. I have ways of doing it. And I think also spirituality helps you keep a longer perspective that everything isn't all cut-and-dried, cause-and-effect, and just because you aren't necessarily seeing the immediate effect doesn't mean you aren't having an effect, and that sometimes you have to do the right thing, even if you aren't having an effect, just because it's right, not necessarily because you're going to win with it.

Needless to say, Starhawk was not talking about Judaism or Christianity. She is a witch. I didn't mention that point previously because I thought readers might discount what she has to say—as I might have a few years ago. It turns out witches don't fly around on brooms (although she assures me she's working on it), but they do practise a religion rooted in women's traditional knowledge and oneness with the earth. Later, I stayed at her very warm, witchy, and beautiful house in the Mission district of San Francisco and found her and her friends to be delightful and down-to-earth.

Starhawk has what I would call *the long view*. I have always had it because of my youth spent as a Trotskyist: When you are on the political margins of society, you learn to have a long view about change. While I have given up a lot of what I learned in those early days, the understanding that change is unpredictable and that fundamental change takes a long time has stood me in good stead ever since.

Another element of the wisdom of spiritual people that I believe is important for the transformations that lie ahead is their understanding of love. Not that the political side lacks love: Che Guevara famously said, "At the risk of seeming ridiculous, let me say that the true revolutionary is guided by great feelings of love." But one doesn't see that slogan on T-shirts or posters as much as *"Hasta la victoria, siempre!"**

As I grow older, I find I am less governed by feelings of anger in my activism and more governed by feelings of empathy and compassion. Sometimes when I see video clips of myself during the pro-choice struggle of the 1980s in Canada, where I was a spokesperson for the movement in a highly polarized and ultimately very successful campaign, I feel a little frightened by my intensity. At the time, I was a very angry person, and it was great that I was able to channel that anger into a struggle that probably needed it. Such intensity was necessary in order to stand up to the powerful forces arrayed against us. The anti-abortion groups can be vicious. We were dealing with death threats, occasional violence, and more-than-occasional attempts to intimidate us—from nasty calls to organizing against me in my workplace. It's hard to imagine how loving my enemy would have done any good at all.

But the problem with intense polarization is that we get stuck in our position, and the other side in theirs, and nothing ever changes. It is a win–lose scenario (and, of course, for women, it was a lot better to win the battle for legal abortion than to lose it). But on many

---

*This was above Che's signature in his last letter to Fidel Castro. It means "Until the victory always."

issues, dialogue works better. What's worse is that this kind of intense polarization excludes everyone but the converted on each side. The more politics is about choosing sides, the fewer people want to be involved. It might work for sports, but when it comes to political issues, it excludes all but the most committed. In addition, of course, such intense polarization can and does lead to violence.

In the essay "Truth or Dare," published in *Webs of Power*, Starhawk says, "We rebel to save our lives. Rebellion is the desperate assertion of our value in the face of all that attacks it, the cry of refusal in the face of control." She explains, "When we rebel without challenging the framework of reality the system has constructed, we remain trapped. Our choices are predetermined for us."

Anger and rebellion are necessary elements of resisting an unjust system, but if we get stuck in anger, then we are trapped. Polarization is the death of creativity and, in a time like this when we need maximum creativity and new approaches to new problems, polarization can be counterproductive.

Ideology is part of the problem. Whether religious or political, ideology traps us in a dichotomy of right and wrong. If we suggest that something is happening that isn't explained by our ideology, our religion, or our political party, then we risk being driven out. Pioneer feminist Ursula Franklin once defined patriarchy as "Do what I say, or else." I think that's the extreme form; in its more everyday form, I think patriarchy is "I am right and you are wrong." And that's how politics is done in our society, whether at the parliamentary level or at the movement level.

Here's what Van Jones has to say about anger:

> The question that any activist has to ask him or herself is fundamental. Am I going to burn diesel fuel or solar power—inside? So much activism is fuelled by anger, by alienation, by frustration, and so we have a politics of confrontation, a politics of accusation. And that can take you so far. I would submit that, just like dirty fuel, there are serious downsides and limitations. I

think we need to be burning solar, in other words, not a politics of confrontation so much; although that sometimes is important, but a politics of confession, a politics of invitation, a politics that says, these problems that my community is facing are so severe and they're an indicator for your community's problems as well, and for your grandchildren's problem—let's work together to solve them.

PART OF MY LEARNING about this more compassionate approach came from the Hollyhock Centre, which is also where I first met Van Jones.

In the spring of 2004, I was invited to speak at an environmental leadership workshop at Hollyhock, an educational retreat centre in British Columbia. In my usual rushed schedule, I was flying in and out the next day, but I fell in love. Cortes Island is one of the most beautiful and magical places I have ever been, and Hollyhock is a fitting retreat for the location. When filmmaker Bill Weaver asked me to stay for his gathering, Media That Matters, I was truly sorry that I couldn't.

"How about next year?" he asked, and I agreed

Media That Matters brings together about thirty media activists from the United States and Canada. While there is a theme, the participants set the agenda themselves through a system called Open Space Technology. The people I met at Media That Matters were engaged, politically aware, and committed to changing the world. Many of them were environmental activists, others focused on alternative media or media democracy, and still others were filmmakers or writers with an activist approach. Few of them identified with the political Left.

The first night, we watched a film called *The Silent Killer* by John de Graaf, which challenged the views of environmentalists on some substantive questions. People were angry but too polite to challenge him in the public showing that night. The following morning, however, one of the facilitators raised the discussion that had been taking place in the hot tub and around the site after the film. John Stauber of PR Watch was the first one to speak.

"I've known John [de Graaf] for thirty years," he said. "He is a man of tremendous integrity and commitment. He has done some great films and important work. He is a kind and thoughtful man, and I love him. But I hated this film." He then proceeded to take apart the film piece by piece. The discussion proceeded in the same tone. Support for the man, criticism of the film.

The filmmaker was able to answer his critics without defensiveness. It became a conversation about what happens when you discover facts that contradict your initial opinion when making a documentary. It was a deep and fascinating talk with no rancour, even though people were speaking about their deeply held views and beliefs.

What do these people know that I don't know? I thought. Ever since I had written *Imagine Democracy*, I had been trying to get this kind of discussion going in the various meetings and gatherings that I attended. It had been mostly an exercise in frustration, despite considerable effort, and yet here it was happening with what seemed like little effort.

I decided to challenge myself and see what I could learn there. That afternoon I went to see a showing of *Scared Sacred*, a film by Velcrow Ripper about stories of hope in what he calls "the ground zeros of the world." Earlier that day, in discussing de Graaf's film, Velcrow had commented, "A filmmaker who doesn't give a message of hope these days is being irresponsible." His film was stunning. I was so moved by it that I was speechless at the end. So I went to his workshop on spirituality.

I expected to see people sitting in a circle, holding hands and chanting "Om." Instead, there was Velcrow, with his laptop open, Googling names or organizations that people mentioned every time someone answered the question of the workshop: "What does the word *sacred* mean to you?"

I was last, and I answered, "Sacred is something that is constructed to be unquestionable." And I decided sometime later that I should stop holding my political framework as sacred. I opened my mind and my heart to new ways of seeing the world.

Velcrow and I became fast friends. At that first meeting, we talked endlessly about spirituality and politics. I noticed that every time I challenged his views, he would say, "Uh-huh" and nod his head. Then he would return a couple of days later with an argument, either a defence of his views or sometimes an acknowledgment of the point I had made. It struck me that no matter how deeply I challenged his views, he was willing to consider what I had said. He was actually listening to me. That conversation has fed this book as well as his new film, *Fierce Light: When Spirit Meets Action*.

It was at Hollyhock that I learned how to disagree kindly. Reaching people at a heart level is much more persuasive than beating them over the head with a good argument. It's true that at Hollyhock they sometimes go to the opposite extreme and silence opposition in the desire to have a positive atmosphere. The worst example of that I have ever seen was at a spiritual conference, the one in downtown Toronto where I first met Starhawk. This was the kind of spirituality that has always made me a little crazy, the "We are all one, Ommmm" kind. They didn't actually chant "Om," but they may as well have. In my workshops, when I tried to raise the inequalities in the world that pointed to the fact that, however much we all want to be one, we are very divided, a wall of silence came up around me that I would have needed dynamite to break through. I always have a metaphorical stick of dynamite in my back pocket—that comes from years of debating—but in this case I chose not to use it.

I am not saying that everyone who has a spiritual practice has a lock on how to work from a caring, inclusive place rather than an angry, dominating place. I am saying that I have learned a lot about good democratic process from people who come from a spiritual practice. While I remain skeptical of the idea that changing consciousness one person at a time will do enough to change the world, I have always understood that changing consciousness is essential to changing concrete reality. Marx argued that for the working class to rise up against their capitalist masters, they needed to overcome the false idea that their interest was the same as that of the bosses. In the women's movement, our first action was to form consciousness-raising groups, where we learned, just by talking to other women about our problems, that these problems were not unique to us. They were social problems faced by all women.

I used to think that getting involved in a movement for change, such as the pro-choice or the anti-war or a participatory strike, was the way that consciousness could change, but now I realize that there are many paths to that goal. Through these efforts we understand collective power, we feel *Ubuntu*, our connection to one another, and know that together we can overcome the odds against us. In the last decades, these struggles have too often dead-ended in defeat, leading to cynicism rather than deeper involvement. Certain kinds of spiritual practice can also bring a change in consciousness to lead to social and political change. And as I will argue throughout this book, just as in nature where biodiversity is needed for survival and growth, so it is in our human society. We need diversity on every level.

5

FEMINISM
The Personal Is Political

WHEN I BECAME PRESIDENT of the National Action Committee on the Status of Women (NAC) in 1990, I was stunned by the diversity of the five hundred member groups that formed Canada's most powerful women's organization. I couldn't believe that everyone from the Women's Temperance League to the women's committee of the Communist Party of Canada belonged to NAC.

Partly because of its unity across massive divides, the women's movement in Canada was a powerful force. Yet today, while I see as much need as ever for feminism, the women's movement in Canada, the United States, and Europe is in decline. At the same time, feminist ideas and practices are among the most influential in the new movements and struggles described in these pages. Turning the world right side up doesn't just mean that people, ideas, and practices from the Global South need to be in the forefront; it also means that women, and women's knowledge, ideas, and practices, need to be at the forefront.

One of the most surprising experiences of my political journey while researching this book was a workshop I gave in Berlin on the impact of feminism on political parties. All but one of the participants were men, most of them young men. When I asked why, the young men responded that of all the movements and political currents of my generation that had influenced them, it was feminism that had influenced them the most.

I HAVE BEEN SOME KIND OF FEMINIST as long as I can remember. Even when I was a little girl, I never accepted the restrictions people tried to place on me because of my gender. I flirted with the organized women's movement in the 1960s by participating in an underground abortion referral system at McGill University. Free love was everywhere, which to a woman meant that if you said no to an invitation for sex with a man, you weren't cool. Nevertheless, it was almost impossible for a single woman to get the birth control pill, and abortion was completely illegal. When I moved to Toronto in 1967, I participated in a few meetings of the Toronto Women's Caucus, but I couldn't relate to what I saw as an anti-male approach. So I was more drawn more to the Left than to the women's movement.

I became active in the women's movement a decade later, falling into the pro-choice movement only after I quit the small far-Left group I had worked in throughout the 1970s. As a result, I missed the stage of consciousness-raising that the movement went through and got involved at the high point of feminist mobilization in Canada in the early 1980s.

The women's movement gave me both an opportunity to use my talents in a mass public campaign and the possibility of personal liberation. As a young woman, my major activity was rebellion against whatever was expected of me, and that led me to behave as much like a man as I could. The vicious faction fights of a sectarian Left just reinforced those tendencies. It wasn't until I became active in the women's movement that I realized how much of myself I had buried beneath the macho behaviour I had taken on.

One of the reasons the women's movement is so powerful is that it has both a personal and a political impact on women. "The personal is political" wasn't just a slogan, it was a lived reality. To liberate women, we had to liberate ourselves—our minds, our bodies, and our emotions.

Consciousness-raising was one of the most important innovations of the women's liberation movement. Small groups of women would gather in someone's kitchen or living room and talk about their lives and their challenges. As young women, they were focused on relationships with men and with their own bodies. Lesbians were still mostly closeted at the time. As women talked about sex and relationships, they came to see that they all faced similar issues. A woman would talk about the problems she was having with her boyfriend and realize it wasn't just her boyfriend acting like a jerk, pretty well everyone's boyfriend was acting like a jerk. It was a social problem. Young women struggled with the men in their lives, demanding that they also do the dishes, take care of the kids, and pay attention to their partner's pleasure as well as their own. At the same time, these young women were organizing political actions around abortion, equal pay, daycare, and, somewhat later, violence against women.

Many women were already part of the youth movement, fighting against the war in Vietnam and in solidarity with the civil rights movement. It was through the discrimination they faced in that movement that they realized even the revolution wouldn't free women unless they did something in the here and now to liberate themselves. Refusing the make-the-coffee-or-run-the-Gestetner (copy machine) role became a political act. There was a handful of women leaders, such as the Students for a Democratic Society's Bernardine Dohrn and Black Power leader Angela Davis, but almost all of the youth movement's leadership was male.

Movements were very radical in those days and so were the women. The initial platform of the women's liberation movement included universal daycare, free abortion on demand, free and accessible birth control, and equal pay. The movement wanted to change gender roles completely so that there would be no difference between men and women in any sphere, at work or at home or in love. In the co-operative child-care centres of the time, boys would be clad in dresses, girls in pants. In the late 1960s or early 1970s, it was as radical to dress a little girl in pants as a boy in a dress. It is some measure of what the women's movement achieved that now it's normal for a woman to wear pants, but a man wears a dress only if he wants to be a woman or make a statement of some kind.

"The personal is political" was the slogan and the most important innovation of feminism as well as its most powerful idea. The idea of personal change going hand in hand with political change is now central to almost every new movement described in these pages.

Even today, though most women have broken out of the restrictions of my youth when I was told "women can't be doctors or lawyers," we still obsess about our bodies, our fading youth, and our ability to attract and hold a man. Of course, our continued feelings of inadequacy are not only in our heads. They are reinforced every day by the culture, by media, and often by individual men and women. But while we are changing the culture to be more egalitarian, we have to continue to work on the oppression or domination that every one of us has internalized. In our culture, the idea that one group is superior to the other is bred in the bone, and the result is both a sense of entitlement among those in the dominant group and a sense of inadequacy among those in the dominated group, whether male/female, white/black, settler/native, or straight/gay. Struggling to rid our minds of those feeling of inferiority or inadequacy was central to the women's movement, the black power movement, and the gay rights movement.

A lot of people use the term *healing* when they talk about the importance of dealing with personal issues at the same time as political ones—and it is a useful metaphor. But I believe that acting to change the world that injured us is just as important to healing as focusing on the wound. The women's movement intuitively understood this. We had to confront our own internalized oppression as well as a world that was fairly hostile to our ideas, and we did it through our connection with one another, through the movement, and through sisterhood.

Understanding relationships between the personal and the political is the genius of feminism and a major reason its influence continues to be felt, however weak the movement itself might be at the moment. The influence of feminism is present on many levels in the new movements that are emerging. It can be seen in women's leadership, in flattened structures, in consensus decision-making, and most of all in an understanding that the personal is political.

The women's movement of my generation worked hard to find new forms of organization, not always successfully. It has to be said that the more successful our demands on government, the less likely most of us were to develop these new forms of organization. Nevertheless, some of these more egalitarian structures continued and developed further as feminists became active in a wide variety of organizations, taking with them their experience and new ways of doing things. The environmental movement and the peace movement of the 1980s, for examples, practised a form of consensus politics honed in the earlier feminist groups.

Moreover, the way the feminist movement created its wide body of knowledge about women was different from the method used in existing disciplines. When I was going to university in the mid- to late-1960s, there was almost no scholarly work available about women. Women's studies and feminists in other disciplines created a massive body of work over these decades. Instead of starting from theory and interpreting reality through that theory, feminism started with the reality of women's lives and developed theory out of that reality.

There are other ways that the new movements have been influenced by feminism. The early women's movement put demands on the state, but they did not wait for the government to provide the services that women needed. Women's groups set up women's centres, telephone crisis lines, rape crisis centres, daycare centres, and women's shelters, although they got almost no government funding. Women tried to live the change we were fighting for through our relationships, our organizations, and the kinds of services we thought women needed.

But as the women's movement gained support—and therefore power and influence—it focused more and more on demanding that the state provide what was needed. Thus, it is not surprising that the rise of neo-liberalism, with its turn away from the social programs so essential to feminist organizing, resulted in the serious decline of the women's movement. Second-wave feminism* in the Global North may not be dead, but it has lost its influence and visibility.

On the other hand, global feminism is getting much stronger. At the United Nations Conference on Women in Beijing in 1995, the Quebec Federation of Women proposed a global feminist initiative called the World March of Women. In 2000, women in countries around the world marched together to demand an end to poverty and violence. In 2005, through a complicated global process of consensus, they developed a Women's Global Charter for Humanity. It's important to note that the charter was not just about women's rights but also about feminist solutions for humanity. Feminism in the Global South or among marginalized groups, such as indigenous peoples in the Global North, is never only about women. In an interview, Lorraine Guay, one of the founders of the World March of Women, explains the impact it had:

> In Latin America, Brazil, for example, the March enabled a women's movement more founded on popular movement. In the South, I found the big UN conferences were positive, as women used these events to put pressure on their governments. But in some countries it structured an elite women's movement made up of thinkers, of women in big organizations, rather than a feminism rooted in the daily life of women. In other countries they used the march as a way to advance demands they already had. We can't say the march won these gains, but that it added

---

First-wave feminism is the term academics use to refer to the movement for women to win the vote at the turn of the twentieth century. *Second-wave feminism* refers to the fight for women's equality waged by my generation of women. Young feminists today call themselves *third-wave*.

power to their demands. In other countries, the demands were accepted 100 percent. In three Asian countries, the women were able to develop the first bill on conjugal violence. In India, they were even able to put it to a first reading.

As the women's movement in North America was in decline by 1999 when the anti-globalization movement first reared its head in Seattle, most young feminists of that generation in North America and Europe worked more with mixed global justice groups than with feminist groups. As a socialist feminist, I have always understood that women's equality can never be achieved in a capitalist system that is based on entrenched inequality. However, capitalism is not the only system of domination and inequality. The interlocking systems of capitalism, patriarchy, and colonialism produce the inequalities and injustice we seek to correct. Unless we challenge all those systems of domination, we will take two steps backward for every step forward.

Some time ago I was worried that women's issues were getting lost in the anti-globalization movement, so I asked famed *No Logo* author Naomi Klein if she shared these concerns. She answered, "There is a sophisticated and complex understanding of the role that gender and race play in corporate globalization, but women's issues that fall outside that analysis get lost." At the time I didn't appreciate what she was saying. But now I see just how profoundly the critique of patriarchy has influenced the movements that have developed in the twenty-first century. It is not only that they are challenging the Type A leadership so common in patriarchal structures, it is also that they are challenging the need for specific leaders at all. Flat structures, networks rather than hierarchy, and consensus all result from a profound critique of patriarchal patterns of domination in decision-making.

Yet there is a confusing relationship between these new movements and the women's movement. The fact that women's rights were central to the U.S. argument for invading Afghanistan and later Iraq, even though Iraq had the best record on women's equality in the Middle

East, built hostility to feminism in some places. As Gita Sen of
Development Alternatives with Women for a New Era (DAWN)
argued in the article "Gender Justice and Economic Justice,"
published in the journal *Development*:

> The irony for some women is that, on the one hand, the
> supporters and promoters of a globalized world economy are
> often also the ones who support the breaking of traditional
> patriarchal orders. On the other hand, some of those who
> oppose globalization do so in the name of values and control
> systems that strongly oppress women. The challenge for women,
> therefore, is how to assert the need for both economic justice
> and gender justice in an increasingly globalized world, in which
> at the same time we witness the proliferation of diverse forms of
> moral conservatism that systematically target women's self-
> determination.

The most dramatic example of this contradiction that I've seen
came during the U.S. invasion of Afghanistan. During that time I was
a guest on a Winnipeg CBC radio phone-in show when a caller
berated me for not supporting President George W. Bush's attack on
Afghanistan. "As a feminist," he said, "you must admit that, without
the bombing, women would still be enslaved there."

We are now years into the war, and it is hard to argue that women
are better off in Afghanistan. The Revolutionary Association of the
Women of Afghanistan (RAWA), the brave organization that has
consistently fought for women's rights in Afghanistan risking considerable danger to educate girls during the Taliban regime, did not
support the U.S. invasion and hasn't seen much progress in women's
rights to this day. In Iraq, there is no question that women are much
worse off under the U.S. occupation than they were under Saddam
Hussein. During Hussein's rule, women had access to education and
good jobs, despite the terrible repression and lack of political freedom.
Iraqi feminists are proud of their history. Because of the exodus of

men during the Iran–Iraq War, Iraqi women achieved professional positions during the 1980s that would have been the envy of women in Canada at the time. In 1989, almost 11 percent of the Iraqi parliament was women, a figure higher than the British House of Commons at the time. Today, Iraqi women can barely leave their homes for fear of violence and the influence of fundamentalists who want to restrict their rights altogether. Just one statistic tells the story: In 1987, approximately 75 percent of Iraqi women were literate; however, by year-end 2000, the percentage of literate women stood at less than 25 percent.

In the meeting I had with Iraqi activists in 2006, they told me how young men had to pick up women from their homes and accompany them to the university to protect them from attack. Every time a spokesperson from one of the Iraqi feminist organizations spoke on the radio, she had to move from house to house to avoid violent attack and even death. The United States is doing nothing to deal with these issues, and there is almost no discussion of them in the context of the American occupation. The idea that the United States is supporting women's rights in Afghanistan and Iraq would be laughable if it wasn't so tragic.

In the Middle East especially, many of the most effective forces opposing the drive of the West for more and more profit (often at the expense of human life) are the most reactionary when it comes to women's rights. If progressive global movements fail to recognize the twin dangers of neo-liberalism on the one side and fundamentalism on the other, they will not address the concerns of half of humanity. It is all too easy for issues of women's equality to fall off the agenda.

In a statement published after the event in 2002, DAWN challenged the World Social Forum to take up gender issues. As the women's group says,

> A final word to other development NGOs and networks. Unfortunately, there are still far too many at global and other levels whose commitment to gender equality is weak, and whose

beliefs and political practice are fraught with patriarchy. But for too long, the tendency among even the more progressive development NGOs is to leave gender equality to be struggled over by women's organizations alone.

Fortunately, when the WSF moved to India and Africa, where women play such a strong role in social movements, women's issues and concerns came much more to the fore. In Latin America, women are starting to play a much larger role. Women leaders are particularly strong in indigenous communities. The massive landless movement in Brazil now has gender equality in all of its leadership bodies. The more horizontal and participatory the structure, the more women are likely to participate. As well, Michelle Bachelet, president of Chile, has brought a feminist perspective and practice to her presidency, facing tremendous sexist attacks in the process.

In North America, too, third-wave feminists are reinventing the movement with what was an exciting and innovative conference for young feminists called Rebelles 2008 in October 2008 in Montreal, and with groups such as Code Pink, a feminist direct-action anti-war group emerging from the anti-war movement in the United States. And while Hillary Clinton's performance may have been modelled on the Old Boy's Club, she nevertheless raised the importance of female leadership. In the conflict of the 2008 Democratic primaries, gender was suddenly on the mainstream agenda again. At the same time, the stunning nomination of Sarah Palin—a charismatic politician who opposes almost every policy that advances women's rights—as vice-presidential candidate for the Republicans has re-ignited a debate on what progress for women really looks like.

As class and race divisions among women grow, it is increasingly difficult for women to self-identify as a group. This division was writ large during the contest for the Democratic Party nomination. Gloria Steinem wrote for *The New York Times*, after Barack Obama's dramatic victory in the Iowa primary:

Gender is probably the most restricting force in American life, whether the question is who must be in the kitchen or who could be in the White House. That's why the Iowa primary was following our historical pattern of making change. Black men were given the vote a half-century before women of any race were allowed to mark a ballot, and generally have ascended to positions of power, from the military to the boardroom, before any women (with the possible exception of obedient family members in the latter).

I was shocked that Steinem wrote this piece, but it seems that when it came to the possibility of a woman in the White House, too many of my generation of white feminists forgot what they learned about the relationship of race and gender. I think it is outrageous to argue that women are more excluded from politics—or anything else—than black men. I can argue facts and figures, but what's the point? For women of colour, gender and race are completely intertwined. They cannot see their gender before their race or vice versa. In Canada, at least, and I thought in the best part of the women's movement in the United States, of which Steinem is part, we understood that overcoming racism is just as important as overcoming sexism in achieving women's equality. From my perspective, the victory of a black man who presents as a consensus-builder and not a polarizer is just as much a feminist victory as the victory of a woman who represents the political establishment. Many young feminists and most feminists of colour saw it that way too.

Of course, many women may have seen Clinton as the better candidate, but arguing that it is more important for a woman than for a black man to become president is counter to the notion that there can be no hierarchy of rights if we are to achieve equality. The gap between the generations of women in the United States was never clearer than during the Democratic primaries.

In English Canada, feminists spent many years struggling with the differences among women. The efforts of marginalized women to be heard in the women's movement have been central to its development. Young feminists begin with an understanding of difference that took us many years of blood, sweat, and mostly tears to develop. My generation of feminists put on armour to enter the battlefields created by patriarchy. To challenge the way power is practised, we needed to challenge the men who held it. We ended up challenging the men, but not sufficiently the way power is practised.

My generation of feminists failed to achieve its goal of eliminating patriarchy. Despite the significant changes that feminism has realized in the lives of women, men, and children, the system of male domination remains intact and is reinforced through continuing male culture in the workplace, in politics, in the media, and in still too many families. This culture is not perpetrated solely by men: Many women in positions of power adopt the same methods of control as do their male colleagues. Our notions of leadership, for example, are still very masculine. And certainly the fact that so little value is placed on raising children or caring for family, friends, and community is a sign that, although economically we have moved radically from the family wage that allowed a male breadwinner to support a woman at home and from the cultural attitudes that supported male superiority that were so prevalent in my childhood, in terms of the institutions of power, we have not moved very far at all.

At the beginning of the second wave, we were openly and actively challenging that male culture. However, as our influence increased, we focused more on demands for reform and less on the deeper cultural and structural changes that would undermine patriarchy. Too many of us accepted a place within the patriarchal structure. The pressure to succeed as a woman in a traditionally male role almost always trumps the desire to change the way things are done to make room for other women. For one thing, all the pressures push women in that direction; for another, we have no blueprint of any kind for making changes to deeply ingrained hierarchical structures. The more power that an organization has, the harder it is to change. If patriarchal structures are to change, men need to undermine them. Otherwise, women who want power have little choice but to participate in them—and, as in the cases of Clinton and Palin, to beat the men at their own game.

In the spring of 2008, I had a speaking engagement at the Ontario Police College. I was speaking to the coordinators of the domestic-violence units across the province. The police are a group considerably outside my comfort zone. Steve Hibbard, the deputy director of the school, kicked off the conference with this story:

> A young woman who is having a very tough time in her life goes to her grandmother to confide in her. Her grandmother puts three pots of water on the stove and brings them to a boil. In one she puts carrots, in the next an egg, and in the third, coffee beans. She tells her granddaughter that there are different ways to deal with adversity. The carrots, strong and bright, become weak and limp in face of the adversity of the boiling water. The egg, hard on the outside but soft on the inside, becomes hard right through. And the coffee beans transform the adversity, sharing their essence with it and producing a delicious drink. "Which will you be?" she asks.

He went on to say that he was an egg. Like most cops, he had never talked about his feelings and, after working for thirty years dealing with the most horrendous cases of violence against women, he had suffered a lot. "It hurt my relationship with my wife and my children," he told the group. "I have suffered all of my life, including serious depression, because I didn't know how to talk about the pain. So I ask you, when you are discussing harm reduction [a theme of the conference], think about the harm you are doing to yourselves, and how we can change the culture of the police so that we can express that pain."

I was blown away. All my stereotypes were shattered. For a man in authority in a patriarchal institution such as the police force to open his heart and admit vulnerability was an act of transformation. And why was I there at all? Because a woman from my generation was in charge of the training and took the risk of inviting a feminist to talk to them. Change happens in many ways.

How do we play the game but still change the rules? As the poet Audre Lorde so famously said, "The master's tools will never dismantle the master's house." But neither can we make change exclusively from the outside. The success of the second wave was in its ability to work both inside and outside the system. Once you are inside a system, however, the pressure to conform is tremendous. Feminists of my generation began as kick-ass radicals, but were slowly co-opted. Italian philosopher Antonio Gramsci identified this process of co-option of movements for change as a central feature of capitalism. He used the term *hegemony* to describe this process and explained it as the way that capitalism maintains its ideological hold.

The new movements represented in this book are exploring new ways of decision-making that entail co-operation rather than domination, inclusion rather than elitism, and new kinds of leadership that involve recognizing and supporting ability and strength in others. Today, we have the benefit of much more work, both academic and practical, in making decisions differently, in realms ranging from popular education to participatory democracy. We know much more about creating egalitarian structures. Speaking truth to power, it turns out, is not enough. We must change the very nature of power. How to do that is a central challenge for the movements of today.

6

EMBRACING DIVERSITY
The Ground of Our Being

THE FIRST GLOBAL MASS MOVEMENT in history was the anti-slavery movement. In what could be seen as a model today, freed slaves joined with progressive activists in England in the late-nineteenth century to organize opposition to the horrors of the slave trade. But it wasn't until after the Second World War that human rights became codified into law. In reaction to the Nazi genocide, the first United Nations Declaration of Human Rights was adopted in 1948. Throughout the next four decades, charters and human rights bills guaranteeing equal rights to everyone, regardless of gender, race, sexual orientation, language, or disability, were periodically adopted—often after major struggles by the group facing discrimination. But every one of these human rights struggles ran up against the same brick wall of the inequality that is endemic in the systems of patriarchy, colonialism, and capitalism under which we live.

The pillaging undertaken by colonialism was only possible because of the racist attitudes that were promoted to justify it. Black and Aboriginal peoples were called savages who threatened the pure Christian society unless they could be "civilized," mostly through denying them their language and culture, or slaughtering them if they resisted assimilation. Racism is the ideology that justified colonialism and imperialism by entrenching the notion of a superior race, civilization, and religion, along with the assumption that the others are inferior.

The ideology continues under capitalism, creating a racialized underclass that is divided from other workers, not only by poverty but also by racism.* Though perhaps in a less explicit way than under colonialism, it also justifies foreign wars.

Overt racism also continues. At Ryerson University, where I work, there have been numerous incidents of obvious racism, including the establishment of a white supremacy Facebook group called "I'm a White Minority @ Ryerson" and racist and Islamaphobic emails attacking student leaders who are involved in anti-racist organizing. Since September 11, 2001, Islamaphobia has become an almost acceptable form of discrimination. When Hillary Clinton's campaign suggested that Barack Obama was a Muslim, he simply responded by saying he was a Christian rather than by also pointing out that there would be nothing wrong with being a Muslim and no reason why a Muslim couldn't run for president of the United States.

In response to the terrorism of the few, we have created a fear of anyone who is from the Middle East or practises the Muslim religion, going as far as calling the so-called war against terrorism *a war of civilizations*. In fact, the more extreme language of the war against terrorism recalls the language of the early days of colonialism. Fear of the Other is a convenient, if base, tactic used by governments from time immemorial to divide and rule.

In Europe, the prejudice against Muslims has occasionally reached a fever pitch in societies that used to consider themselves tolerant. Speaking at rallies is becoming a lost art, but Muslim activist Abdul-Rehman Malik has a wonderful ability to reach the hearts of his

---

Racialized is the newest term used by academics to identify the diverse group of people who face discrimination because of skin colour. In the past, they have been called visible minorities or people of colour. Both terms have been criticized because, in a global context, they are the majority, and white is also a colour.

audience, which is the secret of all great oratory. In a speech to the anti-war movement in Britain, Malik called Islamaphobia "the new McCarthyism" and said,

> The obsession with Islamaphobia is more about Europe's own identity crisis. It doesn't know who it is. No one can define the values, what we are supposed to be integrating into. Just when they were saying it was the end of history, global Islam shows up and upsets the apple cart. We have become such a powerful demographic force that in a way the very presence of Muslims has changed the way we look at the whole society. No longer are we divided into petty racial or ethnic camps or ideational [ideological] camps. We have become a wide-open space, kind of a post-secular society where everything is staking claim to the public square. And what this [anti-war] movement has been able to do is provide a space for us to allow the greatest number of people to stake their claim to the public square and their right to be heard. But we as a movement have to have some kind of vision.... What is the prize?"

Perhaps the prize is a world in which all forms of diversity are embraced and valued rather than a world in which we value ourselves only by seeing ourselves as superior to others. If European identity was formed by colonialism defining the white race as superior to those Europe was exploiting, perhaps the arrival of hundreds of thousands from the Global South to Europe is the opportunity to turn the world right side up.

I recently attended a meeting at which an Aboriginal woman, in talking about the apology by Prime Minister Stephen Harper for the residential schools in Canada, said, "We have a prophesy that white people and indigenous peoples are tied in a knot by colonialism, and each one of us suffers as a result. Now is the time to untie that knot and find freedom for everyone."

But we are a long way from untying the knot. Both overt and systemic racism continue to be major problems. In the United States, African-American men are criminalized to an extraordinary degree. According to a Human Rights Watch report in 2003, blacks comprise 12.49 percent of the national population but 42.91 percent of people in state and federal penitentiaries and 49 percent of those in prison. Some 9 percent of all black adults are under some form of correctional supervision (in jail or prison, or on probation or parole), compared to 2 percent of white adults. One in three black men between the ages of twenty and twenty-nine was either incarcerated or on parole or probation in 1995. And 13 percent of the black adult male population has lost the right to vote because of felony disenfranchisement laws. Racial disparities in incarceration increased in the 1980s and 1990s, as the number of blacks sent to prison grew at a faster rate than the number of whites. Nationwide, blacks are incarcerated at more than eight times the rate of whites. In some states, the ratio is as high as thirteen times.

"The rate at which black men are incarcerated is astonishing," says a report by Human Rights Watch called *Punishment and Prejudice*. "According to Department of Justice calculations based on Census Data from 2000, if current rates of incarceration remain unchanged, 28.5 percent of black men will be confined in prison at least once during their lifetime, a figure six times greater than that for white men." These high rates of incarceration reflect the disproportionate impact of government policy, such as the war on drugs, on African Americans.

Targeting Blacks: Drug Enforcement and Race in the United States, a recent report written by Jamie Fellner for Human Rights Watch, documents persistent racial disparities among drug offenders sent to prison. "Most drug offenders are white, but most of the drug offenders sent to prison are black," says Fellner. "The solution is not to imprison more whites but to radically rethink how to deal with drug abuse and low-level drug offenders."

The report finds that, across the thirty-four states, a black man is 11.8 times more likely than a white man to be sent to prison on drug charges, and a black woman is 4.8 times more likely than a white woman to be sent to prison on the same charges.

IN CANADA, as our policies on social assistance and crime move closer to those of the United States, through draconian cuts to social assistance over the past decades and increased emphasis on law and order rather than prevention, we see similar dynamics in the growth of gangs in the inner city and the increasingly high incarceration of young black and Aboriginal men. These are human rights issues, but unless we understand the interconnection of economic and social policy with racism, we cannot solve the problems. In fact, as the Human Rights Watch report suggests, the impact of racism on poor young black men is getting worse during the same period that overt racism against black people has lessened so much so that there is a black man in the White House.

Non-white lives are also not valued in the same way. Only occasionally do we see newspaper articles in Canada about the high rates of suicide by Aboriginal youths. Suicide rates are five to seven times higher for First Nations youth than non-Aboriginal youth. While such a statistic might be front-page news if it occurred among non-Aboriginals, writers in the mainsteam media neglect what to them appears to be old news on an intractable issue.

Paramilitaries are responsible for many deaths of indigenous peoples in Mexico, but we never hear about them, even though Canada and the United States are close partners with the Mexican government through NAFTA and are now negotiating an even closer relationship through the Security and Prosperity Partnership (SPP).* The statistics from Iraq and Afghanistan reported in the mainstream media are always about the deaths of Canadian or American troops,

---

*The SPP is an agreement being negotiated by the United States, Canada, and Mexico that will further integrate the three countries, going beyond NAFTA and including common security policies.

rarely about the number of Iraqi civilians that have been killed (up to ninety-five thousand, according to www.iraqbodycount.org). We've already seen the rise of violent racism in Europe in response to the influx of immigrants from the Global South. Islamaphobia, combined with the war on terror, justifies treating them as second-class citizens, even imprisoning them without charge and without due process.

And it's not just white racism that's the problem. Poor people in South Africa have turned against immigrants and driven them out of the country. Too many conflicts around the world rooted in economic or political factors manifest themselves through racial, religious, or tribal differences.

Why, despite a generation of human rights law and a global consensus to end discrimination based on race, religion, and ethnic origin, is racism still such a problem?

Economically, too, race determines much of one's status in the world. Ryerson professor and anti-racist activist Grace-Edward Galabuzi, in his book *Economic Apartheid*, shows that people of colour in Canada consistently face lower employment and lower wages than white Canadians, even in the second generation. Racialized groups have lower wages and higher levels of unemployment than white workers. The wage gap is about 25 percent. In 2001, the unemployment rate for people born in Canada was 6.4 percent; for immigrants overall it was 7.9 percent; for immigrants of colour, 12.1 percent; and for visible minorities in general, 12.6 percent.

The growth of overt racism is a serious concern, but racism is no less pernicious when it simply denies possibility and, therefore, hope to generations of young people of colour. In Canada, immigration accounted for 70 percent of the growth in the labour force between 1991 and 1996, with more than 75 percent of that coming from the Global South. Groups such as No One Is Illegal work to stop deportations and point out the hypocrisy of a world where capital can go wherever it wants but labour is seriously restricted. The U.S. economy depends upon undocumented workers and guest workers, the precariousness of whose work and lives is completely unacceptable.

Migrant workers who are forced to leave their homes and work in richer countries to provide for their families are almost all people of colour and face terrible discrimination with few rights. In addition, our society is almost entirely racially divided. The higher up one goes in society, the fewer faces of colour are seen. That Canada has a black woman as Governor General or the United States has a black man as president are important symbolically but don't change the reality of day-to-day life for most people of colour.

It must be said that the political Left in North America and Europe, outside of the anti-war movement, has thus far failed to attract many people of colour to their ranks. The women's movement in the United States has been divided by race. In Canada, after some bitter struggles, there has been much more racial integration of the leadership of the women's movement, but that integration coincided with the decline in the power of the women's movement. Today, most North American and European cities (and none more than Toronto, where I live) are global cities in which people from every part of the world are living together. Overcoming racism is absolutely central to any progress toward social justice.

While the civil rights movement created legal equality for African Americans in the United States, in reality they are still far from equality. We saw most brutally when the curtain was pulled away from the deplorable conditions faced by poor African Americans in the United States during the rescue and reconstruction efforts in New Orleans following Hurricane Katrina.

When Hurricane Katrina was discussed at the U.S. Social Forum, Monique Hardin from the U.S. organization Advocates for Environmental Human Rights said, "New Orleans is a man-made disaster. Bush is the man and Bush is the disaster. Reconstruction on the Gulf Coast is a massive privatization scheme to destroy people of colour and poor white people."

Dr. Beverly Wright, who grew up in New Orleans and is now a prominent local leader, spoke from the floor, saying, "Our parents and our grandparents fought to buy a house to pass on to their family, and they are trying to take that away from us when they talk about turning the place we lived in East New Orleans into a green space. They're not talking about turning the place rich white folks lived into green space."

Another community leader said, "Katrina is both a reality and a symbol. If you work in justice, if you work in health care, if you work in housing, you are in Katrina."

One of the most powerful speeches was from Javier Gallardo, a guest worker from Peru, who was attending for the New Orleans Worker Center. He explained that, when African Americans were displaced, hundreds of workers, like him, had been brought in from Latin America for Gulf Coast reconstruction, and their employers' names are on their passports. Their ability to stay in the United States is dependent on the employer. He described a practice in which, when the employer is finished with the workers, he sells them to another employer for two thousand dollars each. "What is that?" he asked. "We call it modern-day slavery. They want to divide us, but the old slaves and the new slaves can join together and together we can defeat them," he continued to thunderous applause. The "old slaves–new slaves" metaphor wove its way through the rest of the forum in the powerful idea of a black-brown alliance, which veteran activists said would transform left-wing politics in the United States—especially in the South, where the vast majority of the working class are now black and brown.

This new form of slavery, indentured work—the phrase *guest workers* is simply a polite term—is becoming a massive issue in North America and Europe. Guest workers are in the country at the pleasure of their employers. For these workers, standing up for their rights not only means losing their jobs but quite possibly being deported as well. In the United States, more than thirteen million families are headed by undocumented workers, a fact that has mobilized the Latino community across the country in a major political battle. In 2006, millions of people protested a proposed law that would raise penalties for illegal immigration. It was one of the largest demonstrations since the Vietnam War, organized almost entirely by the Latino communities in 102 cities. Van Jones, the human rights and environmental activist from Oakland mentioned in previous chapters, talks in an interview about the Katrina principle in dealing with inequality in society:

> I would argue that we have an opportunity now to embrace the Katrina principle. We saw an American city drown, and we saw people left behind to suffer and struggle on their own. After decades of "sink or swim," "individualism is the way," "everybody's got to pull themselves up by their bootstraps"—after hearing that for decades, we finally got a chance to see what it means, what the sink-or-swim politics mean, when we saw people sinking and not getting help. And I think that was a real watershed moment, for lack of a better term, in the lives of a lot of people. We're better than that. We don't believe in that. We believe that we don't leave behind the most vulnerable, that we want to take care of the most vulnerable in our society again. And I think it's important that we don't let that go, that we don't lose that heart moment, and that calling that all of us heard.
>
> Looking at those TV screens, looking at those faces—different coloured faces than maybe we're used to seeing on the news, and yet moving past the racial division, past the racial hatred, and saying, "My God, can't we do something to help these people? Can't we do something to help?" In the floodwaters of Katrina, we knew that we needed to take care of our most vulnerable, that we need to include our most vulnerable; we can't leave people behind to suffer. Well, there are people who are drowning on dry land, drowning on dry land in Harlem and Watts and Newark and Oakland, California. Let us order our affairs so that nobody will be able to accuse us years hence of having done to whole communities what was done to the people of New Orleans, that we did not leave our most vulnerable behind. That's our moral obligation in the new century.*

---

*From the transcript of an interview with director Velcrow Ripper for his film *Fierce Light: When Spirit Meets Action* (2008).

Over the years, I have had a lot of experience in combating racism. My first efforts were in the mid-1970s with a committee called the Committee Against Racism and Political Repression, which launched an unsuccessful campaign to defend Caribbean activist Rosie Douglas against deportation from Canada. During the 1980s, I worked in a multiracial coalition for employment equity. When I became president of the National Action Committee on the Status of Women, one of my priorities was to make NAC more representative of women of colour, Aboriginal women, and women with disabilities. We instituted affirmative action for our voluntary board by designating certain spots for these under-represented groups. There was a debate over this, mostly about what groups to include, but the motion passed by a large majority. We sought out women of colour to run and, by the time I stepped down three years later, women of colour and Aboriginal women held 40 percent of the seats on the board and the next president, Sunera Thobani, was South Asian and an immigrant. The reaction to her election outside the organization was shocking. A Reform Party MP claimed—falsely—in the House of Commons that Thobani was an illegal immigrant. Lots of debate also surrounded the view that she couldn't represent Canadian women. Inside NAC, too, there were divisions about her election; about half the executive felt that a white woman who had been vice-president was more qualified.

What has changed since then is that we can have a woman of colour who was a refugee take a position as Governor General (as symbolic as that is) and no one dare say she doesn't represent Canadians. The women's movement in Canada was a pioneer in forging this road to diversity. It was painful because we didn't know a way to do it that didn't involve a lot of anger, accusation, and feelings of guilt. We have learned a lot since then in how to deal with racism without so much conflict, but, as one young black woman said recently in a meeting: "We have to learn how to rid ourselves of internalized oppression and internalized superiority."

Working in the employment equity coalition in the 1980s at the height of the often bitter struggle of women of colour to gain their place inside the women's movement, I noticed that we didn't have the racial tensions in the employment equity coalition that we had in the women's movement, even though there was probably less of an equity analysis in the coalition. I think it was because the coalition was formed mostly by people of colour and people with disabilities, whereas the women's movement had largely been established by white women, and women of colour were wanting in. In every group in which I have participated in increasing the representation of people of colour and Aboriginal people, the rubber always hits the road at the point when the representation is achieved and the new people propose changes to better reflect their ideas and their needs.

When women entered the workplace, the organizations had to change to accommodate their presence. It is the same with racial and cultural diversity. The resistance to what are often positive changes for everyone comes from thinking that those already there know best—just like the colonialists of old. If you asked a fish how it breathes under water, it would respond: "Doesn't everyone?" That's what it's like to be white in a white-dominated society. We don't notice how different it is for everyone who isn't white.

Akua Benjamin, who has been a leader in the black community in Toronto since the 1970s, reflected on her approach to fighting racism in my oral history of the Canadian women's movement, *Ten Thousand Roses: The Making of a Feminist Revolution*:

> One of the things I learned coming out of the UN Conference on Racism in Durban in 2001 was that you cannot take up issues of difference, whether it be race, gender, or poverty, without a process of healing. A lot of work in activism is about structural change. It's about getting a policy change, putting a program into place. So we never recognized sufficiently how we ourselves need to heal from all the history of difference that has divided us. First Nations women brought that to our attention.

But in the United States and Canada, where people of colour now compose close to half the population of our cities, social justice and environmental organizations still continue to be dominated by white leadership and an almost entirely white membership, with few questions being asked about why this is still the case.

I first met Shakil Choudhury, at the time a high school teacher, when he presented his *Brown Book* to a day-long meeting of educators from across the country. All the most experienced popular educators in the country were there, and they were tremendously impressed by this young man's approach to teaching mixed groups about Islamaphobia. As an anti-racist educator, now working with his own company, Choudhury has been asking himself some deep questions about why, even on the Left, we seem unable to eliminate racism. In an interview, he told me: "We have these fantastic theories, anti-racist theories, post-colonial theories. If our theories are so good, then shouldn't progressive organizations be the example of how to live in healthy relationship with one another. Shouldn't we be able to see that people are treating one another well and fairly and people are being treated equally and well in these organizations?" But often there is more dysfunction in these organizations than anywhere else.

Choudhury has come to understand that racism is based on emotional reactions, and that those reactions are unconscious. All the great anti-racist theories and statistics about the racialization of poverty or the number of black and Aboriginal peoples in jail don't deal with those feelings. "In those anti-racist workshops, we faced a lot of resistance," says Choudhury. "White people would be reacting. People of colour would be angry, and there was always a polarization that seemed to stop further progress."

Anti-racism work must be about building empathy by dealing with those emotional blocks, he concludes. Choudhury's ideas are controversial and cutting-edge in that he sees a universality in these emotional blocks:

As people of colour, we always think it's about other people, it's about white people, about institutions, about structures, but what I have come to in the last number of years is the understanding that prejudice is universal. There is a common human experience, how our brain functions; we use stereotypes. The difference is when you get a group of people who are in power together and they have the same vision of the world because they come from the same in-group, then racism can play out visibly and invisibly, and that's where the issues of power come in.

What it means to me right now is that we need to develop certain kinds of skills that we don't have and certain kinds of understanding of the world that we don't have en masse. These are critical pieces we need to have to move in a healthy way in the world. I think we desperately need processes that help people develop emotional literacy and awareness.

Using these new techniques in the workshops that he and his partner, Annahid Dashtgard, conduct under the name Anima Leadership, Choudhury finds much less resistance and polarization. Today, Anima is presenting workshops from Amsterdam to Costa Rica, to everyone from government to unions to educational institutions.

It was at the U.S. Social Forum that I first saw this new kind of anti-racist politics. Instead of the confrontations of my generation, there was a unity based on respect for differences. The people most affected by the topic under discussion were the speakers. Instead of academics lecturing about their studies of people, the people themselves spoke about their own reality. Instead of featuring the celebrities of the Left, of whatever colour, the discussions called on local leaders. In a reverse of the usual racial composition of panels in such conferences, the majority of panelists were people of colour and women. When there was conflict, it was handled with grace and a respect for the anger of those who felt offended or oppressed in some way, but with a view to continuing the process and building unity. Perhaps the reason it went so well was that the process was led by a co-coordinating committee composed mostly of people of colour.

Uzma Shakir, an anti-racist activist in Toronto, originally a feminist refugee from Pakistan, tells this story to explain a little about how the world can look different to white people and people of colour: "A chicken and a pig are going for their morning constitutional. The chicken sees a sign in a restaurant window advertising, 'Bacon and eggs special, $1.95.' 'Let's go,' says the chicken. 'Well,' says the pig, 'I don't know. For you it's a contribution. For me it's a commitment.'"

At the end of the U.S. Forum, there was a meeting of social movements. The idea was for different caucuses and issue groups to report back to the whole group on the strategies they had developed, and, because there were a lot of groups, the moderators kept time tight; each group got five minutes. The indigenous caucus sent a woman from the United States and man from Ecuador to report (the indigenous caucus doesn't recognize the borders in the Americas for their nations). The woman took most of the time, and the man from Ecuador spoke for only a minute before the chair tapped him. He continued speaking. She tapped him again, and, when he didn't stop, she removed his microphone.

A few of us chanted, "Let him speak." I figured taking away the microphone was a terrible mistake. I noticed Aboriginal peoples around the audience caucusing and then leaving the room. It wasn't a walkout, but I wondered what was next.

I didn't have long to wait. One hundred Aboriginal peoples paraded onto the stage. (I found out later that they had the agreement of the organizers to do so.) The Ecuadorean man took the microphone and continued to say what he had to say. Everyone cheered.

But that wasn't the end of it. A middle-aged indigenous man then spoke, angrily denouncing the audience for the terrible insult against his brother. He spoke as if no one in the audience had experienced any suffering or struggle and therefore couldn't relate to the sufferings of indigenous peoples. He asked, "How many of you have gone to prison for your beliefs?" Despite the fact that I'm sure a good number of people in the audience had indeed gone to prison and that this was in general a very responsive crowd, no one spoke a word. Everyone was too angry.

At a certain point in his diatribe, an older African-American man stood up and strode toward the front of the room. Pointing his finger, he said, "That's enough, brother. You should stop talking now." The indigenous man retreated behind the crowd on the stage, and I thought the whole conference would blow up. So many times, I have witnessed a wonderful meeting explode at the end because someone says something that angers everyone else. Instead, Tom Goldtooth of the Indigenous Environmental Network and the indigenous rep on the co-coordinating committee stepped forward and, without criticizing the man who had been talking, said, "When the chair took the microphone away, our brother felt silenced. He felt oppressed because we have had five hundred years of being silenced. The warrior stepped forward to defend him because that is the job of the warrior in our culture." He went on to explain that this was a process of healing for them.

Then he asked the Ecuadorean speaker if he felt better. Although he did, before he turned the microphone over, the Ecuadorean felt it was important to hear from the women. A group of about fifteen women stepped forward, and one young woman spoke through her tears, saying, "You are not our enemies." To which many in the audience replied, "Thank you, sister." It was a moving moment.

The chair, a middle-aged African-American woman, spoke. "We are just learning to work together," she said. "And we are going to screw up. I made a mistake, but I am not going away. I am staying right here." There were loud cheers from the audience. What could have been a disaster turned into a moment in which people felt united. I was impressed.

I SAW ANOTHER WAY of dealing with difference in Latin America as well. In December 2006, I attended the Social Summit of the Americas in Cochabamba, Bolivia, where the presidents of most South American countries were meeting to talk about South American integration. Among the several thousand mostly indigenous participants were a group of several hundred gays and lesbians and their youthful supporters from La Paz. Due to the influence of the Catholic Church and traditionally macho culture, gay rights are not very well accepted across Latin America, with the exception of large urban centres such as Rio de Janiero. The young activists organized well, and at the first plenary they entered the hall under a rainbow banner, chanting, "We want to be included." Their drumming and marching was very much in the indigenous tradition, so at first everyone cheered. By the next pass, everyone realized who they were, and the response was more thoughtful than enthusiastic. But instead of the reaction that might have occurred in the 1980s—debate over whether this group would discredit the movement and angry demands from the LGBT group about the homophobia of the majority—there was a quiet acceptance. If we agree with pluralism and autonomy, then we must accept all those who face persecution, whatever the reason, was the thinking. The LGBT group was accepted, and their demands were included with others from the Social Summit.

Going beyond identity politics, these gatherings realize that what unites us is greater than what divides us, but we must honour those differences. It is also essential that we recognize the historic and current injustices perpetrated against people of colour, and in particular against indigenous peoples and people of African origin. It is no accident that the vast majority of the poorest people on earth (including in the North) are people of colour, a direct result of colonialism and slavery. They are poor because Europe, and later North America, took their resources and their labour, either stealing them or paying absurdly low prices for them. White supremacy is a fact of life. No justice is possible without eliminating it.

On March 18, 2008, Barack Obama gave an extraordinary speech on race in response to attacks against him for things the minister of his church had said,

> I chose to run for the presidency at this moment in history
> because I believe deeply that we cannot solve the challenges of
> our time unless we solve them together—unless we perfect our
> union by understanding that we may have different stories, but
> we hold common hopes; that we may not look the same and we
> may not have come from the same place, but we all want to
> move in the same direction—towards a better future for of
> children and our grandchildren.

The notion that we have different stories but hold common hopes is central to understanding the unity among peoples that could exist if we refused to define a group as better or worse based on race, culture, religion, or social class. The notion that human society, just like the environment, functions best in all its diversity is a powerful understanding that is coming from the convergence of the human rights and environmental movements. The idea that we are stronger because of our diversity leads us to embrace that diversity rather than to see it as a threat. The Aboriginal belief that we are all part of the same family is a powerful counter to the divisions created by our culture.

As African-American feminist bell hooks says, "It is difficult to find the place where difference can exist in a context of harmony, where it is not necessary to dominate. But that is the ground of our being. It's where we start."

ONE WAY THAT DIVERSITY CAN EXIST in a context of harmony is by recognizing and defining common ground. In my generation, we often defined struggles around single issues and focusing our attention on winning reforms in that area. The new movements are being defined by the convergence of issues rather than focus on just one.

7

CONVERGENCE
Uplifting Environmentalism

THERE CAN BE LITTLE DOUBT that the most compelling issue of our time is climate change. James Hansen, one of the world's experts on climate change, addressed the U.S. Congress in January 2008:

> We have used up all slack in the schedule for actions needed to defuse the global warming time bomb. The next president and congress must define a course next year in which the United States exerts leadership commensurate with our responsibility for the present dangerous situation. Otherwise it will become impractical to constrain atmospheric climate dioxide to a level that prevents the climate system from passing tipping points that lead to disastrous climate changes that spiral dynamically out of humanity's control.

Over the next few years, governments will be forced to take action to deal with climate change to avoid the dangers that Hansen describes. The question is whether these measures will exacerbate or help to solve other problems, such as inequality and war. One of the most effective networks I encountered while doing the research for this book was founded seventeen years ago in response to a call from the elders of the Navajo nation to protect their land from a medical-waste incinerator.

The Indigenous Environmental Network (IEN) is one of the key organizations in a developing convergence between indigenous communities, environmental organizations, and social justice groups. It is a network of native organizations, communities, and individuals across Turtle Island (the original native name for what we call North America) that have come together to support Mother Earth. According to Clayton Thomas Mueller, a young Cree environmental activist who works on both sides of the Canada–U.S. border with the IEN and lives in Ottawa: "The tribal chairman was one of the main proponents of the waste-disposal site ... [but] through a lot of community organizing and development of accessible materials and support from non-native organizations like Greenpeace, who actually sponsored that first conference, the IEN was founded. At that conference, we determined through community development techniques to organize in native communities. They succeeded in shutting down that incinerator."

In recent years, the IEN has been involved in many battles against the fossil fuel and mining industry in lands claimed by native communities across North America. Their native energy and climate project is an initiative to organize regional networks of resistance against the energy and mining sector that have been allowed to target native lands* during this time of ecological sensitivity. In response to a call for support from a hundred communities, the IEN began to support on-the-ground campaigns on a whole series of issues, most of them related to climate change.

Clayton explains that IEN differs from other environmental non-government organizations (ENGOs) by not being an issue-based organization, but rather focusing on base-building. "We don't go into

---

*I use the term *indigenous lands* or *native lands* to mean not only the small reserves that colonial powers imposed on Aboriginal peoples, but the land they claim as their traditional lands, used for hunting, fishing, and trapping.

a community unless there is a group on the ground and asking for help," he explains. "We do a lot of linking together of communities. Our yearly Gathering of Mother Earth Protectors summits give our communities a chance to work together. We have fundamental protocols. Communities speak for themselves. What we provide can be as simple as economic support for printing, etc., to organizing technical support, or more technical support services regarding environmental issues.... We have lawyers and legal expertise to help communities understand what their rights are."

I HEARD A LOT OF REFERENCES to base-building organizations at the U.S. Social Forum as well. Because of the large amounts of money in foundation funding in the United States, a lot of NGOs have structured themselves around issues and campaigns, forgetting the beginnings of their movements in grassroots organizing. As with political parties, organizing for social change has become professionalized, and social and environmental NGOs have become one strand in a complex matrix of lobby groups vying for media and political attention. Many of them have little reference or accountability to the people most affected by the policies they are promoting, but groups such as the IEN are striving to change this top-down policy-oriented work. Clayton explained it to me in an interview:

> The difference between issue-based campaigns and base-building is that [base-building organizations] are looking at building local capacity and power to deal with these issues and ensuring that solutions being put forward to address the environmental problems won't exacerbate the other problems these communities are facing. The only way to do this is to have these communities speak for themselves. This comes from an indigenous-rights or self-determination analysis.
>
> There are accountability issues with ENGOs. You will get organizations that will swoop in, take all the media, take all the

money. And then they leave when the issue becomes less sexy. So, in many ways, they cause more problems than they solve. Our work is not just built on recognizing local leadership, but it also comes from making sure that anything in the form of policy that IEN or non-native allies put forward is accountable to the communities.

A big part of our work is linking local impacts to policy work. Lots of organizations don't do that, and funding doesn't support that. Most funding focuses on "What's the quickest choke point? Where we can have success?" Base-building takes more time and it takes more resources.

A lot of mainstream organizations do have bases or memberships, but those memberships are often white upper-middle-class people who are out of touch with communities of colour or indigenous communities, and there are a lot of NGOs that have membership bases of support, but they don't necessarily mobilize their base in a way that could constitute base-building work.

Clayton also explains that the lack of accountability is not an abstract problem or even just a problem of the principle of support for native sovereignty; it has concrete policy implications. "When we talk about issues like climate change, these are of such epic proportions that we are talking about a radical shift. The problem with the solutions of mainstream groups is they don't take into account how commodifying the earth's atmospheric carbon capacity and attaching a price tag to that process to be bought and sold in mankind's economic structure (cap and trade, for example),* is fundamentally at

---

*Cap and trade is a market-based system of controlling carbon emissions. The regulator sets a cap for emissions. Permits give a company the right to pollute, and companies are free to buy and sell permits. Those that are able to reduce emissions at a low cost can sell their extra permits to companies facing high costs, which will generally prefer to buy permits rather than make costly reductions themselves.

odds with indigenous communities. It is privatizing the sacred. If we are against the privatization of water because it's part of the commons, then shouldn't we be against the commodification of the atmosphere because it's part of the commons?"

Many leaders of ENGOs argue that the problems are too urgent to work out these major issues of policy and process. Time is running out, they say. Clayton points out that time ran out for many indigenous communities, coastal cities, fishing villages, and much of the Global South a long time ago. The powerful voice of the IEN is a major challenge to the environmental movement in the United States, and is beginning to have an effect here in Canada as well.

One of the most successful leaders of the environmental movement in British Columbia is Tzeporah Berman. She was a major organizer of the 1993 Clayoquot Sound struggle to protect a magnificent old-growth forest from logging and a founder and campaign director of Forest Ethics, an ENGO whose aim is to protect endangered forests by transforming the paper and wood industries in North America. I asked her to explain the urgency of the environmental crisis and how it relates to social justice issues.

At first she quoted the *UN Report on Climate Change*: "'Human activity is causing such a strain on the natural functions of the earth, that the ability of the earth to maintain human well-being is now in question,'" adding,

> In the past, environmentalism was the project of a few who had an affinity for bears and trees, who loved the outdoors. And as we near the end of wild systems and ecosystems, we begin to see that what's left of our forests—only 20 percent of the earth's forests remain intact—are our lifeboat. They are the air- and water-filtration systems that give us the air we breathe and the water we drink.
>
> The other way I would answer that question about the urgency is that the cumulative impact of logging, of oil and gas exploration, the thousands of toxins that we spew into our

atmosphere but end up in our bodies, as well as the threat that's now posed by global warming as a result of increased fossil fuel use around the world—it's those cumulative impacts that threaten the air we breathe, the water we drink, and the food we eat.

The reason we're in such an environmental crisis now is that the earth's ability to maintain human well-being is now in question. What we now know is that if fossil fuel consumption and emissions continue at the rate that they're going [and they're projected right now to increase], it will not only result in catastrophic climate change—a predicted doubling in 2020 of floods, of droughts—but that will result in a hundred million environmental refugees a year by 2020. And so it's not just that our impact on the earth is threatening endangered species, is destroying some of the last forests, and literally killing our oceans—it's that we have now affected the planet to such an extent that it's not stable to hold human populations. So, in my mind, this is the moment when environmental and social justice issues come together by necessity, because the environmental issues have now become a matter of whether or not we value human life as well.

In 1993, Berman was in her twenties and outraged at the clearcutting in one of the most beautiful parts of British Columbia. She and five friends set up a blockade to stop logging trucks in Clayoquot Sound. By the end of the summer, thousands of people joined them on the blockade. One thousand were arrested. The polls were showing that 87 percent of Canadians didn't support the decision to log Clayoquot Sound. Still, the logging continued.

"It was an abject, complete failure of democracy," Berman told me in our interview. "So a group of us got together and said, 'Well, if the government's not going to listen to the people, then who are they listening to?' And we started looking at who was buying the timber, and who was in control here. It's public land, but clearly the government was not in control. At the time, we had an NDP government, supposedly a left-wing government."

When Berman's group tracked who was buying MacMillan Bloedel's products, it found out that the thousand-year-old trees were being made into telephone books for Pacific Bell and toilet paper for Scott Paper and Kimberley-Clark. Berman continued,

> With the naïveté of being in our early twenties, we just donned suits, grabbed a plane ticket, went to London, England, and demanded to see the CEO of Scott Paper. And it worked. They were horrified. They had no idea that they were buying ancient rainforests. They were being sold a bill of goods from the logging industry and the Canadian government, who were telling them that this was all sustainable. Some of the companies agreed to change. They started cancelling contracts with the logging company. Others didn't. We built a coalition—Greenpeace, Rainforest Action Network, NRDC (Natural Resources Defense Council), you name it—we convinced them to help us, and we launched campaigns directed at these corporations.
>
> I remember sitting down with Scott Paper and Greenpeace U.K., and they had mocked up an ad campaign that had Scott's puppies—you know, they always had the cute puppies falling off the staircases—with a little bubble out of their mouths saying, "I kill rainforests!" And Greenpeace just calmly said, "Thirty days to cancel your contract, or these will hit all of the papers in the U.K." And so Scott Paper and Kimberley-Clark became the first two companies to cancel their contracts with MacMillian Bloedel, which were worth three million dollars. And by the end of that summer we had cost MacMillan ten million dollars a year in contract cancellations. And then they wanted to talk.

Berman helped turn this approach into a campaign strategy for Forest Ethics, which went on to use similar tactics to get Victoria's Secret to stop using paper made from clear-cut forest for their catalogue. I asked Berman if she thinks that corporations are the ones with the power and resources to solve the environmental crisis. She replied,

> To solve the crisis? Absolutely not! I think that it's very impor-
> tant. I think that the rise in consciousness on behalf of corpora-
> tions and their willingness to change is great. And we need them
> to change and to see the public demanding them to change. But
> ultimately, we need government legislation to ensure strong
> enough fossil fuel emission reductions, and to ban some of the
> most toxic chemicals in the environment to stop major defor-
> estation around the world.
>
> Ultimately corporations operate to make a profit. And the
> model is unsustainable—there are too many of them, they're too
> big, they're taking too many resources. They exist to get us to
> consume. And in a time when we need to consume less, and
> when we are at the eleventh hour, when we're at such a critical
> moment in our history, we need to ensure that we're protected
> in the commons, and that requires government legislation and
> government action.

Clayoquot Sound was one of the most successful examples of a creative campaign that combined the power of grassroots mobilizing with the sophisticated media strategies of the large ENGOs, but Clayoquot Sound is indigenous territory. I asked about Berman's relationship with the First Nations communities in the area. She recalled,

> When we first started, the First Nations were being courted
> heavily by the logging companies. This was a community that
> had some of the highest suicide and alcoholism rates in Canada.
> They were struggling, and the logging company was offering
> them profits, offering them everything. And the initial meetings
> were rough, you know. It was really, really difficult. And at one

point, the chiefs took a position that unless we supported them—and at one point during our discussions, they had decided to support clear-cut logging in Clayoquot Sound—unless we supported their decisions, they would call us eco-imperialists, and we were going to end up with a huge fight between the First Nations community and the environmental community. And it was hard, but we built trust.

We met and we met, and we talked, and we tried to find common ground. Because they didn't want to log, they just wanted to have healthy communities. And so when we agreed that we, the environmental community, would come together and say to the province, "Not only do you need to protect Clayoquot Sound, but you need to give the First Nations decision-making control over the region," then we had a coalition. And trust me, there were government officials that came and said, "What if we stop the logging, but this other thing, it's going to set a bad precedent...." And we held firm. And we said no. And the result was that the Nuu-chah-nulth First Nation became the first Nation in British Columbia to have an agreement in which they got decision-making control over their traditional territories.

Berman says everyone learned their lesson, and when it came to the battle to protect the Great Bear Rainforest in northern British Columbia, the largest intact coastal rainforest in the world, the First Nations there demanded that the environmental groups share their resources. "And now I have more staff working in the Great Bear Rainforest than I did when we were running a highly public and visible campaign," she said. "We've got economists, we've got foresters, we spend more money on that program than any of our other campaigns, because a lasting solution does take time."

It is easy to forget that the power to stop clear-cutting in Clayoquot Sound or to protect the Great Bear Rainforest came from confrontational tactics. Berman is concerned about that. "One of the most important things is that as we are building coalitions, as we're trying to see people and not positions, as we're connecting these issues, you just can't say you throw out these other more aggressive tactics—the things that are going to piss people off. Because that's where we get our power. We would never have been in the position where we could help the Nuu-chah-nulth, or raise that kind of money in the Great Bear Rainforest, if we hadn't had the conflict that built our power base. So I think we need all of those tactics. And when we are working with First Nations as an environmental community, [it's important] that we respect their position and we don't take their voice. I always saw our job in the Great Bear as giving First Nations leaders an opportunity to tell their story."

It's called *sharing power*, and in the United States an entire movement has grown up—initiated by the IEN among others—placing an emphasis on the connection between social justice and environmental justice and insisting on the leadership of the communities that are most affected, whether indigenous communities, poor people in coastal towns such as New Orleans, people of colour in urban ghettos, or poor white people in Appalachia.

The almost universal recognition of the climate crisis in the United States has meant that a lot of money and media attention are focused there. Just as environmental activists such as Berman are realizing the importance of social justice issues, so human rights and social justice activists are beginning to link their issues to environmental concerns. Van Jones and Majora Carter have taken this convergence to another level. Jones told an audience at Bioneers in 2007:

> I've spent the past twenty years trying to get people in this country to pay attention to what's going on in urban America. Kids are dying, we are going to funerals every other weekend. Not interested. Kids going to school, thirty kids in the classroom, six books, no chalk. Not interested. Police brutality. Not interested. The United States is the major incarcerator in the world. We've got 5 percent of the world's population and

25 percent of the world's prisoners. One out of every four people who is in prison in the world is locked up in the United States. Not interested. Then I said, We want green jobs and not jail for our youth. And they said, GREEN … get that guy a microphone.

Majora Carter comes from the South Bronx, one of the worst ghettos in America. Some 60 percent of the South Bronx, including most of the social and affordable housing, was lost to the construction of highways. Carter calls the South Bronx "one of the regional sacrifice zones created to support hyper-consumption." She noticed that the increasing attention in the media being given to the environment was matched by decreasing news about civil rights. According to Carter, "Environmental justice is the civil rights struggle of the twenty-first century."

Both Jones and Carter talk about the disproportionate impact of pollution and environmental destruction in the ghettos in which they work and live. One out of every four kids in the South Bronx has asthma.

Carter was walking her dog one day, and he dragged her over to a green spot at the mouth of the Bronx River. If a little corner of the Bronx River could be green, she thought, why not build a park along the Bronx River? Since the rate of unemployment in that community is 25 percent, she got the idea of hiring local youth, training them in environmental restoration, and solving two problems in one.

Once she'd accomplished that, Carter went on to develop a broader program, reclaiming the land around an abandoned throughway and building affordable housing, using the labour of local young people in the construction of sustainable housing. In 2001, she created an organization called Sustainable South Bronx. Its vision is to combine environmental and social solutions in creating a more sustainable community that meets economic and social needs as well as improves the environment. "If we can put a cap on carbon emissions," Carter says, "we'd better learn to put a cap on poverty emissions too."

Together, Jones and Carter have founded an organization called Green Jobs for All. They are redefining social justice in a green context. Like any successful social movement leaders, they are, as we used to say in the 1960s, "seizing the time." Jones says the leadership of this new century will come from these places of convergence. Founded in 2007, Green Jobs for All is an example of a new cross-country movement rooted in local projects, with the goal of raising one billion dollars to elevate two hundred and fifty thousand young people out of poverty and into green jobs.

When people say to Van Jones that it will cost ten thousand dollars to train unemployed youth from the ghetto to retrofit buildings, he responds, "The green economy doesn't just count what you spend; you count what you save. What you have to understand is that when you give a young man or woman that extra support, when you take the people who most need work and connect them with the work that most needs doing, when you do that, you save ... the prison costs, the children they leave behind, you save not only money, you save the soul of this country. That is what you save when you invest and give people hope."

Another leader of the Green Jobs for All campaign is Billy Parish, who dropped out of Yale in 2002 to help build a student movement around clean energy and global warming in the United States and Canada. Parish helped found the Energy Action Coalition, a U.S.- and Canada-wide youth anti-global-warming coalition with about fifty organizations. Naming him its number-one environmental hero of 2005 (Al Gore was number two), *Rolling Stone* magazine wrote:

> Working on a laptop and sleeping on couches from San Francisco to North Dakota, Parish has galvanized students across the country to take action on global warming. In July he led a three-day fast at the White House to call attention to the estimated 150,000 deaths caused each year by climate change. He dispatched a bus that runs on biodiesel and vegetable oil to tour summer music festivals and promote fuel efficiency, culmi-

nating in a two-day forum in Detroit. And he has persuaded
more than 120 universities to sign the Campus Climate
Challenge, vowing to lower their emissions of greenhouse gases.

But Parish wasn't satisfied with the limits of this student-based
coalition. Realizing that two-thirds of the youth who were the potential base of his organization were not in school, he decided that a different strategy was needed to reach them. He told me in an interview:

> I came up with really just a seed of an idea, which became the
> Clean Energy Corps—a program loosely based on the civilian
> conservation corps during the Depression at the time of the
> great New Deal programs ... and loosely based on the other
> corps programs since then—Peace Corps, AmeriCorps, and
> others. The first person I called was Van Jones.
>
> There were a lot of local green jobs initiatives but no national
> initiative. We decided to go with a short-term legislative strategy
> that became the Green Jobs Act of 2007, which was part of the
> Energy Bill, and that will authorize $125 million for green jobs,
> training programs, block grants to cities around the country to
> build green jobs training programs. We're also pushing the much
> larger national vision of this program to create five million green
> jobs. It's kind of staggering what we realized we'd be able to do
> with that many people. We're looking at forty million low-
> income homes that need to be retrofitted and weatherized. We
> figured we could do all of those homes in ten years. We looked
> at the school building stock, and we figured we could do half of
> the K–12 schools in the country, major retrofits. Look at the
> transportation systems, rebuilding a sort of mass transit infra-
> structure. Habitat restoration and public parks—just a huge
> amount of work that needed to be done, and if we were able to
> organize this thing.... The model was hard job corps focusing
> on full wraparound services for formerly incarcerated people,
> other sorts of support services to allow them to keep the jobs

and build their skills. So that was the idea of the Clean Energy Corps, and that number, five million green jobs, we kind of made up, as a clean, round number. But that has become one of the main rallying cries in the country now, in the climate/clean energy movement.

Green jobs as an economic strategy is spreading rapidly across the United States. In April 2008, the Blue Green Alliance, a partnership between the United Steelworkers (USW) and the Sierra Club, launched the national Green Jobs for America campaign. The goal of their campaign is a serious commitment to clean, renewable energy to make the United States more energy independent, help end dependence on fossil fuels, and create more than 820,000 new green jobs nationwide. Van Jones got a standing ovation at their recent conference. The Apollo Alliance, which is a more conservative coalition of environmental organizations, business, and labour, is also talking about green jobs. Barack Obama included the goal of five billion dollars for green jobs in his acceptance speech at the Democratic National Convention and continued to feature the idea coming into the election.

When I asked Parish why the idea of a government-sponsored jobs program would take off in this era of neo-liberalism, he responded,

> There aren't really that many big ideas that progressives have been pushing that are truly unifying across a broad range of issue areas. So I think that's one of them. We've been able to attract support from a number of unions, environmental groups, civil rights groups, business groups, seniors groups, just a wide range of organizations. Part of it is also just the recognition of how urgent the climate situation is, and that we need to be thinking much bigger than we have in the past. And for enviros in particular, it comes from a recognition that's slowly been growing, about the fact that it's a problem how white and upper-middle class the movement has been, and unless we do a much better

job of trying to build bridges and make the movement much more diverse than it is, we're not going to be able to see the gains that we need.

And, of course, in face of the economic collapse, Barack Obama is looking for ways to kick-start the economy. The idea of green jobs gives him a ready program. The great thing about the Green Jobs campaign is that it can be funded by many sources, including various levels of government, private foundations, and even corporations who want their green record to go beyond "greenwashing."

It is also an excellent investment for union pension funds. There is an enormous amount of wealth in union pension funds; in the United States, they are now worth more than seven trillion dollars, and estimations are that Canadian pension funds are about 10 percent of that. There has been a debate for a couple of decades about using these huge concentrations of wealth to support progressive change rather than supporting the existing economic system, which damages workers' rights on multiple levels.

About ten years ago I asked the CEO of the massive Ontario Teachers' Pension Plan, which alone has $108.5 billion in net assets, why he wouldn't use at least some of that money to invest in economic alternatives that would be better for teachers and their families. He answered that his only responsibility was to the retirees, not to the workers. But as Leo Gerard, a Sudbury miner who is now president of the United Steelworkers International, told the left-wing Canadian news website www.straightgoods.ca:* "It is time for labour to harness its share of this capital and develop strategies that will help rather than hurt workers." Certainly there is no doubt that green jobs are a productive strategy for union pension funds and a positive way for unions to go beyond protecting their own members to using their power to create positive solutions for society as a whole.

---

*Leo Gerard interview, October 2008.

The Green Jobs campaign is a good example of the value of thinking outside the narrow boxes in which much of the Left and the social movements have been stuck after years of fighting defensive battles against the Right. This creative thinking can lead to the vision for a future society that will inspire new generations to work for change. Breaking from single issues to seeing the common ground where multiple problems can be solved is critical to new politics. Finding ways of working together that share resources, power, and knowledge is—and will continue to be—fundamental.

Another feature of this kind of convergence as seen in the example of Green Jobs for All is a bottom-up network structure with a diversity of participants rather than a traditional top-down coalition structure.

8
———

NETWORKED POLITICS

A New Grammar of Democracy

WHILE THE NEW LEFT OF THE 1960S, feminism, and various New Age projects challenged authoritarianism, the political Left never managed to change its authoritarian and patriarchal mode of functioning. The Left believed that to be effective and take on a centralized and authoritarian power, they, too, had to concentrate power. For the social democratic Left, the pressure of the media to conform to highly managed political interventions and, eventually, to highly managed political conventions was deadly to internal party democracy. As early as 1979,* British socialist feminists were making the argument that the political Left needed to transform itself, following the example of the new social movements, most importantly the feminist movement.

But the problem goes beyond patriarchal modes of functioning to our very notions of power. The Left has always seen power as being located in the state and in the corporations. The way to change the world was to get state power and make changes to state and economic structures. The women's movement, anti-racist groups, and the environmental movement introduced the idea that we must also

———

*See Sheila Rowbotham, Hilary Wainwright, et al., *Beyond the Fragments* (London: Merlin Press, 1979).

change our personal behaviour if we want to change the world. All these movements broadened the idea of politics into the realm of the personal relationships between people and the relationship between humans and the environment. Power was understood as something each of us exercises in our lives as part of a dominant group, including our human dominance over nature and its creatures. These ideas of power were influential in organizations and in community, but somehow didn't change our ideas of political change. Today, we are seeing the beginnings of that kind of change in the notions of transformative power. Hilary Wainwright writes in her saucy U.K. magazine *Red Pepper*:*

> Closely associated with an understanding of transformative power are the distinctive understandings of knowledge influenced by movement-based politics. In good part as a result of this politics and—not unrelated—developments in the philosophy of science, we are increasingly aware of the plural sources of knowledge: as tacit, practical and experiential as well as scientific. We are working increasingly with complexity, ambivalence and uncertainty....
>
> A recognition of the many perspectives from which a single phenomenon can be understood must be reclaimed as tools for analyzing and changing a complex real world.
>
> These new understandings of knowledge point towards an emphasis on the horizontal sharing and exchange of knowledge and collaborative attempts to build connected alternatives and shared memories. They stress the gaining of knowledge as a process of discovery and therefore see political action, the exercise of transformative power, as itself a source of knowledge, revealing unpredicted problems or opportunities.
>
> This recognition of the importance of experiential and practical knowledge deepens the nature of debate. It implies

---

*www.redpepper.org.uk/Rethinking-political-parties. Also available on paper by subscription.

debate driven not so much by the struggle for positions of power as by a search for truth about the complexity of social change, a production of collaborative knowledge that itself becomes a source of power.

An early example of this kind of collaborative knowledge emerged from a decimated labour movement in the United States in the 1980s. Then president Ronald Reagan had waged a relentless attack against trade union rights that had seriously weakened not only the labour movement but the rights of workers. The mainstream labour movement was stuck in business unionism,* and unable to change its tactics to meet the new challenge coming from neo-liberalism.

Some progressive unionists decided to take another route, going around the power of the leadership of the labour movement rather than confronting it head on. These union activists understood that organizing the workers in the new economy—including those in precarious work, part-time and contract workers who are rarely organized—would be central to rebuilding the union movement. They also understood that making allies within the community would be the key to success. They created an organization called Jobs with Justice.

I first learned about Jobs with Justice at the World Social Forum in 2002. I noticed them because there were so few U.S. groups at that Social Forum and because they were working with some Canadian groups I knew. A few years later, at a leadership training session I attended at the Rockwood Institute, I met Sarita Gupta, who is now the executive director of Jobs with Justice. I asked her how Jobs with Justice organizes. She said,

> Even though we are a national network, each of our local groups
> is locally autonomous. Because of our commitment to local

Business unionism refers to trade unions that see their role strictly in economic terms of organizing and negotiating, as opposed to *social unionism*, a term that refers to unions that also work on a variety of social issues, such as women's rights, usually in coalition with community groups.

autonomy, our national office doesn't say, "Here is the campaign that everyone is going to work on." Our leadership has resisted the normal model of national organizations. We felt that in order to build a strong grassroots worker movement in this country, we have to make sure the organization is accountable to local struggles.

We've built a network that's collaborative and not competitive because we understand that we are part of a broader movement, learning from one another. There is a big culture of peer-to-peer learning. Instead of the experts in the national office swooping in to help the national campaigns, we look to one another to help, so our coalition in Boston will help our coalition in New York City.

Our structure is hybrid. We have national stakeholders, but also each of our local coalitions have institutions around the table as a steering committee or whatever governing body works best for them. We also have activists who sign a pledge card saying, "We are committing to be there for someone else's struggle as well as our own at least five times in the next year." We have a hundred thousand people who have signed these cards and are the base of mobilization. Those activists are playing a very big role in helping to organize and ensuring we are actually speaking to people.

Early on we structured it that way and resisted the notion of paid staff. Larry Cohen, who is one of our founders from the Communications Workers, said, "If we are going to do this right, then I will commit as a union that our organizers will give 10 percent of their time to helping get the coalition up and running." This helped us resist hiring full-time staff. Now it's twenty-one years since we were founded, and we are slowly moving toward hiring. But everything we do considers staff and volunteers. For example, we never just do training for the staff, we always include activists and community leaders, so that collective learning is happening in a cross-section, not just for the staff.

People who work with Jobs with Justice come together around an issue or set of issues and make decisions for that particular struggle. It starts at the local level, where the ongoing work takes place. Volunteers can participate at multiple levels of commitment, and decisions are made by consensus.

Like Clayton Thomas Mueller from the IEN, Gupta calls this action *base-building*. She explained, "People take the pledge to support others very seriously. Part of our ideology is around this movement work. We believe that through taking collective action, people are transformed, and their vision of the world or what is right or wrong changes, and their commitment changes."

Gupta told some stories to illustrate the depth of solidarity they have managed to organize. In Washington state, Jobs with Justice was involved in a huge campaign of janitors who were organizing to form a union. At the same time, there was a stagehands' strike of IATSE. The stagehands called for community support to shut down a major theatre where there was going to be a huge show, and janitors came out in support of that struggle. Then, when the janitors went on strike, the stagehands came out in force to support them.

"There was this notion of solidarity and reciprocity," said Gupta, "but it was deeper than that. The stagehands said, 'It helped us a lot when these janitors who worked so hard all day came out on our picket line.' It was deeper. That's the connectedness that we strive for at Jobs with Justice."

She added, "In St. Louis a couple of years ago, there was a terrible case of police brutality. People at the table said, 'We are taking on a police accountability struggle,' and there was a racial divide. Unions initially resisted organizing solidarity, but they could hear what the community allies were saying, and finally St. Louis Jobs with Justice played a huge role in that fight for police accountability."

Gupta points out that the organization is rooted in local struggles. It is at those local tables, as she calls them, that relationships are built. These relationships permit differences to be worked out. Then the national organization can help to mobilize across cities to support a particular local struggle or organize a national campaign that is supported across the board. At the moment, Jobs with Justice's national campaigns include a push to strengthen labour laws to regain rights lost under Reagan and a demand for public health care insurance.

It makes sense that Jobs with Justice was founded by some of the organizing departments of local unions, since this locally based, relationship-building, networked approach has always been that of organizers trying to get new people involved in the union. The organizing departments of unions have always been closest to the ground and to grassroots workers. It's not surprising, then, that Jobs with Justice, a new kind of labour organization that works with the unions, is at the same time outside of them, working with the community.

Given the failure of the Left, the labour movement, and the social movements to creatively resist neo-liberalism, it makes sense that when a new generation emerged to fight corporate globalization, they created horizontal structures and demonstrated an abhorrence of any kind of top-down leadership. In the demonstrations against the various summits of the WTO, FTAA, G8, and the rest of the alphabet soup of global-governance institutions, young demonstrators set up affinity groups and spoke circles* that made decisions by consensus.

These affinity groups have morphed into a new kind of movement politics that is most advanced in Europe. It is called *networked politics*, and it is tremendously effective in a number of ways. Many of the most visible protests in Europe, such as the Spanish response to the 2004 Madrid subway bombings, the rebellion of immigrant youth in the suburbs of Paris in 2005, and the mass upsurge in France in 2006 against a new employment bill that discriminated against young workers, were all organized through informal networks. When formally organized political forces wanted to set up a coordinating

---

*A spoke circle is a meeting of people from each affinity group, usually during an action, to make consensus decisions and share information. Like the spokes of a wheel, they come together and then spread, thus strengthening the network.

body in Spain to institutionalize these semi-spontaneous uprisings, none of the young people involved were interested. Not only do these groups resist any kind of formal structure, they also opt out of the corporate global media system by refusing to have identifiable leaders or spokespeople.

Jeff Juris, an American activist and academic from this new generation, explains "that none of these practices or ideas are necessarily new; these discussions go back to the debate in the early part of the twentieth century about different kinds of organization [between anarchists and socialists]. But technology facilitates more decentralized practices, and allows for scalability. In the debate between vertical and horizontal forms, the horizontal forms perhaps have more of an advantage than they used to, so they are diffusing relatively widely."

The World Social Forum is probably the largest and most complex political network in the world. Its Charter of Principles contains three principles of horizontality. One is respect for diversity that not only values and celebrates political, social, and cultural diversity but sees the need to constantly extend the network to new actors. The second principle is that no individual or organization can speak in the name of the network. People may speak for themselves or for their own organizations, but no one speaks for the WSF. The third has to do with the inevitable decision-making process that comes from this form of organization, and it insists on consensus.

Before you roll your eyes and say that this could never work on a large scale considering the complexity of modern society, we should look at a very similar network that has taken on mighty Microsoft and produced an amazingly successful computer operating system, as well as numerous programs that many believe are of much higher quality than the corporate product. Open source software functions like a network, in many ways similar to the World Social Forum.

The open source system, also called Linux, was created by Linus Torvalds, whose approach has been characterized as "release [program codes] early and release often; delegate everything you can; be open to the point of promiscuity." In theory, this could result in products and projects that were chaotic and contradictory. However, Linux competes successfully with Microsoft, which is based on the old proprietary methods, and continues to grow.

Contributors to open source projects are motivated by the challenge of writing new code, building on the creativity of others, and the chance to act as partners in the project, rather than by personal financial gain. Challenge and the opportunity to collaborate must be available before a person can start an open source project, or a project founded on the open source model. While people pursue their individual interests, they are doing so while promoting the good of all. Thus, while each person is actually following his or her own agenda, the end result also benefits everyone else involved. In a way, open source turns the neo-liberal ideal of self-interest as a motivating force for the market on its head, liberating the creativity of each individual but in the context of a collective project, in which sharing knowledge and building on the knowledge of others becomes the goal—rather than profit and competition.

This is a particularly exciting idea, because one of the acknowl-edged strengths of capitalism is its capacity for innovation, and we are always told that money must be the motivating force for that innova-tion. Open source proves that challenge—rather than money—can be the motivating force for innovation.

The metaphor of "open source" is also becoming a key element in the new ideas about democracy. The code is legible, transparent, and open. It can be modified by anyone and favours individual autonomy, participation, and control over giving power to a representative or a particular group. Openness, as an ethical principle, also refers to reciprocal listening, communication, connectivity, and inclusion.

Jai Sen, a veteran activist from India who is theorizing this idea of open space, says,

> The central idea here is that an open space, rather than a party or movement, allows for more and different forms of relations among political actors, while remaining open-ended with respect

to outcomes. It is open in that encounters among multiple subjects with diverse objectives can have transformative political effects that traditional forms of movements, coalitions, and campaigns, with uniform themes and goals, exclude. By the name itself, it also seems to offer scope for a much wider range of actors to take part and contribute, including those not necessarily involved with politics or movement; so it is more inclusive.*

Of course, neither the software movement nor the anti-globalization movement lives up to these ideals, but both demonstrate that individuals and groups working together as equals, without power being distributed in a hierarchical way, can be very effective at producing the results that the group desires.

Given the strength of unions and left-wing political parties in Italy, Spain, and France, it is significant that the most advanced forms of networked politics have emerged in these countries. In 2007 in Berlin, I attended an intergenerational discussion among activists and intellectuals who were looking at the political meaning of these new forms of organization. Organized by Hilary Wainwright, who even more than thirty years ago was making a democratic critique of the Left, by Marco Berlinguer, an Italian activist researcher who is the coordinator of Transform! Italia, and by Mayo Fuster I. Morrell, a Catalan activist researcher on techno-political tools†, the periodic discussion brought together the most open-minded of my generation of the Left with leaders and thinkers of the anti-globalization generation to identify, and critically examine, the nature of the new politics.

This group had met a year earlier in Barcelona and had produced a pamphlet of their discussions, in which activist Sophie Gosselin reported on the movement of young people in France in 2006 to protest a new law "casualizing" employment.

---

*Jai Sen, "Opening Open Space: Notes on the Grammar and Vocabulary of the Concept of Open Space," discussion draft (May 2007).
†www.transform.it

> In March 2006, a new wave of social protest rushed across
> France giving new generations the experience of politics, self-
> organization, collective decision-making, conflicts of interest,
> power relationships, purposeful use of information and
> language—in short, what is called "democracy."

It began when a group of students at the University of Nantes
called a general assembly and voted to occupy the university,
stopping classes while they organized a protest against the proposed
law on *first employment,* a term used in France to refer to people hired
for the first time. The law proposed lower salaries and less job protection for these new hires. There's nothing new about a university
occupation, but using email and www.indymedia.org, the students
spread the word across France, and what followed was a virtual insur-
rection. General assemblies in one university after another decided to
stage occupations. These protests followed on the heels of the revolt
of immigrant youth in *la banlieue* (suburbs) of Paris the year before,
and the students made alliances with unemployed and part-time
workers, sending the struggle into the neighbourhoods. University
occupations spread into flying blockades of stations, roads, shops,
and airports. Instead of the general strike called by the leadership of
the trade union movement, work was stopped by grassroots activism
in the streets through blockades of transport. The rapid growth of the
protests provoked a broad-based political crisis in France and the
government turned to the trade union movement to negotiate a
compromise.

Sophie Gosselin continued,

> The hiatus between "representative" organizations and informal
> groups highlighted the tension that currently drives social strug-
> gles, the tension between traditional structures, which stem
> from the struggles of the 19th century and the emerging forms
> based on network practices.

The formal student bodies and unions were criticized by the student assemblies. Trade unions had taken on the role of speaking for the movements with the government, but were really speaking for their own organizations, not for the movement as a whole, so mistrust was amplified.

Not able to find leaders or spokespeople, the mainstream media focused on the spectacle and on the debate about whether to employ blockades as a tactic. Meanwhile the movement used blogs, websites, and email lists not only to distribute information but as a means of self-organization.

Students at Nantes created a union called Sud étudiants [South Students] that functioned parallel to the existing student unions. Its job was not to represent students but rather to provide tools, such as techniques and finances, for the self-organization of students, in a similar fashion to the IEN in North America. There are different levels of membership in Sud étudiants based on levels of commitment, from the most active and engaged to those who are interested only in a single action of the network. Leadership is based on activity, not on being recognized by the media as a spokesperson.

Said Gosselin:

> One of the conclusions, which emerged from my interview with these students, is that the movement was centred on the re-appropriation of democratic space by the new generations.... The crisis of representation is related to the obsolescence of the traditional model of political organization, which supposes a homogeneous body (the nation, the people, the workers, etc.) creating its own image, delegating power to some representative authority. Central to this [new conception of democracy] is the space—the "agora," as the open space in the heart of Athens was known. We had multiple new spaces in which to speak, where everybody is considered equal, spaces in perpetual transformation according to new bonds and networks into which cells enter.

The uprising of 2006 in France could have been the equivalent of May–June 1968, when students ignited an upsurge across France that defined a generation of struggle throughout the Western world. The impact of the 2006 uprising is less clear, because one of the features of this kind of organizing is that it is impermanent and doesn't leave behind institutions to continue the work of the initial struggle or to be co-opted by authorities.

Marco Berlinguer explains what he sees as the de-institutionalization of society:

> "The principle of de-institutionalization" has several dimensions: We observe an increasing reduction of the role of institutions in structuring, mediating, or representing the social relations of which we are part. This trend has many negative sides: the growth of the precarious economy, criminal activities and networks, the abandonment of entire territories marginal to the priorities of the market, and the destruction of social regulation and protection.
>
> On the positive side, this principle recognizes the degeneration of the traditional political institution. It also points to the potential of and capacity for self-organization. It suggests a challenge to rethink the shape, the role and even the very concept of political institutions in light of more advanced conceptions of democracy.

Lawrence Cox, an Irish activist and sociologist, said at the Berlin seminar that we must redefine the way we see power itself. Instead of seeing it as located in the state or in the corporation, we have to see power as something in all of our relationships. "Then every single movement we do is a laboratory in which we are experimenting with the grammar of democracy. If we get together in a circle and balance the presence of women and men, we are somehow thinking about how the future grammar of democracy will be."

This is an exciting idea, because it means each of us can change the theory and practice of democracy through how we interact in our organizations.

Thomas Paine, a father of the American Revolution and an important democratic theorist, pointed out in his 1792 essay *The Rights of Man*:

> It appears to general observation, that revolutions create genius and talents; but those events do no more than bring them forward. There exists in man, a mass of sense lying in a dormant state, and which, unless something excites it to action, will descend with him, in that condition to the grave. As it is to the advantage of society that the whole of its faculties should be employed, the construction of government ought to be able as such to bring forward, by a quiet and regular operation, all that extent of capacity which never fails to appear in revolutions.

Perhaps the young activists across Europe and North America are practising a form of democracy, which, while short of revolution, does manage to liberate the genius and talents in ordinary people by using open space, horizontal structures, and self-organization. The question is how does this liberation of human potential interact with existing power structures to transform them?

In 2008, the Networked Politics group produced a paper for the Organizing Committee of the World Social Forum. It was a discussion paper for a debate about the direction and structure of the WSF, and it compared the new networked politics to social networking sites on the internet, such as Facebook, Flickr, MySpace, and YouTube. Anyone can join these sites very easily, and the only requirement is that they reveal a little something about themselves.

> This implies a new relational model that is distinct from that of a traditional community. It is rather based on a kind of weak cooperation which is not a pre-requisite for joining a platform

but occurs afterwards. The motivation to cooperate is driven neither by self-interest, nor by a community feeling. Instead, the possibility for weak cooperation involves first a sort of conversational model where people expose themselves in order for the collaboration to start. One participant calls this relational model "public individualism," noting its application in current modes of activism in the Western world. There we have passed from a type of activism favouring long-term affiliation—"stamp on a card" activism—to one that is temporary and contingent—"note on the fridge" activism.

Of course, the problem with "note on the fridge" activism is that it doesn't take much to take the note *off* the fridge. As one global justice activist put it:

> I think it is all very well to learn as we walk, but what happens when your walking comes to the edge of a cliff? If you haven't talked about things beforehand, what happens is what I think happened to the anti-globalization movement. When the going was good, everything was easy. But when we had problems, because we didn't have prior agreements, we just all went home, because we didn't know how to react to a stone in the way.

Some answers to that question might be found in the experience of Jobs with Justice. At first, the powerful U.S. labour federation AFL–CIO saw them as a threat. By building relationships with the union locals at the local level, Jobs with Justice managed to slowly develop a relationship with the national leadership that had been hostile to them. "Even today, I can go and talk to the national director of the Ironworkers and say, 'We are working with Ironworkers locals in six cities around this and that issue,' and it makes a relationship at the national level much more likely," explains Sarita Gupta. It also changes the power relationship between the union and the organization. It is building relationships at the local level that permits working out conflict.

Jobs with Justice also collaborates with the extraordinary network of workers' centres in the United States. There are about two hundred workers' centres around the country organizing precarious workers, with a special emphasis on immigrant workers and workers of colour. Many of them were established by the workers themselves, because the labour movement wasn't interested in them.

"People in the labour movement would say, 'Why are we helping day labourers, they are taking our jobs?'" Gupta recounts. "Working with those fears, speaking to them and moving people to support day labourers takes time and patience and a lot of struggling with each other. We are now positioned to have some of those harder conversations between people who have said, 'Forget it, unions are sellouts' and the unions themselves. There's a shift in energy right now that we all have to work together. The AFL–CIO now has a national co-coordinator for workers' centres, something that was unimaginable even ten years ago."

At the international level, we have also seen the tremendous impact of networked politics. The desire of the Chinese government to bring positive attention to the Beijing Olympics was initially thwarted by a small group of Tibetan activists and their allies in Canada, who used the internet and their connections with similar groups around the world to organize protests against the international relay of the Olympic torch. This same group brought international attention to the issue of human rights for Tibet by dropping a banner from the Great Wall and blogging about their experience. On one level, this was an act of courage, using the relative privilege of Canadian citizenship to risk speaking out in China against the Chinese regime. On another, it was a sophisticated media stunt that was amplified through the internet but also made an impact in the mainstream media.

This kind of tactic was pioneered by Greenpeace as a brilliant way of focusing light on an issue or a polluter, but the difference today is that a one-off publicity stunt can stimulate a movement. The banner on the Great Wall no doubt created a focus for the pro-Tibetan European activists, who then picked up the call to protest against the

Olympic torch. An important feature of this kind of organizing is that no one controls it. That's one of the big differences between horizontal and vertical organizing. While the Canadian activists may have initiated the idea of protesting, others who may have no contact with them outside of a website or an email picked it up and ran with it.

Here networked politics combine with people's globalization to ensure a level of international solidarity that we have rarely seen in the past. In the last year alone in Toronto, communities from Burma, Kenya, Tibet, China, Pakistan, and the Middle East have organized demonstrations, rallies, and meetings that have been supported by church, union, student, and other activists across the city to support a struggle for human rights or against war in their home countries. Some of these have been large and impressive. I was asked to speak at the Burma demonstration, and was amazed at the size and spirit of the event. It was certainly the first time in my life that I have spoken at a rally after chanting by Buddhist monks.

Another wonderful example of networked politics was the work of the Sierra Youth Club at the United Nations Climate Change conference in Bali in 2007. Thirty young people from across Canada paid their own way to Bali to make sure there was a strong youth presence there. Along with youth from other countries, they organized two weeks of activities, focusing on media events. During every lunch break, they performed a variety of creative actions, and every day at 5 p.m. they named the Fossil of the Day. Rosa Kouri, a twenty-three-year-old environmental activist, was active at the conference.

"We can play up the youth card because we are so innocent and approachable," she told me, "so we actually got a space from the UN. We did it super theatrically and we had a song to the theme of *Jurassic Park*. We gave the media something dramatic and fun to cover, and we got on CNN."

But the young activists didn't focus only on the mainstream media. When they realized that Canada was a major block to agreement, they put together a petition in collaboration with www.avaaz.org, a website specializing in online petitions. Avaaz is member-driven, and

3.2 million strong, another example of networked politics online. Within thirty-six hours they had fifty thousand signatures on their petition asking Canada not to block agreement. On the global petition, Avaaz mobilized three-hundred thousand signatures in just seventy-two hours.

"People understood the urgency of it," Kouri recounts. "Joanna Defoe tried to present a petition to John Baird [Canada's Minister of the Environment], and his head of security wouldn't even let her present the petition, so that was ridiculous. She was really upset and trying hard not to cry. We did a video of her saying she didn't understand why they wouldn't even take the petition, and that video went on YouTube and got a ton of reaction from Canada."

At midnight the night before the last day of the conference, it seemed that if Canada continued to block the agreement, it would fail entirely. Kouri continues,

> It was the morning in Canada, so we sent out a call-out asking people to phone the [prime minister] or the cell phone of the PM's spokesperson in Bali, and sent it out to all our networks. It was so urgent. We told them they had six hours. So many people called that the PM's switchboard went down and so did the spokesperson's cell phone. I think we made a huge impact with that. We had a sign that said, "This will follow you home" and we unfurled it when the Canadian delegation walked in.
>
> We had the petition and the call-out and the videos and we posted a thank-you online too. I think we had a huge impact, especially on the news. It's sad to me that the best you can hope for is news, but that's where the issue is at. Government is fundamentally committed to not doing anything, so we have to expose that. We wouldn't be able to do what we did without the environmental policy experts. A few of us make sure we are not crazy radical youth who don't know what we are talking about, but we are crazy radical youth who *do* know what we are talking about.

And that's another aspect of networked politics: Everyone does what they do best. In this case, the ENGOs focused on lobbying and policy and left the direct action to the youth. The ENGOs didn't burn any bridges, but they willingly shared their expertise with the youth so their actions could be more credible in assisting the lobbying going on inside.

There is nothing new in the strategy of using more radical action to make space for more moderate action. In the civil rights movement there was Martin Luther King, but there was also Malcolm X. In the women's movement, too, we had radicals and moderates. But in those days we had savage debates about whose tactics were more effective, who was a sellout, or who was discrediting the movement. Today, there is an acknowledgment of a diversity of tactics and often an acceptance and appreciation for each group and individual as they do what they do best.

The Obama campaign used the principles of networked politics both to fundraise and to organize. The most sophisticated online fundraising operation in the world, www.moveon.org, was assisting him, and obviously he has brilliant online strategists from the generation that grew up with networking online. While the campaign machine itself was probably organized in a fairly traditional, professional, top-down manner, they were organizing a grassroots campaign. If you signed up as a volunteer, you could get a list of phone numbers of people to call and a script of what to say. No one monitored what you were doing; you didn't have to join the Democratic Party to do it or go to a meeting to be trained. They just assumed that if you supported Barack Obama and wanted to volunteer time, then they wanted you involved.

In the kickoff of the presidential campaign, they contacted every supporter from the primary races to get involved in a day of action. The message read:

> A year ago this week, our grassroots supporters organized a nationwide canvass in more than 1,000 cities to introduce people to Barack Obama.

Since then, we've had an unprecedented primary season that built a grassroots infrastructure in all 50 states—not just for Barack, but for all of the Democratic candidates.

Now it's time to bring all of that energy together for our common cause of change.

All across the country, Democrats, Independents, and even Republicans are tired of the politics of the past and are looking for new solutions to the challenges we're facing.

That's why we're launching a nationwide day of action on Saturday, June 28th, called "Unite for Change"—and asking you to host a Unite for Change meeting in your neighborhood. In all 50 states, supporters like you—seasoned veterans and first-time volunteers alike—will host house meetings to reach out and bring together folks who supported all of the Democratic candidates (and those who are just tuning in to the process now).

The goal is to come together and use the common values we share to build a united volunteer organization in your neighborhood that will register new voters and build support locally.

It's going to be an amazing time, and hosting your own event is easy. We'll provide all the tools and resources you'll need. Here are the details:

Unite for Change Meetings
Saturday, June 28th
Host one in your community

That's it. Anyone who got that email could host a meeting for Barack Obama. Notice how the email message gives credit to the grassroots supporters for beginning the process, and how easy and fun it makes it for someone to host an event at their house. Just like the Sud étudiants in France, the IEN, or Jobs with Justice, the Obama campaign provided the tools and resources and left it up to the individual to handle the meeting. That kind of confidence in supporters is rarely seen in a traditional campaign, in which control over the message and the campaign is of paramount importance.

It wasn't just online that this open, friendly approach governed the campaign. According to an October 8 article in his blog at huffington post.com, electoral campaign expert Zack Exley explains that the genius of the Obama campaign was in combining the openness of networked politics with a sophisticated electoral machine. "The Obama campaign is the first in the internet era to realize the dream of a disciplined, volunteer-driven, bottom-up-AND-top-down, distributed and massively scaleable organizing campaign," writes Exley. Instead of staff recruiting volunteers to knock on doors, they spent their time identifying volunteer team leaders and training them to organize others, thus vastly increasing the volunteer operation on the ground. The slogan of the organizing campaign was "Respect Empower Include."

Jeremy Bird, the Ohio general election director and one of the driving forces behind making teams a national strategy, said, "We decided in terms of timeline that [our organizers] would not be measured by the amount of voter contacts they made in the summer—but instead by the number of volunteers that they were recruiting, training, and testing. The regional field director for southwest Ohio, Christen Linke Young, said,

> I feel like people are committing more time this election because there's a community thing going on, and they're part of something that's local and social. But we're also more effective at harnessing volunteers because the teams do a lot of the training and debriefing themselves—it scales well. Everyone who goes out canvassing comes back with at least one story of someone they impacted. The team leaders are trained to give people time to tell those stories, and so everyone gets a sense of progress, and they learn from each other how to be more effective next time.

But when the openness of the Obama campaign met the vicious attacks of the McCain campaign, they were forced to a certain degree back into the old model of the battle of Titans. Nevertheless, they kept the positive message and the friendly, open approach to their supporters right up until election day.

Internet expert Jesse Hirsch says the Obama campaign will transform electoral politics in the same way as the Kennedy-Nixon debate, which marked the moment that television took over electoral campaigns. According to Hirsch, this is the moment that the internet will take over. Hirsch is not an Obama supporter, but he is impressed with his campaign's understanding of the online culture. "The whole language of his site, it's community, it's friends, it's social inclusion, it's social movement, it's the cloud campaign in the sense that there's a commanding control mechanism that's keeping tight control of the messaging and the candidate, but the rest of it is this feel-good kind of cultural milieu, where they're getting you to work, and they're getting you to donate, and they're getting you to fundraise, and they're getting you to do all the things that a normal campaign would do. But the language, the tone and the culture are all social. It's all social networking, it's all community building, it's all the internet love-in, as the Facebook thing is."

While no political party in Canada managed to take the risk of losing control required to use the internet in the same way as the Obama campaign, environmental and social activists who were concerned with the danger of a Conservative majority did. There were two websites at which voters could determine if they were in a swing riding where voting for the opposition party with the best chance of winning according to the latest polls would defeat a Conservative candidate. In an extraordinarily creative and apparently completely legal initiative, another group set up a Facebook site at which voters could swap votes—if I was in a safe riding for my party, I could swap my vote with someone who wanted to vote for a minority party but was in a swing riding where voting for one of the bigger progressive parties would defeat the Conservatives. Using Facebook style, they introduced voters to one another so they could chat and decide if they trusted one another enough to swap. All this is necessary because

Canada has five parties and a "first past the post" electoral system that means that a right-wing party can get as little as 35 percent of the vote and still form the government.

Networked politics has its weaknesses, of course. While open source is a great challenge to the capitalist dogma that only money and competition can create innovation, as a governance structure it has shortcomings. Jesse Hirsch points out: "Open source's problem is governance. They don't have a governing structure. They don't have a dialogue about governing structure. They have a dialogue about how to manage code, which is a type of governance structure. But they don't have a dialogue on how to manage labour, on how to manage decision-making." As a result, the open source community is really a series of fiefdoms, with benevolent dictators and a series of camps.

Participants in the World Social Forum are having a major debate about the advantages and disadvantages of open organizing, with critics saying that it is time the WSF moves away from such openness into action.

Diversity of tactics is a great idea when it comes to valuing different skills and strengths, but it can be highly problematic. When the Black Bloc in Quebec City decided that throwing stones was a good tactic to delay the police's assault on the crowd, their actions may have greatly aggravated the tear gas retaliation from the police, which lasted two days. There was no discussion about the wisdom of this tactic. Protestors were given the choice to enter a "green zone," in which violence was less likely, but when things heated up, the police didn't respect any of the zones created by the organizers.

Consequently, the event was depicted in the media as a violent demonstration. The reality is that most of the aggression came from the police, but one or two photos of masked stone-throwing protesters was enough for the state and the media to blame the mostly peaceful demonstrators for the violence. Over time, in informal discussions, the movement concluded that such tactics were no longer acceptable, and they largely stopped, especially after a protester was killed in Genoa. But in a network, and especially across networks, there is no clear method of resolving serious differences except to walk away. Some of the work being done on dialogue and consensus can help to solve these problems, as long as it is acknowledged that the problems exist.

The challenge is to figure out how the networked politics approach can impact on the hierarchical institutions that have most of the power in our society. Open source shows that on the economic and creative level, networks have as good or better outcomes than hierarchy. Obama shows that introducing even an element of networked politics into a highly structured political system can vastly increase people's participation and the campaign's creativity.

Recognizing the weaknesses of networked politics does not in any way take away from its considerable strengths. It is the network with roots in the ground, on which any lasting transformation of power will take place.

9

LEADERSHIP
The Political Is Personal

WHAT DOES LEADERSHIP MEAN in an era of networked politics? One thing we learned in the women's movement is that whether or not we want leaders, we get them. Leaders are people who influence others, either through force of personality or because of their position—or both.

I've been a leader as long as I can remember. In high school, I organized the student input into the school announcements. That's what passed for activism in the early 1960s. In university, I worked on the *McGill Daily* student newspaper. When the student council moved to fire the editor and everyone was packing to go, I got up on the desk and said, "We have to fight this thing. We can't just give up." And we took over the Arts newspaper, built it up so that it had a larger circulation than the *Daily*, and got back the *Daily*.

But there are two specific moments that I remember that helped shape the kind of leader I became.

When I graduated from university in 1967, I wanted to be a journalist. It's hard to believe today, but in those days we thought mainstream journalism was a place where your work could change the world. Together with my male comrades, I applied for an entry-level job writing radio news at a private radio station.

The man doing the hiring said to me: "I'm sorry, we don't hire girls here."

And I said, "Why not?"

"Well, the men swear in the newsroom, and they wouldn't be comfortable with a girl," he replied.

So I said, "I don't give a shit if they swear."

And, of course, I didn't get the job. I often tell this story, especially to young women, to show them how far we've come, but there's another lesson to be taken from this story. What I really should have said is: "Well, that's the most ridiculous thing I've ever heard." I should have said, "I'm a good writer and I can do this job well and you're not going to hire me because the men are uncomfortable with a woman? That's ridiculous."

But I didn't say that. Instead, I started to learn that if I wanted to be a writer in that newsroom, I was going to have to act like the men. And that's how I learned to lead. I learned to lead from men, positively and negatively.

A few years later, I had a male mentor. He was far ahead of his time in terms of supporting female leaders. In the early 1970s, he recognized a leadership quality in me. He told me: "You know, Judy, if you speak with confidence, people will believe everything you say."

He said this to me just before I was about to chair a public meeting of about five hundred people. I'd never really done any public speaking before. His remark stood me in great stead, because it really is true, but it also showed me a kind of leadership: a male, or a patriarchal, style of leadership. It is a style that says you have to hide your vulnerability, hide your fears, hide your doubts, hide all of that, be absolutely sure of yourself, and express an opinion, whether you have one or not, and really be willing to go to the wall to defend it.

I became very good at doing that, and in many ways it took me far. I learned from my father, I learned from my mentor, I learned negatively from what happened to me when I didn't lead like a man. And I was so good at it that I became a public figure even though I was a crazy left-winger.

What we've learned is to pattern our leadership after a model. Almost all of us have learned this, either consciously, as with my mentor, or unconsciously, in the way I internalized the lesson in applying for the job in the radio station. We all learn to lead by modelling ourselves after men, or women who lead like men.

Now *that* is a provocative statement, and I offer it because I think it's almost totally true. If you look at the most recognized women leaders— let's say, in politics—they have become very good at playing the game that men have created for leadership. Former deputy prime minister Sheila Copps is a good example. Frances Lankin is another: She was the most successful female minister in Bob Rae's Ontario government, maybe the most successful minister, and is now the executive director of the United Way of Greater Toronto. Speaking with me in an interview about being a woman in politics for my last book, she said,

> The male structure in which government works is very hierarchical. The pressure of the place drives some of that. If you're a minister, on any given day you have to get up and running fast. I came into government having worked in a consensus model, and at first we tried to work in government that way. I had to move quickly to match the style of that world. Very top-down, directive, and not consensus-oriented.
>
> I've found myself a lot in my life having to work in ways that I don't like. You get a strong training when you work in a male way of doing things, and it sometimes takes over how you are as a person. I sometimes wish I could have worked more in a women's collective and had more balance. I think this is why I've been successful in a man's world. I take pride in that, but not in thinking that I've changed things to make it easier for women coming along. I think there's a lot of work for women to do to change the way in which institutions are run.

Indeed there is a lot of work to do. In this book, you have read many ways in which we can encourage the leadership of people who are not usually encouraged to lead—participatory democracy; horizontal structures; sharing resources with marginalized groups; training—but here I want to talk about how those of us who have power, whether personal power, positional power, or the power of privilege, have to change ourselves to encourage leadership in others.

I am not sure whether Frances Lankin has found a way to change her leadership style now that she is out of politics, but I know that, for me, it has been a long and ongoing struggle. When I became president of the National Action Committee on the Status of Women in 1990, it didn't take long for me to realize that my way of leading, while it was effective in the world, was oppressive to other women. It stopped other women from being able to express themselves. One of the characteristics of patriarchal leadership is that it allows only two kinds of response—one is submission and the other is rebellion.

We are trained to submit to power in the family, at least in those families that still function in this patriarchal way. In school, we are taught to submit to the will of the teacher, and at work to the boss. It is no wonder that people look for that kind of leadership in community organizations too. One of the most important elements of the new ways of organizing we are discussing in this book is that most of them reject this patriarchal style of leadership.

It's not just progressive movements that are questioning this style of leadership. Most advanced management training today accepts the idea of emotional intelligence (EI), as systematized by Daniel Goleman. Goleman claims that emotional intelligence is a much better predictor of successful leadership than other factors more related to traditional leadership values, such as assertiveness. Here are the key elements of EI, according to Goleman:

1. Self-awareness—the ability to read one's emotions and recognize their impact, while using gut feelings to guide decisions.
2. Self-management—controlling one's emotions and impulses and adapting to changing circumstances.

3. Social awareness—the ability to sense, understand, and react to the emotions of others, while comprehending social networks.
4. Relationship management—the ability to inspire, influence, and develop others, while managing conflict.

Now these sound more like the things women are thought to be good at, not what men are thought to be good at. Just as industry has adopted many of the organizational principles of networking in organizing work, so progressive management is now using EI to do management training.

MANY OF US DON'T LIKE TO ADMIT we have power. And because most of us don't recognize our power, we tend to exercise it badly. Both the tendency to refuse to recognize leadership on the one hand or eating the leader on the other were problems in the women's movement, reactions that stemmed from the idea that we shouldn't have leaders at all. Some people have personal power. They are natural leaders. Wherever they work, whatever they do, people listen to them, and look to them for solutions. Natural leaders exist in both genders, in all classes, and in all cultures, but the dominant culture tends to recognize only leaders that fit the model of the patriarchal leader. This recognition reinforces tendencies to lead through domination, rather than through the many other ways of leading, such as inspiring, mentoring, nurturing, serving, supporting, etc. The exceptions to this are people of such tremendous personal power and integrity that they are universally recognized as leaders. When I ask any group to name leaders they admire, they always say Martin Luther King and Nelson Mandela. Neither man led in a dominating way, but they are still patriarchal leaders of a benevolent, fatherly kind. Barack Obama is providing another model of male leadership: strong and intelligent but also vulnerable; calm and centred, refusing to be drawn into anger and division; caring and finding time for his children, even at the height of a presidential campaign. If anyone ever doubted the importance of leadership, the impact of Obama's presidential campaign, not only in the United States but around the world, should put those doubts to rest. People need inspiration and recognition to get engaged in working for change. A leader such as Obama is not only an important role model but also gives people courage to be their better selves and hope that change is possible.

Most leadership is positional leadership. If you are anyone's boss or supervisor, if you are a parent, if you are on a committee that makes decisions that have an impact on other people's lives, if you are a teacher, if you are a police officer, if you are a politician, you have positional power. I was amazed how people related to me as a candidate when I ran for provincial office in the 1980s, even though I didn't have a hope in hell of winning. Many people invited me into their homes to ask if I could help them solve some problem they were having with the bureaucracy, assuming that because I was running for office, I had the power to do that.

Robert Gass was making a very good living at management training when he decided that the Left needed better leadership, so he founded the Rockwood Institute. I was lucky enough to attend their year-long Leadership from the Inside Out training in 2006. It was transformative for me in many ways. Gass uses knowledge from psychology, management training, and meditation to interactively teach leaders how to be as skilful as possible. He doesn't really separate the person from the work, realizing that a lot of what makes us less effective as leaders is experience from our childhood or what he calls *core wounds*. When someone taps into that insecurity (called *triggering*), we tend to overreact. Just learning not to act when triggered can be a powerful tool to being a better leader, not to mention a better friend, parent, or partner. One of the things I learned from the Rockwood training is that the best way to lead is from a place of being yourself. It's much more effective, especially in an era when people are as skeptical as they are. The buzzword is *authenticity*. I've been effective as a leader, there's no question about that, but I've paid a terrible personal price. I covered up who I was,

I was stressed all the time, I was sick a lot, I was upset a lot, and because of that I got angry a lot, which sometimes made me difficult to work with, and also set me up as a lightning rod for an entire generation of right-wing men.

I also think I wasn't as good a leader as many people think I was. In NAC, when I started to pull myself back a bit, I learned to listen. Arlene Perly Rae once said of her husband, former premier of Ontario Bob Rae: "His idea of listening is stopping and giving the other person a turn to talk." And that was kind of my idea of listening too, in the old days. I had to learn to really listen.

One of the things about diversity is that you really need to listen to whatever group of people is marginalized in society, or to a person who is a member of the group of people marginalized in society. You really have to listen to understand what they're saying, and not immediately see it through your own lens. That's difficult to do well—and an important skill to learn. At a tribute given for me when I stepped down as president of NAC, the comment that meant the most to me came from Carolann Wright-Parks, a black activist who was always challenging me. She said, "What I like about Judy is that she has big ears. She listens." But I think that's just the beginning of learning how to be a leader. If you can be a leader from who you are, not only will you benefit from it by feeling less stressed, less unhappy, less tired, all of that, but you'll also have a much more positive influence on others. You'll create situations in which others feel able to lead, and you'll allow for more diversity in leadership, because others will begin to understand that they can be leaders.

A couple of years ago, a friend approached me with a problem in the university department she was working in that was a very polarized situation. I said, "Do you think you can provide some leadership here in solving the problem?"

And she said, "Oh, no, I don't think I could do that." But having talked to her, I knew she had a really good analysis of what was wrong.

So I said, "Why not?"

She responded, "Well, I really don't like confrontation."

I replied, "Well, let's pretend that I'm the chair of the department, and tell me how you would approach it, coming from who you are. How would you talk about this?"

My friend answered, "I would say, 'I feel quite marginalized in the department, and I've talked to a couple of other people of colour here and they feel quite marginalized too. And this is why... '" and she gave a couple of examples of some things that had happened.

She believed that she had to go in aggressively and say, "You've done this! You've done that! And you're responsible for this! And why haven't you talked to this one? And why haven't you talked to that one?" That's how the women she saw as leaders in the department would have handled it. They'd have polarized it, duked it out, and whoever was left standing would win.

But in fact, the way she proposed to deal with it—her natural way of dealing with it—was much more likely to solve the problem. It's very hard to fight when someone says, "I really feel marginalized, and I've talked to other people...." You can't say, "No, you *don't* feel marginalized!" By modelling a different type of leadership, you make way for diversity, because you show there isn't just one way to lead. What I've learned is that it's really important to support those different styles of leadership.

So now you're all saying, "Yeah, sure, you're not in the meetings I'm in, you don't have to deal with the [unprintable] jerks that I have to deal with, and they'll just walk all over me." But let me stress that the opposite of partriarchal leadership is not being a doormat. You can be assertive without being dominating. Patriarchal leadership pretends to be very rational: It's about who has the best argument, who knows the most. It's about who's the most accomplished, who's done the most, and so on. It's all supposedly on an intellectual level. It's also about who can yell the loudest, but nobody admits that.

The reality, however, is that most of our relationships at work, just like our relationships at home, have an emotional component to them. They're not only rational. They're *never* only rational, because we're humans, and as humans, we have both intellectual and emotional reactions to things. As well, most of us are afraid of anger, so when anger is the only emotion permitted in a work situation, most people become intimidated and the bullies wind up dominating—not because they are stronger leaders or smarter or wiser, but because they are comfortable with anger.

In groups that work for social change, there are almost always dysfunctional people. In a society in which so many people are wounded, it makes sense that some will find a home in an organization that is trying to change the circumstance that hurt them. Some of the most effective fighters for social change are people who've been wounded a great deal in their lives.

In NAC, there was a woman who was quite dysfunctional, and whom other members did not take very seriously as a result. One day we were having a discussion, and she burst into tears and left the room, which seemed to me to be normal behaviour for someone who's upset. I continued with the meeting, but noticed that the three Aboriginal women on the executive were very uncomfortable.

I asked them what was wrong, and they answered, "Well, this is not how we do things."

And I said, "Okay, well explain how you do things," and they said, "No, that's okay. This is your way, and we'll adapt to it."

"No, no," I replied. "We want you to feel included. So explain to me, explain to us." The Aboriginal women said, "Well, for us, emotions that happen in a meeting are part of the meeting. We think the emotions are part of what's happening, and that you have to deal with them. So we want to know why she's crying."

And I said, "Oh … really?"

Now, at that time, if a white woman had said that to me, I'd have said, "Oh, this is touchy-feely, New Age crap." But because it was Aboriginal women, I said, "How would you handle it then?"

They said, "Why don't we start the meeting with people saying how they feel about being here, what they're bringing, whether they had a fight with their partner the night before, whatever it is, you know, how they're feeling at that moment." (In many situations today, this method of starting a meeting is considered appropriate, but in 1990, when this event occurred, it seemed "way out there.")

And I said, "Okaaaaay ..."

But we did it, and it was amazing, totally amazing, the change that it made in our process.

Believe me, at the time I was not a true believer; I was just the opposite. We all have difficult things that happen in our lives, and we bring them in to work, we bring them into meetings, we bring them into those places where we're supposed to be rational. And we rarely talk about or acknowledge them, unless they are extremely serious.

When we did this exercise, it completely opened the space. We had much better meetings, less conflict, less anger, and far fewer tears. Taking a moment at the beginning of the meeting for people to actually acknowledge how they felt made a huge difference in our process. And it made me start to realize that you can lead from your heart, that emotions are important, and that connecting with people on that level is essential in politics and in work. To be authentic means you have to be present in your head *and* in your heart.

THE COUNCIL OF CANADIANS is a policy-based organization, a super-rational organization, in which politics are done by analyzing the problem, deciding what the policy should be and then either educating and organizing around the favoured policy or protesting against the rejected one. I was the emcee for part of a teach-in the council had organized in Ottawa in 2007 on the Security and Prosperity Partnership (SPP), and at least half of the people there were policy wonks. It was a great teach-in, with lots of information. The people sat there all day, taking in all these facts and information. It was the best of that kind of teach-in I've been at in years.

When I went around to the workshops, I found that some of them were great and interactive, but others were panels with seven people and the audience just listening, like in the plenaries. People were a little overwhelmed with information.

One of the workshops was on street theatre, and there were two incredible, charming, and charismatic young people leading it. I was chairing the last session, so I had the idea to ask them to come up on the stage and do a theatre piece they had planned in the workshop. That's what I thought I was asking them to do. Instead, they did what they had done in the workshop—a movement exercise, with the whole audience of five hundred people, most of whom were union people and policy wonks.

At first, I thought, Oh … my … God, what have I done? But it was my instinct to do it and I learned at Rockwood to trust that kind of intuition. And it was fantastic! At first people felt a little strange, but the facilitators were so engaging that people started to move. And when they started to move, they loved it. The energy level in the room rose, and people felt great. Now they had all this information *and* they felt great.

The organizers had been worried that nobody would come back the next day for the strategy session because the big speakers wouldn't be there. But they did, in part, I think because of this exercise— because people felt drawn together, they moved together, they felt one another's energy, and they felt connected. The experience at this conference wasn't just an intellectual one; it was a physical one and an emotional one too.

In the Global South, people seem to understand this need for connection. At the World Social Forum in Nairobi, I noticed that all the sessions that were focused on poor people in Africa started with singing and dancing. In Brazil, there is a song for every politician, and everyone gets up and sings and dances when he or she comes on the stage and when she or he finishes a speech.

It's important to understand mind, body, and emotion—some people would include spirit as well—and the relationship between them. A mother understands all of those things; she is never just rational. Your relationship with a baby is not on a level of intellect: It's on another level that you're communicating. And most mothers have had that experience and understand it.

Yet as we become leaders in this patriarchal world, we put that knowledge aside. We underestimate and undervalue it. But that kind of understanding is very powerful in a leader, because it gives power in relation to other people—not a power *over* other people, which is what patriarchal power is, but a power *in relation* to others that in turn allows others to have more power themselves. If we are talking about redefining leadership, and about diversity in leadership, then we cannot have the kind of leadership that says "To be a leader, you have to be like me. Or him."

You have to be you in the lead. You are unique, and your leadership is going to be what it is. It may be great, and it may apply in just this place or that place, like anyone's leadership. But in order to have diversity in leadership, we have to accept many different kinds. And the more holistic it can be—the more people can bring their knowledge, their experience, their feelings, their intellect to leading—the more we will all benefit from it.

For me, that's what leadership can be in the age of networking. Each one of us can develop our leadership ability, and those of us who are naturally leaders can learn to step back and use that leadership to help other people take the lead.

With patriarchal leadership, people do not contribute as much as they can. As mentioned, they may either submit, and give the leaders what they want (they could be giving much more, but they give what is demanded, what the leaders know to ask for), or they rebel. A different kind of leadership, more open, more supportive—dare I say, a more nurturing kind of leadership—will get more from people. People give more because they feel more confidence in themselves. And that's the kind of leadership we have to develop.

Glenn Jenkins is a working-class activist from Luton in Britain who has successfully organized a community of poor people to take over social housing and community services in their area. Here's what he said to me about his leadership:

I am awake to the perils of leadership, even though I am a leader. Like it or not, we're in a culture of needing to be leaders or needing to be led. No surprise. School primes you to fit into a pyramid. Be on time, don't rebel. When I started speaking out, there was a lady who said, "You speak well, you are confident and articulate; so is the devil. Why do you think that you have the solutions to all our problems?"

Believe you me, if I was saying that, it would be devilish. What I am saying is that we, the people, are the only ones who can solve our problems. We, not me. The "I" should not be needed here. If I got run over, it would make no difference. Do my best and our best, we as leaders overcome by leading our community to a place where we all start out together. Co-ownership and co-responsibility.

A few years ago, I participated in a workshop at Hollyhock with Van Jones, who is a very powerful leader. The discussion was about a split that had just taken place in COPE, a left-wing civic party in Vancouver. They had won the mayor's seat and most of the seats on the council, and then sabotaged themselves through divisions. Individuals from both sides of the split were present, and they talked and tried in the Hollyhock style to be open-minded and kind to one another. When it came his turn to speak, Jones said, "I hear a lot of grief here." Everyone was stunned. Here he was, an outsider who knew nothing about the issues, identifying what was at the core of the problem: the hurt and betrayal everyone felt that made it impossible to overcome the divisions.

He then talked about his own hurt at attacks from comrades. "I work in the prison system in Oakland, I go to kids' funerals every other weekend, I deal with Oakland cops and prison guards, but nothing hurts as much as when my colleagues attack me or when I attack them." His comments transformed the room, and afterwards people were able to express sympathy to the people who had lived through this split rather than just siding with one or the other.

I used to believe that good leadership meant being accountable to the people you serve, and that is still an important element of leadership. When I was president of NAC, I always tried to see representative leadership as a way of re-presenting what our member groups had told me as much as possible. But now I believe that good leadership is about encouraging leadership in others, and that means stepping aside as well—"co-leading," as Glenn Jenkins calls it.

I am encouraged by the leadership I see in many of the movements described in this book. Men who express their feelings, women who step up and speak out, people supporting and encouraging one another. Just as the new technologies enable more horizontal organizing, new knowledge that comes from psychology and management training can help us to lead in a way that encourages people to speak for themselves and to look for the leader in themselves.

Changing yourself is not all that much easier than changing the world. As I mentioned in the introduction, I started thinking about writing this book at the WSF in 2006. At first, I thought the book would be primarily about what we could learn from the new political changes in Latin America, but somehow I couldn't get myself to begin the project, which is very unlike me.

During the second session of Rockwood a few months later, Robert Gass asked for volunteers for an exercise he called Affirmation. By this time, I had seen how powerful these exercises could be, so when he asked for someone to explore what was stopping us from starting an important project, I volunteered.

He asked us to formulate a sentence that would express what we wanted to do in an affirmative way. I wrote, "I will write a book on new paths to social and political change, with a focus on Latin America." He asked me to say the phrase and then say whatever negative thoughts came into my head. "Who do you think you are?" was the first thought, and then, "You don't even speak Spanish. How the hell are you going to write a book about Latin America?" Then I started to laugh, and he started to laugh and it turned into giggling of the kind I used to get into with my brother when we were kids. My father would get furious at us because we wouldn't stop giggling, and the angrier he got, the worse the giggling. At a certain point, I realized that, underneath that giggling was a terrible fear. Showing fear in front of a group of people was something I had never done before. But I trusted him and the group, and I had seen others show their vulnerability, so I said, "I am really afraid." Robert said, "I have an intuition about that fear. Is it okay for me to say what it is?" I agreed. "I think you are getting ready to throw off an old identity. It has served you well, but you don't need it any more. But it is scary to let it go." I was getting ready to give up my out-front leadership and take the role of an elder, writing, supporting young people's leadership, and playing less of a frontline role myself. It was scary to make that change and this book represented it to me.

The impact on the group was considerable. A number of the people of colour who had also thought, "Who does she think she is, trying to represent people in Latin America?" were impressed that I had the same doubts they had, and everyone was amazed that someone could be as strong as I am and at the same time be so vulnerable.

It freed me to start working on this book. Research and discussion led me to write quite a different book than I originally planned, but it was at Rockwood that I faced the fear that was stopping me from beginning the project.

Fear of change is a very powerful force in maintaining the status quo. The Right uses it in a conscious way through fear of terrorism, fear of poverty, fear of violence, fear of the Other. I am often amazed by how many people fear speaking out or standing up for what they believe in, even in a relatively democratic society such as Canada. Those of us who are working for change need to find ways of overcoming fear through compassion, empathy, and solidarity, and through showing that there are alternatives—and they are not scary at all.

10

COMMUNITY ALTERNATIVES
Living the Change

A CRITICAL FEATURE of the new movements for social justice and environmental sustainability around the world is the fact that they don't just look to governments for change but act to bring about change themselves.

Moema Miranda from IBASE in Brazil spoke at a seminar on networked politics I attended in Berlin:

> If capitalism has been victorious in shaping the global order, then neo-liberalism has tried to complete and seal the process by undermining the legitimacy of politics and effectively disqualifying serious debate of alternative directions in society. The worst scenario now is that we bow to the apparently self-evident fact that we live in a world shaped by forces that cannot be understood or controlled by the population. The only way we can rebuild politics and trust in the possibility of alternatives is to develop proposals that have a meaning for our daily lives, that create hope and that extend confidence in the force of common action.

In Brazil, the movement that has most effectively created solutions at the same time as protesting the policies that make them poor is the

MST (Movimento dos Trabalhadores Rurais Sem Terra, or Landless Workers' Movement). It is the largest social movement in Latin America, with an estimated 1.5 million landless members organized in twenty-three out of twenty-seven states. The MST carries out long-overdue land reform in a country mired in a system of unjust land distribution. In Brazil, 1.6 percent of the landowners control roughly half (46.8 percent) of the land on which crops can be grown. Just 3 percent of the population owns two-thirds of all arable lands.

Since 1985, the MST has peacefully occupied unused land, where it has established co-operative farms, constructed houses, built schools for children and adults, and started clinics. It has also promoted indigenous cultures, a healthy and sustainable environment, and gender equality. The MST has won land titles for more than 350,000 families in 2,000 settlements as a result of MST actions, and 180,000 encamped families currently await government recognition for their land titles.

According to its website, the MST's success lies in its ability to organize and educate. Members have not only managed to obtain land, and therefore a secure food supply for their families, but also to continue to develop a sustainable socio-economic model that offers a concrete alternative to the sort of globalization that puts profits before people and humanity. The MST has been a major presence at the World Social Forum in Brazil, both in meetings and in marches. In addition, before taking political positions, the MST holds extensive debates and discussions across its membership.

Today, the MST is the major source of pressure on the Workers' Party, led by Lula da Silva, to carry out the transformations that its supporters expected from it. In June 2008, thousands of landless rural workers invaded railways, plantations, and corporate headquarters in a wave of protests across eight Brazilian states against major multinational agribusinesses that are responsible for high food prices. They occupied, blockaded, and marched in the most significant uprisings since Lula's election. The MST organized the protests with Via Campesina, a global organization that represents farmers and agricultural workers. The protests were also aimed at electric companies that the group accuses of causing environmental problems and displacing people with the huge reservoirs they create with their hydroelectric dams. It is hard to imagine an organization such as the MST developing in the advanced capitalist countries, but the experiences of self-organization among poor people in Latin America do provide valuable lessons for people organizing in the North.

In Canada in the early 1970s, both the women's movement and the youth movement created alternative services that were not necessarily funded by government. Women's groups started crisis lines, shelters, rape crisis centres, women's centres, and daycare centres, often in women's own homes, without any state funding to provide the services they needed.* Around the same time, I was part of an alternative youth network called Grass Roots that was involved in creating youth services run by young people. In fact, the Canadian government provided small grants for many of these initiatives in a blossoming of democracy that was Pierre Elliott Trudeau's response to the youth movement of the 1960s. Many of these services were later incorporated into the provision of government-funded services, often losing their original radical political perspectives but gaining a permanence and professionalism that the earlier services lacked.

The state response to the uprising of the 1960s and 1970s was to fund a wide range of social services, from daycare to social housing. The movements of these decades insisted that the users of services also run the services, but when the movements went into decline, so did the impetus for user control. This was especially so when it came to poor and working-class people. Services were integrated into the state bureaucracy or top-down social-service agencies, and, as in many top-down structures, the managers were removed from the people they were serving, and the workers were almost as powerless to make change as their clients were.

---

*See my book *Ten Thousand Roses: The Making of a Feminist Revolution* for more on this history.

Though they provided much-needed services, they did so in a way that placed many of the recipients of those services in a subordinate, dependent, and sometimes demeaning position. The experience of receiving those services was often an oppressive one, and the provider, living inside a system that sees itself as helping, was unable to see his or her role as an oppressor.

The Right exploited this by calling social services the "nanny state." Attacks on the so-called nanny state were central to the ascendancy of neo-liberalism, and, in most countries, privatization of public services has been one of the results. However, far from making these services more accountable, privatization has made them even more distant from, and uncontrollable by, the people they are serving. In the public services, cutbacks have meant that workers are doing more for less and are unable to provide the quality of services needed by their clients. The community-based services that survived are under terrible and constant pressure to fundraise, to make up the revenue they need, and therefore are anxious not to offend anyone who might be willing to give them money.

The response of social movements and the Left to these attacks was to defend the services. Instead of acknowledging the problems of top-down service delivery and proposing a democratization of the service, we defended them against assault. Under that assault and a neo-liberal ideology, the social safety net in Canada and many other countries is in collapse.

One example is unemployment insurance. In 1976, almost 80 percent of workers were eligible for unemployment insurance in Canada; as of 1996, the changes in standards for qualification, combined with a restructuring of the workforce to create more part-time and contract work, means that qualified workers have been reduced to 34 percent. The shredding of the social safety net pushes more and more people into the underclass since they no longer have a cushion between jobs. Charity, in the form of food banks, temporary shelters, and soup kitchens, does little more than pick up a few of the pieces.

In *Imagine Democracy*, I argued that these services had to be democratized by giving users and workers a stronger say in how they are run. In London, England, the Greater London Council tried to do just that before they were wiped out by Margaret Thatcher, the Queen of Neo-liberalism. Today, democratization of public services is taking quite a different route than I imagined in 2000.

Glenn Jenkins, the British working-class activist introduced in the previous chapter, has pioneered a new kind of activism in which people who have been displaced by poverty, unemployment, de-industrialization, injury, or anything else get together to build or rebuild their communities.

"They build an industry on the back of every social problem," he told me in an interview. "It happens in development and it happens here. All the good things that are supposed to be going to the ground are sucked up by the layer of providers. It's like vampires. You get a middle-class layer of administrators and service providers who become the beneficiaries of the services. They usurp much of the money, the training, and so on. I'm part of a natural reaction to that and the non-commercial, flat-managed development of autonomous community activity. What's happening is the emergence of a participatory democracy that comes into conflict with the top-down administration. It needs to change, and it's going to take a battle."

Jenkins is an incredibly articulate, funny, and charming fellow. He told me about his group of mostly young people on the Marsh Estates (estates used to be social housing in Britain, now they are half-privatized). They started by squatting in abandoned buildings and organizing raves to give local youth something to do with their energy. He continued,

> I see government money as our money. It's high time that the people of the world organize ourselves not be organized and take back what's ours. Rather than letting them squander that money, we should stand up and fight for it. My first effort was squatting and using our homeless benefit [money that the state provides for housing] that was really a landlord benefit. We

squatted in derelict buildings and got the homeless benefit and demanded that the payments go to us. We learned how to build, using money that would otherwise go into the pockets of landlords. People among us—people call us dropouts, but we call ourselves forced-outs—have no shortage of knowledge or skill. One guy was an experienced builder, but his body was knackered. He's super talented and might be able to do two hours, but not eight hours. He trained us.

From 1993 to 2000, these rave organizers used their homeless benefit to create social housing and jobs for their community, one of the most disadvantaged in the United Kingdom, and they did it through a combination of direct action (squatting), community organizing, and intelligent use of public money. Jenkins said the key is a different value structure. In another generation, he might have been organizing mass protests against government policy. Now, he said, "It makes me feel good to use public money. We have a duty to engage. We can't call it democracy and stick an X on a ballot on the paper every five years and then moan when it turns into a police state. You can't sit back and let Rupert Murdoch make up your mind for you."

In 2000, when the government started to see that much of the money that was supposed to go to the poor remained in the hands of service providers, they decided to establish a series of pilot projects called the New Deal for Communities (NDC). Jenkins and others formed the Marsh Farm Community Development Trust, a coalition of residents, service providers, and the local municipal council, and became one of the thirty-nine communities to win fifty million pounds from the NDC for regeneration.

A battle of conflicting visions ensued, which Jenkins described as community-led or community-fed. Since the municipal council received the money, they had a de facto veto. Council commissioned a report in 2004 that criticized the bottom-up process that had been developed. The report has since proven to be wrong, but nevertheless the council hired consultants at five hundred and fifty pounds a day—more than some people in the Marsh make in a month—to report on the bottom-up process.

"They used it to sack our management team, and imposed what they called *an interim corporate management team* to reshape the trust in their image with all power to the chair, and four out of five chairs were either counsellors or service providers. It was corrupt and dishonest and began three years of them trying to bring in their master plan, dumping the original plan that had won the bid to begin with."

Jenkins explained that the key is "regeneration, and if community economic development doesn't plug the economic leaks there are in our communities … it won't have worked. There's long-term unemployment, and these people don't have much opportunity. Yet, in one year, ninety-four million pounds flows through our estate, more than some small countries. How can there be so much money and so many poor people? It's this provision culture. Regeneration is five million to build a building by people who live miles from here and by rich companies. Unemployed people with building skills watch other people build. If we plugged that leak, and took on that tender, and built that building ourselves, then all those wages, achievement, stay within Marsh Farms, within our community."

Jenkins's group organized and collected a thousand signatures within three days, demanding a vote on the new proposal. Some 64 percent of the residents chose the original plan, and that has paved the way for the development of a multi-functional community hub with community services, a business centre, and social space. It will also contain a series of social enterprises organized by an innovative method developed in Brazil called the Organization Workshop.*

Once again, Jenkins explained,

---

*For more information on the Organization Workshop, see Raff Carmen and Miguel Sobrado (eds.) *A Future for the Excluded: Job Creation and Income Generation for the Poor: Clodomir Santos de Morais and the Organization Workshop* (London–New York: Zed Books, 2000).

It has to be facilitated by local people [Marsh Farm Outreach Team, all live on the estate]. It's an eight-week intense workshop where one hundred to one hundred and twenty people organize a large co-operative enterprise. The people may have no experience in the aspect of work … there are technical mentors and experts. We call it entrepreneurial literacy. Over the eight weeks, the group learns a distinct set of self-management tools, the tasks needed to do the job, and then they get paid to do it once they are finished.

We needed a method that would train people to do it themselves. They automatically go to look for a leader mode. Over the eight weeks we form into a self-managed shape rather than chair and vice-chair.

As with the participatory budget, the Organization Workshop teaches people to rely on themselves rather than looking to others for leadership.

Jenkins's plan is backed up by research from the New Economics Institute that says if just 10 percent of annual spending on public services was redirected to services delivered locally by local people and businesses, the equivalent of fifteen times the total economic benefits would go directly into those communities.

"New community-run enterprise looks for services we already use and spend on but can provide at home," Jenkins explained. "For example, we just found out that we spend 1.7 million on fast food, and at the moment that all goes off the estate. If we provided that here, the jobs would stay in the community and, what's more, we might shop ethically and provide healthier food choices as well.

"It's an emergent culture that's been rising for years, and going to rise—not for private profit, self-managed, and community led. Provision culture has led us for centuries and it has to stop. There is big change in the air," said Jenkins. "It's local and it's global. We call it *glocal*."

ANOTHER EXAMPLE OF A PROJECT that used expertise from Brazil to create a new form of service is FoodShare, an organization in Toronto that I have always admired. It was founded in 1985 by then mayor of Toronto, Art Eggleton, who was concerned about the growth of hunger and food banks after the recession of the early 1980s. FoodShare's original mandate was to coordinate emergency food services and to collect and distribute food. In the late 1980s, FoodShare staff began to share the frustration of many that the problem of hunger was not diminishing. Income inequality and unemployment were, if anything, increasing. Food banks—originally intended as a stop-gap solution—appeared to be here to stay, despite their weaknesses. So FoodShare began to explore self-help models such as co-operative buying systems, collective kitchens, and community gardens, which would have the potential to address short-term issues of household hunger, while also providing longer term benefits by building the capacity of individuals and communities.

The result is a unique organization that uses many of the principles we have been talking about to distribute healthy food. Here is their philosophy, as described on their website:

> Over the years, we have broadened our focus to look at the entire food system—how food is produced, distributed and consumed. We see hunger as just one symptom of a food system that is geared to treating food primarily as a commodity. Most people believe that access to food is a basic human right, because, like air or water, it is fundamental to health and survival. But the question is how to make this right a reality. First, should food be subjected to the same rules of market distribution that govern, say, soap or toothpaste? We believe there is a role for not-for-profit food distribution mechanisms, of which the Good Food Box is one example.
>
> What we've come to realize is that the "what" and "how" of food access is also important. All of our projects are based on the premise that it's not just any food that we're talking about. We

try to promote an awareness that fresh, whole foods are key to health, well-being and disease prevention, and to illustrate this principle through all our programs.

How people get their food is also important. Food distribution systems that involve communities and help to create neighbourhood leaders have a great potential to enhance individual and community empowerment, by leading people to feel that they have some control over this very basic part of their lives. Again, because of its material, cultural and social importance, food is special in its power to mobilize people to action. All our programs are based on this community building principle.

FoodShare tries to take a multifaceted, innovative and long-term approach to hunger and food issues. This means that we're involved in diverse actions: grassroots program delivery, advocacy for social assistance reform, job creation and training, nutrition education, farmland preservation and campaigns for comprehensive food labelling are just a few examples of the areas we work in.

Under the visionary leadership of Debbie Field, a non-profit organization is re-imagining and implementing a healthy, sustainable food distribution system that now feeds ten thousand people and also builds community (including urban–rural links), educates people about healthy eating (including in-school lunch programs), and interacts with government to ensure that public policy meets the same principles. "There are three problems in the capitalist food system," Field explains, "and they're integrated as a whole: We've created a monopoly system where people run out of money and therefore are hungry; we've created a food system that is based on promoting the least healthy food; and we've created an agricultural system that's not sustainable. All three are problems. FoodShare entered, as do most food activists, looking at hunger, but then realized the whole food system needed to be changed."

Field takes a less confrontational approach than Glenn Jenkins:

What FoodShare sees is that everybody's an ally in creating a new food system. We have to create win–wins of how we can incorporate new ideas into the structures that exist. FoodShare has this amazing list of people giving us stuff for free at the government level, from buildings to money. We never make fights with people in City Hall. We win them over to work with us. There's a lot that is wrong at City Hall, usually from the politicians' point of view, or the staff's point of view, but if you wake up in the morning and scream at them and tell them what they should do, then what you end up doing is pulling the knot so tight that they won't participate. And you need them to be active participants. You treat them as someone you want to win on your side, rather than somebody you want to put up against the wall and defeat. I think actually a lot of the crisis of the Left is rooted in male aggressive war analogy.

But Field agrees with Jenkins about creating models of a new society:

It's about problem-solving; it's about women's methodology; it's about a sideways, rather than a hierarchical, approach to decision-making and processing. It's about creating examples of the society you want to model now, so you treat people in a very respectful way. You have very non-hierarchal, very flat organizational structures, lots of consensus decision-making, process as much as possible. Food Share has a hierarchy, in that I'm the executive director and there are some managers, but it's a lot of consulting and trying to build consensus all the time.

When I asked Field to explain what principles guide FoodShare and other new approaches to solving social problems, she offered:

- Propose rather than just oppose.
- Use positive energy; look for convergence rather than difference.

- Integrate entrepreneurial programs with advocacy and service delivery.
- Use market mechanisms as a replacement for charity models.
- Add advocacy to direct service and entrepreneurial activities.
- Accept the women's movement's motto that "the personal is political."
- Integrate individual, community, and social action.
- Consciously promote diversity and anti-racist policies.

As opposed to food banks from which people receive donated food for free, FoodShare charges money or sweat equity for their food boxes. Field explains,

> When people pay for the Good Food Box, they are "customers" instead of "clients" of a passive welfare system in which they cannot have any input. A customer can complain about a rotten apple in their box; a client cannot, and has to be "grateful" for what they get. Out of our $3.7 million annual budget, we generate a third from our own income generation.
>
> Like most leaders of the "new politics," we are not averse to charging for some program delivery, which is hard for the traditional Left, and something that I had trouble with when I first came to FoodShare. I used to fight against the idea that student nutrition programs charged kids and their parents a nominal fee, but low-income women told us they didn't like free because free represented second-class charity. They wanted to pay what they could.
>
> We're in the middle of a knock-down drag-'em-out fight with a guy who is the head of something called Farmers' Markets Ontario. This vision of farmers' markets is what was in Kitchener thirty or forty years ago. So he wants rules at farmers' markets that are much too restrictive for Canadian society, FoodShare believes.

FoodShare is insisting that Toronto's farmers' markets need to be culturally appropriate. They need to have mangoes as well as apples. Local food is important, but it can't be everything. This great guy from the African Food Basket is a partner of ours. He'll say, "I'll go to your farmers' market if it has mangoes."

We stopped the city from implementing a farmers' market policy that was going to say that you have to sell only local. And doing our research, we found out that every city in the United States has that rule. So we're going to have a made-in-Toronto, multiculturally sensitive farmers' market policy.

CREATING ALTERNATIVES WITHIN and alongside the existing system has many names—*social economy* and *social entrepreneurship* are the two I hear most often. Social entrepreneurship is very faddish now among funding agencies, and it definitely has its strength and weaknesses. The basic idea is that you can be in business with more than just profit as your goal. From Van City, a progressive credit union in Vancouver, which provides funding for a multitude of progressive causes, to Bullfrog Power in Toronto, which sells electricity at a premium with a goal of developing sustainable power sources, social entrepreneurs are taking advantage in the best sense of the socially and environmentally conscious marketplace.

There is a large movement of people, mostly in North America, who see the path to change as reforming capitalism from the inside. These are small entrepreneurs who see social good as part of their mission and larger entrepreneurs such as Anita Roddick, former owner of the Body Shop, who use their money and power to promote progressive causes, and others who spend their time consulting with large corporations such as Wal-Mart to convince them to buy organic. Of all the movements described in this book, it's the one about which I am most skeptical. It's great to have enterprises such as Van City that run an ethical business and use a significant part of their profit to fund progressive causes, but they are few and far between because the driving force of capitalism is so far from social justice that it takes a very strong vision to keep social concerns in sight when the focus is to make a profit.

Joel Solomon is the heir to a shopping-mall fortune who is working very hard to change the system from within. I first met Solomon when I was raising money for www.rabble.ca, the news and discussion website I founded in 2001. Even though the priorities of his foundation favoured the environmental and the West Coast, he managed to find some money for our worthy project. Solomon is also the chair of the Hollyhock board.

Solomon believes that it is possible to reform the system by including social and environmental values in business. He described social entrepreneurship in a meeting with me:

> This is an incrementalist strategy to try to go within the DNA of the thing [capitalism], and change some of the makeup, which means the headset, the heart, the culture, and the support network that can allow people to look at business as a place where ambition is expressed as delivery of necessary goods, and services are created, and that looks at bringing externalities back into the economic analysis....
>
> The good part about capitalism in my mind is the way it allows creativity to be expressed—the inventiveness of the human being and the culture; so it captures that but then turns that into the brutal commodification of everything.

Solomon says this effort started in the 1970s with hippie entrepreneurs and church people who wanted to treat their employees better. Then it spread during the anti-apartheid movement, when a lot of institutions such as churches and universities started to see that they could use their investments as a power for change by boycotting South Africa. That action reached its height in the 1980s. These experiences promoted both discussion and new models of business.

"There's been a flowering, and now there are success stories that have built a lot of capital," he explains. "And there's a debate going on among those people, of 'Should we stay local, or should we sell to big guys?' And there are others saying, 'If we don't turn around Wal-Mart, if we don't infect this bigger system from inside, we're not going to succeed.' This is not a strategy of storming the Bastille and bringing it down. We have to change the DNA of it."

I ask Solomon how it helps much of anything for Wal-Mart to buy organic and at the same time pay their workers terrible wages and destroy small business in a predatory manner wherever they set up shop.

"How else are we going to change them?" he responds. "Regulation is unlikely to work, because they are so powerful. Replace them, good luck. Who's shopping at Wal-Mart? Everybody. So what do you do about that? Create an alternative to Wal-Mart where you can pay double? Okay, you'll get a few of the elite who would drop out of the system. But meanwhile, the masses want Wal-Mart. So given that they exist, I'm glad that there are people chipping away. And it's not as simple as just organic." He explained how, when a company is convinced that doing something more ethical or environmentally sustainable is good for their bottom line, they start looking at doing it on numerous levels.

I suppose I'm glad that there are people and organizations focused on trying to make big corporations more environmentally and ethically responsible, but corporations such as Wal-Mart are part of the problem, and it's pretty hard to see them as part of the solution. It may be better for them to sell organic foods cheaply and put them in the reach of low-income people, but why should they get any credit when their average wage for their so-called associates, most of whom are women, is $7.50 an hour in the United States—out of which they must pay for their own health insurance. As was so aptly demonstrated in Mark Achbar's film *The Corporation*, I believe that big corporations are by their nature unlikely to ever place social responsibility even close to profit as a goal of operations.

But what interests me here is the use of entrepreneurship and market strategies for making change. I think we need to expand our minds to see that these projects show people dealing with a problem that government is simply not helping us solve. The old way of thinking about change focused on making demands on the government to solve the problems of society. What Joel Solomon, Debbie Field, and Glenn Jenkins are doing is solving the problems themselves. It is not a question of giving up on our demands on government, but rather seeing the complex interconnections between protest, popular power, and creation of alternatives.

11

INDIGENOUS IDEAS
Diversity of Dignity

AT A CONFERENCE on university–community partnerships I attended a few years ago in Saskatoon, a door that I didn't even know was there was opened for me. Ovide Mercredi, who was the national chief of the Assembly of First Nations at the same time as I was president of NAC, told the academics: "You will never be able to work with our communities unless you accept that there are other ways of knowing than Eurocentric scientific ways of knowing."

When a group of us were discussing his remarks over dinner, one of the professors said, "That's anti-scientific." "No," I responded, "it is not against science, it is simply saying that there are other valuable ways of knowing than science."

One of the most exciting elements of the new movements arising in the Americas is the leadership of Aboriginal peoples. Despite the fact that I had been active on the Left in Canada for more than twenty years by then, it wasn't until 1990 that I first worked in active solidarity with native peoples in Canada. When I was elected president of NAC, there were three Aboriginal women elected on the same executive, and their presence ensured that our organization was closely involved with the major struggles of Aboriginal peoples at the time.

My first formal speech after being elected was in front of the Manitoba legislature in support of Elijah Harper. As mentioned earlier, the native MLA held up the approval of the Meech Lake Accord, which totally ignored First Nations, by blocking agreement in the legislature, all the time holding a symbolic eagle feather.

In the summer of 1990, I worked in solidarity with First Nations in Canada during the Oka crisis, a dispute that arose over a golf course on land claimed by the Mohawk Nation. Mohawk warriors famously confronted the Canadian Army in an armed standoff that lasted more than two months. However, while I understood at the time the importance of supporting Aboriginal struggles and learned a lot about process from the native women on the NAC executive, I saw Aboriginal peoples as a group who had faced terrible oppression and discrimination without really understanding how important their leadership could be.

I started to understand this only at the World Social Forum in Caracas, Venezuela, in 2006. One of the most inspiring talks was from Ecuadorean indigenous leader Blanca Chancoso, who served as one of the directors of the country's largest indigenous organization, CONAIE, and plays a major role in the rise of South American indigenous movements. She talked about the economic and social solutions that indigenous peoples can offer, and explained the impact of neo-liberalism better than anyone I have ever heard.

> They want to base society only on the economy and also on the idea that only certain people are fit to rule. But they are responsible for these terrible circumstances. They have forced people to migrate and disintegrate their families. It is not that we are bad parents. It is that we don't have stable work to take care of our children.... They try to divide us. In Ecuador, they told us that Peru was taking things away from us, but it is the oil companies who are taking things away from us. We do not swallow these stories. We know what is really happening is that they want the best slices of the cake. What we want is a diversity of dignity.

Chancoso added that indigenous peoples have survived many centuries—including the five hundred years since contact—for a reason that has to do with their economic and social knowledge.

In Latin America, many intellectuals who have spent most of their lives within a European political framework are rethinking their views. One of Venezuela's leading academics, Edgardo Lander, said, "The whole Western scientific project implies a separation between body and mind, separation between culture and nature. There is an assumption which is never being discussed, the assumption that the purpose of knowledge is to control."

I met Lander at a Social Summit in Cochabamba in 2006. He impressed me because he said that he thought that Bolivia was the most important progressive process happening in the world today, and he is from Venezuela. Ever since my visit to Bolivia six months before, I had been unsuccessfully trying to convince people of the importance of the election of the MAS in Bolivia and the process they were unleashing. Lander was the first person outside of Bolivia who understood this.

His view is that the indigenous peoples of Bolivia have memory of knowledge that we need to solve the crisis of the world today. More and more thinkers and actors from the Global South are realizing that they have been trapped in European philosophies, not seeing the world before their very eyes. Lander told me that he has no idea how we in the North will see what changes are needed. "You can't even imagine how the world can be different," he said.

It is no accident that, in an historic period in which we need some new solutions to the problems modernism has created, the courageous warriors who survived the genocide of colonialism—whether the outright slaughter, the disease, the small reservations, or the theft of their land, their children, their language, and their culture—are now coming to the fore and providing leadership and wisdom for the struggles ahead.

Solidarity with indigenous peoples today is not just a moral question of righting the wrongs that our ancestors did and that our governments continue to do. Nor is it just a strategic question of recognizing that indigenous peoples around the world are at the forefront of the battles to protect the earth from further destruction from industrialization. It is also the fact that some indigenous peoples have memory of the knowledge we need to survive in a world in harmony with nature and with one another.

One of the most powerful speeches I have ever heard about the importance of indigenous knowledge came from Evon Peter, former chief of the Neetsaii Gwich'in from Arctic Village in northeastern Alaska. Peter is the chair of Native Movement, whose vision is "young leaders motivating the world's peoples toward balanced relations with each other and Mother Earth." He was one of the remarkable speakers at the 2007 Bioneers conference. Bioneers is an American organization that describes itself as a forum for connecting the environment, health, social justice, and spirit within a broad progressive framework. In his speech, he said,

> We still have a way to go before there is an understanding of the diversity of knowledge. Just like in a nature ecosystem, there is a complexity and diversity that allows it to be sustain[ed]. Within humanity, without the full diversity of human experience at the table with an equal power and an equal say, we will not come to the solutions we need to come to. Just because you have the power, or just because you have a lot of money or a big name, does not make you the person who has the answer. We have to all be with one another in order to come to solutions that will truly guide us to where we need to go.

Later, Peter sent me an article he had written on indigenous knowledge for www.indiancountrytoday.com:

> There is only one path that I see for America to truly become a land of life, liberty and justice for all. That path is to heal itself through an uncompromisingly honest acknowledgment and

thorough addressing of its atrocities and lies. Without this, our country will continue to act out of ignorance, fear, greed and an obsessive need to forcefully control human lives both domestically and internationally.

Humanity has experienced time and again how a history rooted in dysfunction and unsustainability feeds the fire of self-destruction. As sure as the Roman Empire collapsed and a drug addict smiles as his last dose ushers him to death, the United States will continue to blindly and in some cases consciously inflict suffering at home and abroad if it does not acknowledge and address the truth of its past and current actions....

There is a path that can free us from this cycle and help to transform the world. It is not an easy path, but it is necessary if we hope to prevent the loss to millions of human lives. We have the resources, knowledge, technology and time to make a transition, but the question is: Do we have the courage and the will to face truth and act from a place of humility, patience, compassion, and conscience? How successful do you think Jesus, Muhammed or Buddha would have been in sharing their teachings with a tainted heart and a distraught, fearful mind?

We must begin by acknowledging and addressing the foundation upon which America was built—stolen land and the genocide of American Indians. The United States has never apologized to American Indian people for these violations. This country has demonized Hitler and erected Jewish holocaust museums, yet refuses to acknowledge its own acts of genocide.

An apology or museum alone would not heal the wounded hearts and disempowered governments of indigenous peoples or the tainted heart of America. There is one great, critical lie that the U.S. government has effectively taught to indigenous and non-indigenous Americans alike—that there is no way for the United States to honor its treaties with American Indians and pursue new treaties with those not yet afforded that opportunity, including Alaska Native and Native Hawaiian indigenous nations.

This great lie is only as true as we Americans accept it to be. There were similar lies told in our country's history to women deprived of a voice and to African slaves. In the case of abolishing slavery it took a radical shift in human consciousness, a courage and will to overcome, and a changing national economy, as well as a forced acceptance upon many Americans who were not ready for the positive evolution of our country. As painful and challenging as it may be for many Americans, we must begin our healing by dispelling this great lie and moving through a process of reconciliation with American Indian nations.

Even though I had been thinking about these issues for a long time, I was deeply affected by his talk. Afterwards, I had to take a walk to let it really sink in. It has taken almost two decades to come to the point of understanding that not only do I have to listen to what people are saying, not only do I have to consciously use my heart as well as my head in the decisions that I make, but also that I might not have all the answers.

And I still have a long way to go. As Shakil Choudhury, a Toronto anti-racist educator, says, "It's a lifelong journey."

Those of us with privilege have bought into the existing system—even me, and I've been a radical my whole life. The leadership of those who aren't in the same place can inspire us to do what we need to do. Those who, as Evon Peter said so eloquently, have suffered terribly under this destructive system and survived are most likely to have the knowledge we need to get out of it. For me, there is no guilt in this at all. It is a conclusion I have come to after opening my mind and my heart to different ways of thinking and being, and seeing that often the people who are mostly likely able to resist the corruption of wealth and ego are the people who benefit least from the system as it is.

Legendary Latin American writer Eduardo Galleano, who has devoted his novels, essays, and journalism to "remembering the past of America above all and above all that of Latin America, intimate land condemned to amnesia," says, "If the world is upside down the way it is now, wouldn't we have to turn it over to get it to stand up straight?" Turning it over means that the people who are most oppressed and marginalized should be at the forefront. It is not just a question of involving them (which suggests involving "them" in something "we" are doing), it is a question of following their lead.

This takes a certain humility, and humility is not my strong suit. But when I put my writing aside for a couple of months in early 2008 to get involved in an indigenous struggle in Ontario, I started to see the power of bringing together the knowledge of the social movements with the knowledge of indigenous communities.

Seven First Nations leaders in two different communities were jailed for refusing mining on their traditional lands. Bob Lovelace, a university professor and retired chief of the Ardoch Algonquins, located near Kingston, Ontario, along with Chief Donny Morris and his five councillors from the remote northern community of Kitchenuhmaykoosib Inninuwug (KI), six hundred kilometres north of Thunder Bay—known as the KI Six—were willing to give up their freedom to take a stand for their people and the land they feel a responsibility to protect. They opposed a powerful industry that threatened them with massive lawsuits, a court that acted in the interests of that industry, and a government that claimed neutrality at the same time as actually supporting the mining companies.

I became involved because a Ryerson colleague and friend, Judy Findlay, the former Child Advocate for the Province of Ontario, had been working closely with KI in a child welfare advocacy organization called the North-South Partnership. I went to a press conference they held on the impact of the jailing on the children of KI and realized that this was a huge issue that needed a larger profile to get the attention of the Toronto media and, therefore, the government.

Lovelace had been sentenced to six months in jail on February 15, 2008, for peacefully protesting uranium mining in the Ardoch homeland. On March 17, 2008, a Superior Court judge in Thunder Bay had sentenced the KI leaders to six months after they were found in contempt of court in a dispute that was virtually identical to that of the Ardoch Algonquins. In their case, they were resisting exploration for platinum mining. KI decided to make an alliance with Ardoch, even though Ardoch is not officially recognized as a First Nation under the Indian Act. (One of the ways that native peoples are divided is through this colonial act that decides who has Aboriginal rights and who doesn't.)

While the jailing of indigenous activists is nothing new, this was the first time that a chief-in-council, Donny Morris of KI, the official leader of the community as recognized by the Indian Act, had been jailed for following the laws protecting indigenous rights. The remote community was left virtually without leadership.

The excuse given by the Ontario government was the archaic Mining Act, which places the rights of industrial development over everything. Mining companies are given automatic licence to explore wherever they want without First Nations' approval, without an environmental assessment, and even without the permission of the owners of private property.

Unlike in many previous Aboriginal struggles, both KI and Ardoch received a lot of local support in the media and from non-native communities in Thunder Bay and Kingston respectively, but they understood that to get their leaders out of jail, they needed to have their issue raised in Toronto.

At the press conference, I realized that none of the local activists in Toronto were aware of the issue, so I proposed a rally at Ryerson University to build action leading to a mass rally at Queen's Park. The first rally on April 9, 2008, was standing room only. Ovide Mercredi and Assembly of First Nations national chief Phil Fontaine were the keynote speakers, but the audience was most moved by the presentations of Ardoch Chief Paula Sherman and Chief Donny's wife, Anne Marie Morris, as well as by the phone call with the KI Six in jail in Thunder Bay. Another moving moment of the rally was when a native drummer from Sarnia told how his father had gone to visit KI about twenty years before to warn them not to let the industrial devastation that had happened to their land near Sarnia occur in the north.

Just before the rally at Ryerson, I got a call from David Sone of Rainforest Action, an American environmental group, telling me that they were planning a tent village at Queen's Park at the end of May to support the long-standing blockade at Grassy Narrows, northeast of Kenora. He asked if we would be willing to join forces. There was some hesitation among local activists in Toronto because of past differences with Rainforest Action, but they finally agreed, and we decided on a rally and what Ovide Mercredi called a "sleepover."

Chief Donny Morris would agree to the alliance with Grassy Narrows only if he could meet with them in person. Grassy Narrows, a community about eighty kilometres northeast of Kenora, has been waging a decades-long battle to protect their land from clear-cutting and their water from mercury poisoning. Twenty-two young people from Grassy Narrows were planning to arrive in Toronto for the rally at the end of an eighteen-hundred-kilometre walk from Kenora that they called the Protecting the Earth Walk. They agreed to stop in Thunder Bay to meet the KI Six in jail.

I had a conference call with Chrissy Swain, the leader of the walk, the night before the group set out for Toronto. She said, "I looked at a map last night. It is really far, and a lot of the youth are scared." But full of the fierce commitment that I have seen at rare moments in social struggles, they left Kenora, with little money or other resources, to show how strongly the youth of Grassy Narrows feel about the protection of the Earth from environmental destruction. Working on a relay system, in which each of them walked ten kilometres a day, with support from First Nations communities along the way, they walked every step of the way.

As support was building, Ontario premier Dalton McGuinty made an announcement that he would amend the Mining Act. But requests for a moratorium on drilling so that the leaders could be released from jail went unheeded. Realizing the power of the jailing of the KI Six, the provincial government wanted them released, but the Six would only leave jail if they were given assurances that there would be no more drilling. This the government refused. So the KI Six remained in jail. They also refused to go from Thunder Bay to Toronto for their appeal, since the only option they were given was to go in shackles, and they felt that was beneath their dignity. They would participate in their appeal through video conferences.

Given the KI culture of face-to-face meetings and the central role I was playing in organizing their support, I decided to go up to Thunder Bay with Judy Findlay the week before the rally to meet them. In that meeting in the jail, Chief Donny Morris said, "When you think of when the settlers first came, they tried to slaughter us. Why? For the mineral riches on our land like gold, and now it is happening again. I have been thinking about what it means that non-Indians are organizing all this support for us. I am thinking about that a lot here. I haven't seen this kind of thing in the past. It's like all of you are becoming Indians. The Canadian government tried to assimilate us for generations and now it is the opposite that is happening. You are all starting to think like us about the Earth."

Then, as a sign that Platinex, the mining company, was feeling the pressure, they agreed to stop drilling so that the KI Six could come out of jail. In a bold move, their lawyer Chris Reid petitioned for them to be released until the appeal, and they were. The KI Six could attend the rally.

We also wanted as many people from KI and Grassy Narrows as possible at both the rally and the appeal. Since it costs about one thousand dollars per person to travel to Toronto from KI, that meant a lot of fundraising. Most of the funds came from the unions and the environmental groups that were involved. We raised more than fifty thousand dollars in a couple of weeks to bring fifty community members from KI, and another fifty from Grassy Narrows, for the rally and sleepover.

BOB LOVELACE, from the Ardoch Algonquins, was being treated much more harshly than the KI Six. He had spent part of his sentence in solitary confinement for going on a hunger strike. He called me on a pay phone from jail so that his voice could be heard at the rally. His speech was so inspiring that more than one thousand people listened to the tape in rapt silence, rare attention even for someone speaking in person at a rally. He said, in part:

> My imprisonment has been an ordeal, but I accept it without complaint or remorse. I know that my imprisonment, and that of my brothers and sister from Kitchenuhmaykoosib Inninuwug, stand as symbols of the oppression that all Aboriginal peoples in Canada have endured, every day, most often in silence, for hundreds of years now. I also know that our imprisonment, and the struggle to free us, represents, for good-minded, non-Aboriginal peoples, the frustration that they feel in trying to put an end to their own colonial legacy.
>
> That no Canadian should be sent to prison for peaceful resistance to the evil of colonialism, and that no Aboriginal person be denied freedom, are our goals. I am humbled by your presence here today, and your commitment to these goals.
> Colonialism is the great burden that is upon us all. Democracy and colonialism cannot long walk hand-in-hand before the disparities in justice, economic opportunities, and morality so sicken human spirits that we will all live without the hope of becoming the nations we wish to be.
>
> There is a great suffering in our abundant Creation, because few have real human privileges, and many do not. Colonialism is at once embedded in our institutions, the law, and in our minds. It sets neighbour against neighbour, while those who benefit continue to control us, and entrench their position. Resistance alone is not enough. We need a change of heart and a change of mind. Revolution is not enough. We need a renaissance of the human spirit.

The calm determination of Bob Lovelace and the KI Six, and the heroism of their communities, which were totally traumatized by the loss of their leaders and the attacks on their communities, inspired extraordinarily broad support. The alliance between the indigenous communities and outside supporters was unprecedented, both at the local and provincial level. In Ardoch, non-indigenous peoples were speaking out in defence of Lovelace and raising money to support him and his community. In Toronto, by the end of May, we had a network of students, unions, churches, anti-poverty groups, international solidarity coalitions, and, of course, environmental groups working full out. Not since the 1980s have I seen an issue into which every single individual and organization put so much work and money.

The protest culminated in that mass rally at the provincial legislature at Queen's Park and the four-day sovereignty sleepover, at which teepees and large tents were pitched on the grounds of the provincial legislature. The seven leaders were permanently released from prison for time served by the Court of Appeal after Lovelace had served three months and the KI Six had served two months of what were supposed to be sentences of six months for contempt of court. Their final exoneration came on the third day of the sleepover and represented a rare and important victory for indigenous peoples.

The integrity and courage of Bob Lovelace and the KI Six inspired First Nations across the country to realize they can say "No" to any development that is not in the interests of their communities or their land, and helped to build the broadest coalition of supporters I have seen in many years. This support influenced the Appeal Court decision as well.

Sam McKay, the KI spokesperson, told a press conference on the Tuesday of the four-day sleepover that he understood why southern First Nations were negotiating with industry, because their water and lands have already been destroyed. But, he argued, "We have a choice. We still have fresh water, clean air, and forests. We can still hunt and fish and trap and we will never give up the right to protect our traditional lands and our traditional way of life."

On June 9, 2008, only a week after the rally and sleepover, the giant paper and forest products company AbitibiBowater decided to stop logging on the traditional territory of the Grassy Narrows First Nation in a tremendous victory for the Grassy Narrows activists

One of the extraordinary elements of this organizing was that the network in Toronto agreed that all major decisions about the rally and sleepover should be made by the three Aboriginal communities. It was difficult figuring out how to make that happen with us in Toronto and the leadership of KI in jail. As I have seen in other struggles, people who had never seen themselves as leaders stepped into the breach, but it took us a few weeks to determine how to ensure that the outspoken organizers in Toronto—such as me—would stop dominating the conversation.

Still living a traditional life, the KI make decisions through consensus. We would ask a question on a conference call and they would sit in the band council office in a circle asking each person their opinion. Silence on a conference call is very uncomfortable: I had to mute my phone to make sure I didn't jump in to end it. At the beginning, we would make a decision, thinking that the communities had agreed, only to get an email a few days later saying that they weren't comfortable with the proposal. We were just too pushy and too quick to come to decisions; in the end, we reduced the number of Toronto people on the call. On their side, they realized that we were serious about them making the decisions, and so they did.

We didn't have agreement on the messaging until three weeks before the event. From the perspective of efficiency, it should have been a disaster, but instead we successfully organized an event called a Gathering of Mother Earth Protectors with clear messaging about the right of First Nations to refuse industrial development and exploitation, and we got support from almost everyone.

One example of how this worked comes to mind. An activist from Grassy Narrows suggested that a way to get around the fact that it is illegal to camp at Queen's Park was to write a letter to the Speaker of the House, who is in charge of the legislature and grounds. The

Speaker was informed that the three communities were holding four days of sacred ceremonies and, of necessity, were going to sleep over at Queen's Park—and, furthermore, they had a permit from the Mississauga of Port Credit, who claim this land.

We organized separately for the rally, which needed a permit because of the sound system. At first we approached Queen's Park security separately from the sleepover group, but then Queen's Park insisted on meeting us together. The lawyer for the two First Nations communities and one of our rally organizers, a professor from Brock University who, in her own words, "looks like a lady from Rosedale," managed to get agreement that we could have teepees and large tents, but not small tents. Some of the Toronto activists wanted to push the issue of the small tents, but the First Nations communities didn't see the need, since they wanted a peaceful gathering. Instead we put some of the community members up in local churches and union halls and others slept in the teepees and large tents. Supporters who wanted to sleep over did so in the open air. It was an amazing experience.

Carmelle Wolfson, one of the young activists who had helped organize the sleepover, wrote at www.rabble.ca:

> The gathering culminated with Grassy Narrows, Ardoch Algonquin and Kitchenuhmaykoosib Inninuwug (KI) First Nations and their supporters grasping hands to make a wish, before offering tobacco into the sacred fire. Then we headed off for the final march. Normally, I would find this kind of stuff pretty cheesy, but somehow it just seemed like the right thing to do. The gesture was a spiritual custom from a Native tradition, but also symbolized disparate groups coming together to form a broad coalition.... A Peruvian from a community with the largest gold mines in South America said it very eloquently at the May 26 rally: "The Andean people are united with Canada's First Nations people to defend their water and their land." He went on to say, "This economic system that's based on greed wants to take away from us not only our land but also

our spirit and our unity. And we're here to make sure that doesn't happen."

Through our solidarity networks we were able to break the isolation that can hinder resistance. Our arms stretched across rivers and highways. There were times when we as activists had tactical disagreements, but we recognized that this issue was too important to walk away from. When we build solidarity instead of division within our movements, we can accomplish so much more. When we held hands at Queen's Park we were told to make a wish. I wished for logging to stop in Grassy Narrows. It looks like I wasn't the only one.

Clayton Thomas Mueller, another extraordinary indigenous activist, mentioned previously in discussing the Indigenous Environmental Network, is currently organizing with native communities in and around the Alberta tar sands, the largest oil extraction project on earth. He says the Aboriginal leadership is coming to the fore at this time for two reasons: "This is a time of prophecy. Many of our indigenous nations talk about this time as a time of great change. This is why we are seeing this come forward now." The other reason is the need of the environmental movement for new strategies and the strength of an indigenous rights argument in protecting the environment.

AT THE 2007 U.S. SOCIAL FORUM, Faith Gemmill from REDOIL (Resisting Environmental Destruction on Indigenous Land) in Alaska said, "Our people have a prophecy that there will come a time in the history of humanity when people are in danger of destroying ourselves. When that time comes, a voice will arise from the North to warn us. That time is now. I was sent here to give you part of our burden to speak up now against the greed."

And indigenous peoples have been organizing together across the Americas and around the globe. On the occasion of the United Nations General Assembly adoption of the Declaration on the Rights of Indigenous Peoples (only Canada, Australia, New Zealand, and the United States refused to sign), the statement of the Indigenous Caucus read:

> One quarter of a century ago the United Nations agreed that the situation of Indigenous Peoples around the world was so desperate and consistently exploited, that it warranted international attention. Within a few years of brief examination and assessment, the United Nations decided that a human rights standard on the rights of Indigenous peoples was required. Simultaneously, the Indigenous peoples of the world were uniting, because of our increasing capacity to communicate to each other, but also out of necessity to achieve an international voice. Together we found out that Indigenous Peoples around the world shared a common situation of loss of control of our lands, territories and resources and a history of colonization.
>
> As Indigenous Peoples we now see a guarantee that our rights to self-determination, to our lands and territories, to our cultural identities, to our own representation and to our values and beliefs will be respected at the international level. The Declaration is a framework for States to link and integrate with the Indigenous Peoples, to initiate new and positive relations, but this time without exclusion, without discrimination, and without exploitation. These rights in the Declaration are already recognized in international law, but they are rights which have been denied to Indigenous Peoples everywhere. They are rights which are seen by Indigenous Peoples as essential to our successful survival, dignity and well-being, and to maintain our strong cultural and spiritual relationship with mother earth and nature. It has, after all, been our determination to defend our identity and our lands, territories and resources which has helped to protect and preserve the biological diversity of the world, the cultural diversity of the world, and the environmental stability of the world. These are the very issues that governments are now

so desperately trying to address, as matters requiring of emergency, recovery actions.

The convergence between the indigenous movements for self-determination and protection of their traditional lands and cultures with the rise in environmental consciousness is one of the most powerful forces for social change in the world today.

Having looked at some of the exciting new movements and approaches to social and environmental change, it's time to look at some new approaches to our more intractable problems: war, economy, and electoral politics.

12

NON-VIOLENCE
Neither Fight nor Flight

"My favourite movie is *Life Is Beautiful*," Refaat Sabbah explains to me. "I love the way the hero protects his son from the experience of the concentration camp. I try to protect my children from the horrors around us, too," he adds with a gentle smile. "I notice my daughter doesn't draw guns and tanks."

We are sitting together in a covered porch in his modest home in a downtown Ramallah neighbourhood. The night before, Israeli troops nearly decimated Yassar Arafat's compound nearby. Sabbah and his wife, Sorida, were up all night. The shelling began at 2 a.m. and continued until 6 a.m. Mercifully, the children, a girl of ten and a boy of three, slept through it. Not so the little girl next door, who has been crying ever since. This is life in Ramallah, the capital of the Palestinian Territories.

Sabbah is the head of the Teacher Creativity Center here, and his wife works with women's groups. They are intelligent, charming, and passionate about life. Like so many activists I meet here, they are also remarkably without hatred or bitterness. Sabbah tells me that he tries to avoid crossing the checkpoints that surround Ramallah so that he won't get too angry with the Israelis.

I am in Palestine. Even the term makes me a little uncomfortable. I am Jewish, born and bred. I went to Hebrew school. My first battle for equality was to insist on having a B'at Mitzvah in my thirteenth year. In those days only boys had a coming-of-age ceremony. My father was a major fundraiser for the United Jewish Appeal (UJA), and most of the money went to Israel. In 1956, he went on a mission to Israel, when such travel was unusual. Israel is supposed to be my homeland.

My 2002 trip to the Palestinian Territories was part of a fact-finding mission organized by Alternatives, a Montreal-based NGO with a twenty-year history of work with groups in both Israel and Palestine. What I saw there was both deeply disturbing and strangely inspiring.

The inspiration came from the people I met on both sides of the Israeli–Palestinian divide. I was already aware of the brave people of the Israeli peace movement, who continue to stand up against the Israeli occupations of and incursions into the West Bank and the Gaza Strip, areas that everyone agrees are Palestinian territories. But I did not know about the diversity of the Palestinian resistance. Here in Canada, we hear a lot about Fatah and Hamas, which are indeed the major political organizations operating in the Palestinian Territories. What I didn't know before my trip is the strong and growing movement of activists in the Palestinian Territories who call themselves *the democratic opposition*. Most of them work through NGOs that provide what is left of the social services in the Palestinian Territories.

A comment that has stayed with me since my visit was from a Palestinian I met who said, "I only wish the Israelis realized that their best hope of security is a strong Palestinian state. The rest of the Arab world hates them. We don't. We know them; they are our neighbours." One of the strangest feelings I had in Palestine was how alike the Palestinians and the Israelis are. In fact, the Palestinians have often been called "the Jews of the Arab world" for their lack of a homeland and the value they put on culture and education. I was open about being Jewish in Palestine and never felt threatened because of it. "I am not afraid of the Israelis," Refaat Sabbah told me at the time. "I am afraid that violence is becoming a positive moral value in our society. And from that we will never recover."

Recently I wrote Refaat to ask him to update me on his views on the situation now. He replied with a beautiful essay entitled "What We Understood but Forgot." I am reproducing some of it here because it is a powerful indictment of a war without end.

> There was a time where, as Palestinians, we agreed that the voice for democracy came from many a source, a belief, a religion, a philosophical view, an education, a political party, an oppressed people, and even a personal experience.
>
> We understood that resistance of occupation came in many a form and that ours would be the rock that defended and did not attack, the education that would be the weapon that we did not own, the boycott of Israeli goods, the defiance to purchasing what was stolen from us, the scarce drop of water left turned into a lesson in survival of plant, animal, and human being.
>
> We understood how to make their jails the other school and our prisoners the students and the lessons those of love for Palestine, patience, strategies, reflection, hope, and endurance. The graffiti on walls became a mode of communication and a file for a history unwritten. The nursery rhymes of children became the stories of land, people, hope, struggle, and a future happy, free Palestine. Our children became the adults who spoke the language of the old wise philosophers on life and politics, teaching us adults the ways of an unbroken spirit....
>
> We were the hope, the lover, the spirit, the educator, the philosopher, the defender of a future Palestine that would be perfect.
>
> We had as a people passed every cruelty forced by them on us, always emerging with a stronger understanding that they are them and we are us, until the aftermath of the second Intifada.

The events took us into a dark path by those who distorted religion and used it in an agenda, allowing for the introduction of a slow poison that would be activated full blast after the democratic elections of 2006 and the cruelty of the international community, causing a deadly amnesia to a nation that forgot what it understood.

Today is a time in Palestine where part of our fight is not that for freedom, rights, democracy, and land. It is a fight of one against another, of oppression and violations, although a minority of us remain untouched by the poison that caused amnesia and continue our old fight for freedom, justice, and rights, as in the Bil'in movement [an Israeli/Palestinian solidarity movement] and many others....

We created jails and turned them into places that breed hate, despair, darkness, and violence, feeding in us what we hated the most about them. The games of our children became that of real-looking plastic guns and war between teams divided into Hamas and Fatah. The wisdom of our teenagers and young adults disappeared as they lost identity, disassociating themselves from friends who belonged to other factions and fighting after university elections, violently injuring each other, allowing more of what we hated of them into us....

We forget that poverty is in hating ourselves and not in asking for our entitlements, which we confuse with charity. We turn our noses up at what the land has to offer us and seek the goods of them, making us the more reliant and less self-sufficient.

We move through life, passing blindly the wall of hatred built by them, the weeping olive trees that have been separated from their owners, and the dusty flag that refuses to fly high, even with the strongest breeze, as if communicating the shame it feels.

Today in Palestine, we have allowed more of them into us, but we are noticing that the poison is exiting slowly and there is big hope that we will remember all we understood once upon a time to come back stronger and better than even the us we were before.

Still there is hope even after so many years of things getting worse. For Refaat Sabbah, the hope is in the joint work of Palestinians and Israelis, which continues despite all the violence and division. His prose poem shows two sides of war. The first is the strength that a people can feel in resistance. The Palestinian resistance is one of the most powerful we have ever seen. The other is the danger in a long-standing war. As Sabbah points out, we turn into them. Violence breeds violence. From Algeria to Vietnam to Palestine we have seen peoples who will never give up their claim to their homeland. Whatever your views are on the Middle East, what is obvious is that war is obsolete in this era.

The situation in Iraq and Afghanistan show even more clearly why violence will never solve any problem. As Naomi Klein points out in her extraordinary book *The Shock Doctrine*, war today is not aimed at solving problems but rather at creating disaster, so that even more profit can be made on the backs of peoples who simply don't matter to the world's dominators.

Massive propaganda tries to convince people in the Global North, and particularly in the United States, that violence is necessary to defend "our interests," and that terrorists are a huge threat to our civilization, but the truth is exactly the opposite. It is the Iraqi civilization that is under threat. The levels of violence and depravity of the U.S. occupiers, while they may not have reached the heights of a vicious dictator such as Saddam Hussein, are seriously beyond any internationally accepted behaviour in war: rendition,* torture, illegal arrests, the holding of people for years without due process, as well as the massive killing of civilians. These horrors are now well known

---

*Rendition is the term for handing a captive over to another country for interrogation without any due process. It is, basically, outsourcing torture.

and, despite the fact that the majority of Americans oppose the war in Iraq, so much of the United States' power is based on its ability to carry out terrible violence that it is hard to see how that will ever change. And just as importantly, the United States has built a huge military industrial complex that needs continual war economy to feed its profit.

During the war in Vietnam, a powerful anti-war movement, combined with strong guerrilla resistance in Vietnam, managed to stop the war, but this time it seems that no movement, no matter how big and powerful, can stop a war without end. A BBC World Service international poll in the fall of 2006 found that 67 percent of citizens around the world and 61 percent of U.S. citizens wanted American troops out of Iraq within a year. The war against terrorism, like the Cold War before it, never runs out of enemies. First Afghanistan, then Iraq, now the focus is turning on Iran and Pakistan. Even when the mythology of the United States as the defender of democracy has collapsed almost everywhere around the world, the United States continues its militaristic domination. Even Barack Obama, for all his positive qualities, continues to talk about military solutions, proposing to pull out of Iraq and instead focus on Afghanistan and Pakistan, where Al Qaeda is more present.

In her essay "Rethinking Political Parties," Hilary Wainwright points out that the refusal of the Blair government in the United Kingdom to end participation in the war in Iraq, despite massive public opposition, has stimulated a lot of new thinking about politics.

> The anti-war movement marked a new phase in thinking about electoral politics. The experience of being a majority and yet in the U.K., Spain, and Italy failing to stop governments which claimed to rule in their name, reinforced people's sense of the corrupt and distant nature of political institutions or, for some, awoke them to this fact. It also led to a greater concern with the nature of political institutions: in the U.K. the creation of a new electoral alliance, in Italy the creation of a more organised

co-ordination between movements and parliamentarians, in Spain, and also in the U.S., movement support—on an autonomous basis—for an electoral campaign.

Anti-war activist Abdul-Rehman Malik also feels that the anti-war movement has been too narrow in Britain to succeed in mobilizing the majority sentiment in the population against the war. At the same time as he congratulates the anti-war movement for including Muslim organizations in its ranks, he notes, "Part of the reason is that the anti-war movement has retreated into its leftist hole. I think part of the trouble is that the Left has had a lot of trouble creating an argument that is going to reach middle England, or middle Canada for that matter. I mean, we have to convince the *Daily Mail* reading public of our contentions. And in many ways I think that by pursuing a very dogmatic line in some cases, allying itself with only certain kinds of Muslim groups that are situated within the framework of political Islam, I think it has alienated some people outside the anti-war movement."

To explore this question of how to stop wars, I sat down with three people from the Christian Peacemaker Teams, James Loney, William Payne, and Sylvia Morrison. I first met the Christian Peacemaker Teams (CPT) at a checkpoint in Palestine, and was astonished at how they were able to de-escalate a potentially lethal confrontation by stepping in and talking to the Israeli soldiers. Their calm centredness and ability to appeal to the humanity of these soldiers was extraordinary. There were other international solidarity groups who put themselves between the Israeli soldiers and the Palestinians waiting in line to cross, but it was only the CPT members that I saw actually transform a potentially violent situation.

The CPT had its beginnings at the World Mennonite Assembly in 1984. One speaker, a theologian named Ron Cider, issued a challenge. What if there were ten or one hundred thousand Christians willing to risk what soldiers are willing to risk—but for peace, not war? After discussion, the idea emerged to have peace teams that were trained in non-violence. They would work in areas of active conflict and try to reduce violence by working with people who were affected by that violence, and by taking the same kinds of risks that soldiers would take. The first training was in 1994, and the first mission was in Iraq just before the war began. Today, there are two hundred trained CPT members, including one hundred and seventy reservists supporting about thirty full-timers in four projects.

They work in some of the most violent places on earth—Palestine, Colombia, and Iraq. They also work with indigenous communities in Canada. When I described my experience in Palestine and asked how they manage to diffuse the violence, Sylvia Morrison responded, "It's hard to say we're not taking sides, but we're taking the side of justice, we're taking the side of peace. So CPT goes there and doesn't treat the military—who are not being just to the Palestinians—as demons, but really speaks to their humanity, really honours them for who they are as human beings, recognizing that the role they are playing is not them, and speaking to them about that role and how it impacts people."

James Loney, who passed the ultimate test of this philosophy when he was kidnapped in Iraq, continued,

> In our best moments, I think, we see that there is a presence of God in every person. So there's a presence of God in soldiers, in paramilitaries, in kidnappers, and in a person who's screaming in your face. And so if you are engaging the person from that place, then it opens up the space, it opens up the possibility. It surprises the person. It puts them off balance. It's unexpected.
>
> And I think that also it's very easy to escalate a tense situation—by saying the wrong thing, or your tone of voice or body language. So we spend a lot of time in training on how to be present in a tense situation, how to communicate with body language. Ninety percent of communication is non-verbal.
>
> It's this very easy thing—if you call me a name, I'll call you a name right back. That's our normal kind of socialization. But if

we're really aware of what our goal is, instead of reacting, we can start to influence things. In a way, it's about exercising a kind of power. That's real power. Reacting is not real power. Being grounded and being clear about who you are and being able to shift things—that's power.

I asked how they keep it up, such a relatively small group of people taking on such terrible violence. William Payne responded,

One of our daily rituals is to gather in some kind of time of reflection or prayer together that tries to access that power that isn't "power over," that dwells within each one of us. And for me, it's in the collective, in working with other people, that we see the third choice, which is neither flight—hiding my head in the sand, escaping the horror of the world the way it is—nor the fist, fighting back, believing that my power over is somehow going to be successful.

I asked James Loney what they mean by the power within. His answer:

What does it mean to have power? For boys and for men, we're socialized into power. It's having lots of muscles and being good at sports and being able to use a gun, and being able to fight and use your fists when you have to, and having a loud voice, and throwing your weight around, and no one's going to tell me what to do. These are all different forms of power as domination.

What about the power of love and forgiveness and nurturing and patience and being able to sacrifice, or the power to accept suffering instead of inflicting suffering? Is that what power is? I think that if we're really attentive in ourselves, this is the kind of power that we're trying to exercise—because we all need to be powerful—we all want power and we need to be powerful. Every two-year-old is trying to find out how to be powerful. And our identity, the formation of our identity is how do we have access to power through this identity, what we belong to, who we belong to, what we are? There is a power that's available to us that I, as a person of faith, as a Christian, think comes from God. This is the power of love, which is the power to forgive, to heal, to nurture. It is not the power of domination. It is not the power of violence.

And when we live out of that power, that's when we are our best selves. And we know it; we feel it. When I get really angry and I'm triggered into this reacting thing—if I'm really attentive, I know I'm suffering. But if I'm not reacting, and I'm grounded in who I really am, I know, I have this sense of being grounded, and this sense of … I'm not suffering. It's hard to describe. I wish I could think of a story to illustrate it. When you get into a fight, and you hit somebody, that really hurts. Your fist will swell up, and it cuts, and it really hurts. And we never see that in the movies. We just see the person fall, we don't see the swollen, sore hand, the injury that comes from violence. And when we do that, we harm ourselves.

Sylvia Morrison continued,

It's a kind of sustaining power, a kind of power that you don't learn. It is just in you. And you feel it. One example of that power for me is in working with violence. There are many times when we talk about that violence that is physical and violence that is out there, but there are times when we are dealing with violence within, and the conflicts we have even within and among ourselves.

There was a particular instance when I was doing an anti-racism training. There was a group of thirteen of us. I was one of two persons of colour in the room; everyone else was white. And we're talking about racism. And I am a participant in the room, but, since I'm a person of colour, people also expect me to be the teacher. And we're having this conversation, we're really trying to break this thing down and look at racism, and we'd gone through a roleplay and we're now debriefing it. And we felt like, okay, white people are really getting the point of whatever that teaching moment was. And just as we thought we were done with that, and now we were going to move on to the next, one white woman in the room said something that was so painfully racist that the other white people felt it too.

There were times when, doing a racism workshop as a woman of colour, I would know how to not allow myself to feel, so I could talk about racism intellectually and go there, because I can. So as not to feel pain, I would not go to my feeling place. But this time I decided, maybe I should allow myself to go to my feeling place and see what that was like. So I just allowed what was being said to wash over and through me, and trust whatever was going to happen to me as a result of that.

And what happened was profound. Because there was a power within me that allowed me to sustain that, to feel that, and when the feeling got to a certain place in my body, I knew that "Okay, I can take no more of this, walk out." Prior to that, walking out would have had me thinking, "Now they've really just destroyed me. Now I've lost my voice. Now I won't be able to speak any more." But this time, I allowed the feeling to rise up and I allowed myself to feel that and do whatever I needed to do with that. What I needed to do was walk out of the room.

So I walked out of the room, and I walked back in three minutes later. The room I walked back into three minutes later was completely different than the room I walked out of. Because me walking out did something for the white people in the room that speaking for hours from my head or my heart or wherever was not doing for them. I walked back in, and people were sharing with one another experiences of what they had done wrong, and who they saw do what, and what they should do different. And I thought, "Oh my gosh!"

So prior to that day, allowing the power within to sustain me, I would have felt like that was weakness. But it wasn't. It was transforming for the others, and it was for me too. Because I realized that I can be okay if I allow myself to feel that. Because then I learned something more about myself and about other people in the room.

That story reminded me of a scene in my friend Velcrow Ripper's film *Fierce Light* in which well-known environmentalist Julia Butterfly says, "When I realize I can feel the pain of the world is when I know that I am still all right." And she shows us the pain she feels as she is speaking. This powerful woman, who sat in a tree for two years to save a rainforest, who is strong, brave, and articulate, demonstrated a power in herself that everyone could see, though she was speaking through her tears. I thought of how, in our patriarchal world, tears are a sign of weakness and anger is a sign of strength when maybe the opposite is true. Maybe finding this power in ourselves, the power to love rather than hate, the power to feel suffering rather than shut it out, the power to feel compassion rather than anger, is the power we need to change the world. That's the power within that Gandhi called soul force and that Velcrow Ripper calls fierce light. In his film, you can see it in almost every person he features, from Desmond Tutu to actor-turned-environmental-activist Darryl Hannah, to Carly Stasko, a young Canadian anti-globalization activist.

I also remembered interviewing Rosa Kouri, the twenty-three-year-old environmental activist mentioned previously. Describing her reaction to the police violence and tear gas at the Quebec City protests against the FTAA, which she experienced as a teenager, she said, "It made me conscious of the militant inside me that I can't trust. Maybe not the militant but the 'I am right and they are wrong and I will conquer them,' because it was so easy to be in that place and want to fight. This person in the mask in front of me is my enemy. Realizing what it was to feel that way. Someone is aggressive to you and you want to be aggressive back. But it's not something to welcome in activism. It sounds cool, but if this work is to respect the sanctity of life, then you have to imbed those values in the way you work with people."

Kouri's words made me think about the role of riot police, masked and banging on their shields. They not only dehumanize themselves, they provoke a fight-or-flight reaction in demonstrators. At first you feel the fear and then the anger. But, as Rosa Kouri says, if you act out of the anger and strike back, you become like them and nothing changes.

I was very stimulated by my conversation with the CPTers. Clearly the anti-war movements have not yet managed to stop the war, despite the massive protests, but it is also hard to believe that practising non-violence on a personal level will do much to end war. Progressive religious people have always preached that you must love your enemy, an idea I have found very difficult to understand, let alone embrace. But perhaps this new generation of activists, having come into a world where violence so obviously solves nothing, and benefiting from the knowledge that the interpersonal violence of sexism, racism, and homophobia is no longer acceptable, can come to the spiritual understanding of non-violence without belief in a higher power but through the belief in using their own power in a respectful way.

NEVERTHELESS, MILITARISM remains strong. It is the first time I can remember in Canada that the military is being celebrated as a fighting machine and not as peacekeepers. In the United States, the power of the war resisters is simply not as significant as it was against the war in Vietnam, perhaps because of the class differences. Middle-class boys were being drafted for Vietnam, and people with power personally knew the young men who returned in body bags. Moreover, the media is much less open today than it was during that war.

For example, the Winter Soldier hearings at the George Meany Center in Silver Spring, Maryland, from March 13 to 16, 2008, presented a remarkable anti-war testimony from veterans of the Iraq and Afghanistan wars. Most of the mainstream media ignored it, to the point that I began wondering whether there was a deliberate blackout. Named after the famous Winter Soldier hearings from 1971 that focused on the real story of the Vietnam War, the testimony detailed the horrific conditions under which U.S. soldiers are fighting and dying and Iraqi civilians are suffering.

I watched online while veteran after veteran told his or her story of shock and betrayal, anger and sadness, at what they found when they went to Iraq. I wept through almost every presentation. These were young people who joined the military because they believed in protecting their country from terrorism, and they found out that they were inflicting more terror than anyone else. Almost to a person, they concluded that this war should never have happened. "Democracy Now!," Amy Goodman's amazing radio show on www.pacifica.org, was the only media outlet to broadcast these extraordinary hearings or even report on them in any depth. You can still watch them at http://ivaw.org/wintersoldier.

Edward Tick is a registered psychologist who works with veterans of the Vietnam and Iraq wars who are suffering from post-traumatic shock. He calls it a soul wound, an identity disorder—a social disorder, not a mental illness—and says the soul of these soldiers has been battered and ravaged. The only way they can heal is to accept the suffering that they have created and to make amends. Tick organizes trips to Vietnam for vets to meet with Vietnamese survivors and to participate in building hospitals and schools. His techniques are so successful that a speech he gave at the Walter Reed Hospital was broadcast to U.S. military bases around the world.

Tick says that Vietnamese soldiers don't suffer post-traumatic stress, because their religion, Buddhism, prepares them for the role of warrior. I think it's more likely because their war was to resist an imperialist invader, and so for them it was a just war. Yet when Buddhist leader Thich Nhat Hanh returned to Vietnam in 2007, after forty years in exile for refusing to take sides between the North and the South, he led huge gatherings throughout the country that were designed to heal the wounds and divisions of the past.

Pretty touchy-feely, you may be saying to yourself. What about all the bad people in the world who want to inflict violence on others, who get off on it, or are ideologically driven to it? My response to that question is that our governments are using violence now against such people, whether in Iraq and Afghanistan or in prisons, and yet the violence has not been reduced. Or as James Loney says, "I think that before we say that non-violence doesn't work, I'd like to see 10 percent of the resources that we put into war be used for a hundred years for non-violence, and then we might be able to make a judgment that this doesn't work."

Much more daunting is the military industrial complex that is such a significant part of the economic structure of the United States—and the world. War has always been part of human history, but it seems to me that if it ever made sense, it no longer does. I don't know how it will end, but what I do know is that we have to do a much better job of modelling non-violence and peaceful ways to resolve conflict. In May 2008 at Hollyhock, I heard a powerful story about ending violence. A fisheries activist told the story to a workshop. It comes from a dispute about the lobster fisheries that occurred around the same time as the famed Burnt Church struggle, when a terrible confrontation between native and non-native fisherman took place in Nova Scotia. In September 1999, the Marshall decision of the Supreme Court of Canada affirmed the treaty right of Aboriginal peoples to make a moderate livelihood from fishing, hunting, and gathering, with no reference to the hunting and fishing seasons set by the government. In October, the people of Esgenoopetitj (Burnt Church) attempted to exercise their treaty rights by fishing for lobster. Non-native fishermen responded by cutting their lines and destroying $210,000 worth of traps belonging to the people of Esgenoopetitj. The situation was tense, with fishermen ramming boats and making threats with firearms. Two Mi'kmaq men were seriously injured during an altercation.

In southwest Nova Scotia, a confrontation on an even greater scale was brewing. More than five hundred non-native lobster boats gathered in Yarmouth, in the belief that their industry and livelihoods were threatened by the Supreme Court decision. Pressure mounted daily. At a series of mass meetings, politicians indulged in blatant fear-mongering that further inflamed the crisis. At one of these meetings, the fishermen's representatives proposed that they meet with the chiefs of the local bands to try to find a solution, and the fishermen agreed, but on the condition that this would be the last attempt.

I asked Arthur Bull, an activist in the area, if I could tell the story in this book, so he went to the chiefs involved and edited my version of what I had heard according to their advice:

> In this highly charged atmosphere, the fishermen's reps set up a meeting with the two chiefs—Chief Frank Meuse of the Bear River First Nation and Chief Deborah Robinson of the Acadia First Nation—and their staffs. This meeting was to take place in secret at an inn outside Yarmouth, without any government bureaucrats, lawyers, or press present. The morning of the meeting, everyone showed up but one person—Chief Frank Meuse. Tension filled the room as the representatives waited in silence. When Chief Meuse finally arrived he was carrying an eagle feather. He asked the group's permission to try something different—that the eagle feather be passed around the circle and that each person speak not for him or herself but for his or her grandfather or grandmother.
>
> What happened then surprised everyone. Every person told stories about the most personal and difficult issues and experiences in their lives. Most people broke down at one point or another. It took a long time for the feather to go around, and once it did, Chief Meuse then asked permission to pass the feather around to "go to a deeper level." The storytelling continued in an even more intensive way, and it took most of the morning to complete the circle. Once the feather had completed

its circle, everyone rose and hugged each other, and it appeared that the meeting was over.

At this point, someone said, "But what about the lobster problem?" Everyone sat down and, in about fifteen minutes, worked out a compromise that involved the number of traps and boats on the water. Once this was done, Chief Meuse went out and came back with some crayons and paper and everyone worked on a banner, colouring in the letters. The word on the banner was Peace. A couple of days later there was another mass meeting of fishermen in Yarmouth. The fishermen's reps sat at the front of the stage and were joined by Chief Robinson. When she stood to speak, to explain the compromise that had been worked out, she received a prolonged standing ovation from the fishermen in the room.

As well as putting First Nations' fishermen on the water, there were many other outcomes of this meeting. Acadia First Nation became active in the commercial fisheries without any violence. Bear River First Nation went on to play a lead role in a series of cross-cultural projects about indigenous/non-indigenous co-operation on community-based fisheries management.

More and more activists are realizing that non-violence is the only practical approach to winning battles. In the period after the events of September 11, 2001, any confrontational tactics were painted by media and government as terrorism. In the last ten years, they have tried to criminalize any activist who uses confrontational tactics. As we talk about transformational tactics, we have to talk about replacing violence with non-violence. This does not mean pacifism. Martin Luther King was for non-violence, but the movement he led practised direct action and non-violent confrontation.

The women's movement has always been against war. The Voice of Women for Peace, founded in 1960 in Canada, developed incredibly brave but non-violent methods for resisting war. At the height of anti-communist hysteria, they invited Soviet women to Canada to sit down and discuss issues with women here. They saw that understanding one another and connecting to one another as human beings is the best way to avoid war. During Vietnam, they did the same. Today, Code Pink in the United States continues that tradition.

I have no idea of how we will end the scourge of war, but I do know that the more people who give up the need to have power over others by any means, the more likely there will be an end to war. The more people who try to understand the story told by others, the more likely there will be an end to war. The more people realize that it is not acceptable to make money from destruction, whether of the environment or other human beings, the more likely there will be an end to war. The more each of us gets in touch with ourselves, our neighbours, and the people around us, the more likely there will be an end to war. The more that women and men who are providing leadership have broken from the habits of patriarchy, the more likely there will be an end to war. The more justice and equality there is the world, the more likely there will be an end to war. The more we try to understand the other side, the more likely there will be an end to war. Go ahead and add a sentence of your own. It's not that hard to dream about it.

13

IS ANOTHER ECONOMY POSSIBLE?
Green Jobs, Fair Trade, and Networks

WHILE LOCAL COMMUNITY PROJECTS, small businesses, and even national campaigns to re-introduce ideas of social justice and environmental sustainability into the economy are critically important, probably the most daunting challenge for those who want to change the world is the creation of large-scale economic alternatives. Since the fall of the Berlin Wall in 1989, any talk of developing an economic alternative to capitalism has been met with derision. Almost everyone has been persuaded that the market works best to produce economic wealth. This hegemonic belief system has been dramatically challenged by the global economic meltdown of 2008. The most ferocious ideologues of free market fundamentalism, such as U.S. Treasury secretary Henry Paulson, are turning to the government to bail out the private sector. If they had let the market work its own way during this crisis, the economic price would have been far too high to pay. In a supreme irony, British Labour Party prime minister Gordon Brown reached into the deep past of that party for a socialist solution to the problem. Nationalizing the banks was the only measure that calmed the roller-coaster ride of stock markets around the world. The debate about the price we have paid for neo-liberalism is now on the table like never before.

Neo-liberal ideology believes that the market works best in regulating everything, including education, health care, prisons, social services, and so on. Despite massive resistance against the dismantling of the welfare state, especially in Europe and Canada, there has been significant erosion of public education, universal health care, and especially any kind of social safety net for the poor and unemployed. Privatization and cutbacks, in addition to so-called free trade agreements, have preoccupied the energy of the trade-unions and many social movements. They have become mired in defending the status quo, rather than envisioning a better system.

One silver lining in the global environmental crisis is that it has forced recognition, even among neo-liberals, that the state once again has to play a regulatory role in ensuring that private enterprise does not continue its destruction of the planet. The current financial crisis of capital combined with environmental disaster means that the elite consensus against regulation and state intervention in the economy has collapsed. The Chicago school, with its guru Milton Friedman's belief in the market über alles, has lost its grip.

Governments are bailing out financial institutions, and all the talk on the business pages is suddenly about regulation instead of leaving everything to the market. In a wonderful opinion piece in *The Globe and Mail* in the midst of the crisis in September 2008, Robert Skidelsky, a political economy professor from Warwick University, said, "A few geniuses aside, economists frame their assumptions to suit existing states of affairs, and then invest them with an aura of permanent truth. They are the intellectual butlers, serving the interests of those in power." The pendulum has started to swing back from the extremism of market fundamentalism, but with the exception of the proposals for a green economy, there is not much political leadership on the Left to propose new economic solutions. Barack Obama is proposing some modest solutions to protect homeowners and small businesses, but with the exception of his apparent adoption of the Green Jobs campaign and his rhetoric about caring for what he calls middle-class Americans and not big business, he is not making proposals that will fundamentally change the economic system.

Activist Van Jones has thought about this issue:

> The three big challenges that the human family is facing are: radical social inequality, radical environmental destruction, and deepening despair. They kind of define the new century. And so we're trying to move an agenda that says we can have a green growth economic model, where you really restore the earth and you heal the earth and you honour the earth, and you make that the basis of your economy. You could put people to work doing that so you can solve some of the economic problems. And you begin to restore hope. When you talk about solar power, and bio-diesel, and wind, and organic agriculture, all of these positive economic activities could be the basis for a new politics of hope and economic opportunity.
>
> It's hard to see it, though, if you're not coming from a heartful place. Your mind is going to tend to divide those issues up into analytically separate categories. You have this analytical category and that category and how do these categories relate? But your heart will say, "We don't have any throw-away children, we don't have any throw-away resources, we don't have any throw-away species, or neighbourhoods, or nations. It's all sacred. So let's treat it that way." And that's the way out of these crises.... We are no longer faced with an information problem or a technology problem. It is a wisdom problem. That is our problem. All the technology exists right now to save the earth in terms of renewable energy, organic agriculture, permaculture— all that is in place. The information is there, the technology is there—the human heart is not ready, you see.*

---

*From an interview with director Velcrow Ripper for his film *Fierce Light: When Spirit Meets Action* (2008).

But there are human hearts that *are* ready, and it is from them that we begin to see some alternatives. In the United States, the most promising movement is Green Jobs for All, discussed in Chapter 7, whose goal is five million new green jobs. Obama is talking about adopting at least some of their proposals, and no doubt the movement for green jobs will keep up pressure on him to do more. In his new book *The Green Collar Economy*, Van Jones outlines a sweeping proposal to transform the casino economy that benefits mostly the rich to a green economy that will benefit all. In Europe, a lot of the alternative economic strategies are based in reclaiming privatized state services—but then turning them into something more democratic, and, therefore, much more functional.

In a recently updated edition of her book *Reclaim the State*, Hilary Wainwright talks about an example in Italy that combines resistance against privatization with the development of new economic ideas. She writes:

> Recently many municipalities have become involved with a wave of very popular, powerful and deeply rooted territorial movements who are presenting an alternative model of development. This alternative is based on sustainability, democratic control and the development of social capacities. With the global shake up of traditional hierarchies of government and the new interweaving and cross-cutting of the local, the national and the global, the story of these municipalities and territorial movements is suggestive of new institutions and new political relationships.

One example Wainwright studied in detail was the town of Grottammare in Italy, where a group of activists, including a couple of city councillors, organized the community to resist ideas about tourism that were based on large projects. "We argued for a tranquil tourism that was about nature, culture, and human relationships, not consumerism," said Massimo Rossi, one of the councillors. In a story that is becoming familiar, they introduced their ideas to the community in a participatory project.

Wainwright describes it:

> Their first task was to develop an entirely new urban plan to introduce care and vision into a town which was becoming cluttered with concrete and was losing its magnetism for tranquillity-seeking citizens of Milan and Rome. (Since "Participation and Solidarity" took office, the numbers of tourists has more than doubled, from 254,000 to over 500,000.) They combined a professional efficiency: surveying the threats to the environment, taking sewage treatment back into municipal ownership: calling open assemblies in every neighbourhood [to implement participatory democracy].
>
> Massimo Rossi later became governor of the province of Ascoli Piceno and, as part of the extraordinary slow-food movement born in Italy, he used his leverage to bring together restaurateurs and food shops in the historic town of Ascoli and to organize linkages between them and networks of local farmers and food producers. And this experiment with a form of networked economics has an international dimension: he is arranging linkages with China. In these ways the Italian radical municipalities attempt to combine the development of participatory forms of budgeting, administration, and planning with the development of a local—and as far as possible democratic—economy. As Glenn Jenkins would say, it's glocal, and given the importance of tourism to so many local economies, it could be transformative.

The slow-food movement itself is another example of an alternative economic approach that has grown virally. Started in Italy by the charismatic Carlo Petrini, who became known for organizing protests against the opening of a McDonald's on the Spanish Steps in Rome, the slow-food movement not only resists fast food, it is creating alternatives to it. It has expanded to 83,000 member organizations with chapters in 123 countries, in a network with a global reach. Totally decentralized, the slow-food movement is an international effort to promote local and organic food and protect heritage seeds against the predatory policies of big agriculture. In the introduction to his book *Terra Madre*, which describes sixteen hundred of what he calls *food communities* around the world, Petrini writes:

> It is the translation into written words of a network that self-generates, grows, develops, giving life to a close-knit web of solidarity, exchanges information and in some cases protests. *Terra Madre* brings together those who work in food and support sustainable agriculture, fishing, and breeding with the goal of preserving taste and biodiversity to work towards increasing small-scale, traditional, and sustainable food production.

The slow-food movement is a good example of the new form of international solidarity in which knowledge is freely shared across borders. The growth of the movement and its impact on food production is an example of how, in this age of networks and people's globalization, a good idea can not only spread but build and support itself across borders. Here is the slow-food movement's mission statement:

> We believe that everyone has a fundamental right to pleasure and consequently the responsibility to protect the heritage of food, tradition and culture that make this pleasure possible. Our movement is founded upon this concept of eco-gastronomy—a recognition of the strong connections between plate and planet.
>
> Slow Food is good, clean and fair food. We believe that the food we eat should taste good; that it should be produced in a clean way that does not harm the environment, animal welfare or our health; and that food producers should receive fair compensation for their work.

> We consider ourselves co-producers, not consumers, because by being informed about how our food is produced and actively supporting those who produce it, we become a part of and a partner in the production process.

Obviously the slow-food movement is not coming from a left-wing perspective at all. Slow food has been criticized as being more for the elites than the masses. But it is part of what has become known as the *food security movement*. This movement is not only rethinking food production, distribution, and preparation but it is putting it into practice at numerous levels, from community gardens, to the occupation of unproductive rural land, to farm-to-table distribution systems, to protection of heritage seeds, to local farmers' markets, to the hundred-mile diet, to permaculture (an idea that self-sufficient communities are possible and desirable, especially in terms of food and energy production). It is a massive global movement that has grown mostly virally not only to address the crisis of food and hunger around the world—a crisis that is worsening by the day—but also to create an alternative system that makes more sense economically, ecologically, medically, and sensually than agribusiness and fast food.

THE SLOW-FOOD MOVEMENT combines for-profit, non-profit, and governmental initiatives into a creative global solution to the economic, social, and environmental destruction created by agribusiness. This model—combining community-based initiatives supported by public resources and entrepreneurship, as well as larger scale public enterprise—is similar to the green jobs initiative and may be a new approach that combines capitalist entrepreneurship with socialist planning; the market with the community; environmental sustainability with economic growth; a needs-based economy with creativity and initiative. Could it be that instead of the triumph of capitalism against socialism, we may end up with a system that combines the best elements of both with a new awareness of local and community-based solutions that are environmentally sound?

Another movement for alternative economic solutions, the social economy, has emerged from just these local needs and interest. I discussed some examples of it in Chapter 10. There is little talk in the media about the social economy, even though it is a significant part of the economy in many countries around the world. In Quebec, the social economy is quite significant, with more than ten thousand collective and community organizations taking part. Nancy Neamtan explains the principles of the social economy in a paper called "The Social Economy: Finding a Way Between the Market and State," for *Policy Options* (July/August 2005). She lists the following guiding principles of the social economy:

- It aims to serve members or community, rather than working for profit.
- It is independent of the state.
- It has democratic decision-making process in its statutes and requires both users and workers to participate.
- It sets a priority on people and work over capital in the distribution of revenue and surpluses.
- It bases activities on principles of participation, empowerment, and individual and collective responsibility.

At the moment, the social economy is completely integrated into the capitalist economic system in Quebec, but its advocates, including Neamtan, believe that the model they have developed has the potential to replace much of the for-profit top-down economy.

Probably the most visible element of a social economy is the rapidly growing fair trade movement. Over the years we have learned that there is nothing free about free trade. In fact, what is called *free trade* is really free only for investors. Capital moves quickly and easily across borders, while workers are displaced and forced to move under restrictive immigration rules and conditions. International free trade agreements such as the FTAA and the GATT, and the World Trade Organization, which enforces free trade even when there are no agareements, have been exposed by the global justice movement and by governments of Global South countries as anti-democratic agreements that favour the rich countries over the poor, and corporate interests over democratic decision-making.

Fair trade, on the other hand, is based on relationships between the producer and the consumer, in which the producers are ensured a fair return for products, and consumers are willing to pay a premium to make sure they are not exploiting people who are already living a subsistence existence. The fair trade movement began with NGOs such as Oxfam combining their advocacy against free trade with the sale of fair trade products.

As consciousness of the importance of fair trade became more widespread, a host of small businesses popped up selling a variety of fair trade products. Then big corporations such as Starbucks were forced into the game through a combination of consumer and NGO pressure. There is a lot of debate about how fair fair trade really is, but what is clear is the process of change that is overtaking what looked like an impenetrable system of power.

Brazil has been working very hard since Lula da Silva's election to undermine the inequality of trade deals, such as the FTAA. The FTAA is pretty well dead due to the pressure of South American countries. The WTO is on life support, given the refusal of India and China to agree to compromises proposed by the Northern countries. The balance of power between North and South in trade has profoundly changed as a result on the one hand of some of the changes in South America described in these pages and on the other of the growing economic power of China and India. Now both the United States and Canada are using bilateral trade agreements with friendly countries as a substitute for more global trade deals.

The meeting of the G20, which is scheduled to deal with the global economic meltdown, could very well be a moment when the governments of the Global South insist that solutions not be at the expense of their citizens and also improve the massive global imbalance of resources that neo-liberalism has created.

The Bolivian Alternative for the Americas (ALBA) is a trade deal developed among Cuba, Venezuela, Bolivia, and Nicaragua. Recently, Dominica and Honduras have applied to join. This deal puts human need and environmental sustainability at the centre of trade, and respects national sovereignty at the same time as promoting social solidarity, with richer nations providing resources to poorer ones.

In May 2008, twelve South American countries came together to formally launch the Union of South American Nations (UNASUR). Argentina, Brazil, Bolivia, Chile, Colombia, Ecuador, Guyana, Paraguay, Peru, Uruguay, Venezuela, and Suriname assembled at the Third Summit of Heads of State of South America to sign the treaty that established the union. This is a hugely significant economic and political development—barely noticed in the North—that seriously challenges the dependence of South America on investment from the International Monetary Fund (IMF) or other neo-colonial lending institutions.

Consciously modelled on the European Union, UNASUR will have its permanent headquarters in Quito, Ecuador. Its presidency rotates annually, its first president being Michelle Bachelet of Chile. The new organization announced a common market, freedom of movement within the community, general economic development, and co-operation in intra-regional integration.

Economic development should also benefit from the creation in 2007 of the South American Bank. Headquartered in Caracas, it began with an initial outlay of US$7 billion, with Venezuela contributing US$3 billion and Brazil US$2billion. The bank will finance developmental projects aimed at promoting economic integration, reducing material inequalities, and balancing investments across the region. Telesur, a regional television network that provides a Latin America alternative to CNN, is another project supported by the countries in this trade bloc.

While it falls short of the more egalitarian relationships among countries represented by the ALBA group, UNASUR is nevertheless a serious challenge to the hegemonic power of the United States in the region. When right-wing thugs were threatening the Morales government, UNASUR issued a strong statement supporting democracy in Bolivia that would make it clear to the United States that support for the anti-democratic forces in Bolivia will not be tolerated by other countries in South America. Meanwhile, Bolivia's Evo Morales and Venezuela's Hugo Chavez continue to argue for a more progressive South American integration. In his speech to the 2007 Summit of Presidents, Morales said, "Our integration is and has to be integration of and for the peoples. Trade, energy integration, infrastructure, and finance need to be at the function of resolving the biggest problems of poverty and the destruction of nature in our region."

IT IS ALSO IMPORTANT to see what governments that are trying to create more egalitarian societies are doing on the economic front. Both Venezuela and Bolivia are using oil and gas revenues to develop their countries economically. Bolivia is still in a battle to the death with the Right, and has been unable to carry out the small local industrializations they had planned, so I will focus on Venezuela.

One of the most interesting experiments in Venezuela is the promotion of co-operatives. Now, co-operatives are nothing new: We have worker and producer co-ops in Canada that are more or less integrated into the capitalist economic model. But in Venezuela, the government is providing long-term, interest-free loans to groups of workers so they can set up their own businesses and make all the decisions about how to run and operate them. As of 2006, there were 106,000 co-operatives formed by the 300,000 graduates of the Vuelvan Caras Mission job-training program, which began in 2004.

Co-operatives are a key strategy in the efforts of Hugo Chavez's government to involve excluded sectors of the economy. Venezuela is one of the most urbanized countries in Latin America. By the time of

Chavez's election, Caracas was surrounded by barrios that housed nearly half its population. The huge gap between the rich and poor in Venezuela is typical of most so-called Third World countries, as is the large number of people who participate in the informal economy. Worker co-ops are an important initiative that offer the poor more organized and better-paid work. The co-ops in Venezuela combine with the *missions*, discussed in Chapter 2, to promote what Chavez calls "endogenous development."

But, as is the case in Brazil, Chavez has not managed to democratize large state-owned industries, such as the oil industry. Bringing worker control and participation to these larger economic enterprises will be a key test of the democratization of the economy—and central to any genuinely democratic society.

ODDLY ENOUGH, the place where there has been a democratization of sorts of a large-scale industry is a place where socialism has little influence, the internet. Another extensive global experiment in economic alternatives is open source software, as discussed in Chapter 8. The open source software movement is not only giving Microsoft a run for its money on operating systems but it is also putting forward a new approach to the production of knowledge and technology, based on sharing rather than competition. In the open source model, people pursue their individual interests at the same time as they are promoting the good of all. Unlike the capitalist model of production that insists on private ownership of knowledge and technology, and competition as a way of ensuring creativity, open source bases its motivation not on money, but on the challenge of producing better code. This model also differs from centralized state socialism in that each individual involved has autonomy but contributes to a collective project.

The Economist predicts that open source will spread:

> There is a prediction that open source as a form of economic
> production will continue to grow steadily in the future. One

reason for this is that companies are now managing their intellectual property in ways that facilitate sharing. Another reason is that projects are becoming increasingly complex. Open source allows for a task to be broken down, worked on by self-organized specialists, and then reassembled. It also allows for companies to use each other's innovations in order to keep their products competitive. Another reason is that more companies are now working together on projects, and it is therefore more efficient to develop projects jointly and share the intellectual property created.*

Of course this isn't in any way a challenge to capitalist modes of production because even if there are flat structures for the development of knowledge inside the corporation, that knowledge is still proprietary to the company, which then owns the final product whether or not there is some sharing among corporations. In fact, the book *Wikinomics*, by internet guru Don Tapscott, provides an instruction manual for corporations on how they can use networks to improve their creativity and productivity, all within the frame of proprietary intellectual property.

In the discussion we had at the Berlin seminar on networked politics, Carlo Formenti, an Italian professor of new media theory, pointed out that rather than an alternative to capitalism, the open source movement represents a new form of capitalism. "There is a moment of transition of the business models. We are entering into the Google era. It is no longer the Microsoft era of intellectual property. We can see a new form of capitalist domination. You have a capitalism that needs community, a capitalist community. Web 2.0 is a fantastic way of putting to work hundreds of millions of people for Google, YouTube, MySpace. It's a very interesting transition point."

Unlike many of the *hacktivists* who participated in the discussion, Formenti doesn't think that open source is any kind of new economic

---

The Economist 377 (8449) (October 22, 2005): 12–14.

or governance model but rather that "we have some ways of using this space that capital gives us. In a situation of transition that I'm not sure will last a very long time. I think there are little windows of opportunity. Perhaps we can use these windows but not for much longer, I fear."

Nevertheless, it seems to me that the basic value of open source is that the best code or programming comes from the free sharing of knowledge rather than the buying and selling of it. While I am aware that the people, mostly men, participating in the open source movement are not consciously anti-capitalist, the basic value of open source is social, not capitalist. Like the online encyclopedia Wikipedia, for which thousands of volunteer researchers put untold hours into posting items, or the social-networking sites such as Facebook, YouTube, or MySpace, in which millions put their energy into totally voluntary work, we see that the basic human motivator is not greed but rather social connection and sharing with others.

For me, this is incontrovertible evidence that if a sustainable economic system, based on human need, were organized in a democratic and mostly decentralized way, it could produce wealth, provide jobs, and share that wealth much more equitably. There is little doubt that this kind of socially progressive economic system is unlikely to emerge in the way some of us thought it would—from the top-down planning of a progressive government. But what we are seeing, through both the social economy and the burgeoning green economy movements, and also online, is a challenge on multiple levels to an economic system based on greed and competition. Moreover, the global economic crash of 2008 has torn away the curtain from the casino economy. The Wizard of neo-liberalism has been exposed as a fraud. It is up to us whether we allow a minor fix to the system or support and extend the economic and social experiments that are questioning its very foundations.

File sharing has produced a massive alternative distribution system for music, television programs, and films that, at least in the case of the music industry, is seriously threatening the role of the middleman in the distribution of artistic products. Of course, the problem is that the artists are also receiving nothing for their work, except insofar as their popularity in downloads affects their popularity in the market-place. But there are now programs to allow artists to sell their music directly and collect payment.

Hacktivists call this file sharing *piracy*, in a romantic reference to the pirates of old, who stole mostly from the rich. They are so politi-cal about it that there are actually Pirate Parties, actual political parties, in several countries. The first one was founded in Sweden.

In an unpublished master's thesis at Ryerson University, Fenwick McKelvey describes how an anti-copyright organization called Piratbyrån in Sweden created an online mass movement by setting up a file-sharing site called www.thepiratebay.org. One of its leaders sees Pirate Bay as "a sort of organized civil disobedience to force the change of current copyright laws and copyright climate." According to McKelvey: "Pirate Bay defines file sharing and piracy as copying and sharing, not theft or taking. They argue that copying is part of digital communications. People naturally copy when using the computer and copyright holders do not understand this basic fact." In a 2004 decision, the Supreme Court in Canada agreed and ruled that file sharing is not an infringement of Canadian copyright as long as the material downloaded is for personal use only.

If Jesse Hirsch, the CBC's internet expert, is cautious about open source, he is positively euphoric about piracy. He told me in an interview:

> This is a civil disobedience movement that is successfully taking billion-dollar industries down to their knees. It's forcing them to abandon investments in copyright controls. Nobody, not government regulators, not the EU ... nobody's been able to stand up to telcos [telephone companies], copyright consor-tiums, the entertainment industry, and still keep going, but the pirates have. You have to just pause, take your hat off, and go, "Yeah!" What can we learn from that?

You know what we can learn from that? Anonymity. The power to control your identity and the power in hiding it. Because the kings—the real legends to that community—are to this day anonymous. And let's be clear: pseudonymous. There's this guy, Axxo. Just last week, Axxo announced his return. Axxo went into retirement in November. Because Axxo is releasing all the new movies in DVD quality before they're in the theatres. Before they're in the theatres! So Axxo is a celebrity. People love Axxo.

Hirsch explained that Axxo was enough of a threat to Hollywood that the studios started releasing their own titles early, under his name but with poor quality. "And that's why he retired, because they were releasing lousy versions and his reputation was being ruined."

Now this could just be a criminal activity, except it's not very profitable, and I get the sense from talking to all the young people I know who are deeply into the benefits of piracy that they see it as a political act, not as a crime. Hirsch continued,

Open source has its own contingent of people who would never be political about anything except open source. And it's their only avenue of political expression. Piracy is the same thing. A lot of these pirates know this is civil disobedience. They really believe that they are revolutionaries in the classic historical sense. But they would never come to it through anywhere else. If this had not been a forum for them to express their ideas, they'd probably be nerds in computer class thinking they want to get rich.

But they really believe in changing the world. It's weird how some people become politicized. For some people, it's war, right? For some people, it's gender; for some people, it's sexuality; for some people, it's intellectual property. Go figure. But hey [the pirates feel], it's their movies, their music, and they believe it should be free.

And piracy is just the beginning; Hirsch told me about something called a brightnet, which is the opposite of a darknet. The whole concept of a darknet comes from the National Security Agency, the military industrial establishment. It runs darknets. These darknets make sure one group online can't see another group online. It was designed to make sure the NSA website was insulated. Hirsch continued,

> Brightnet is the opposite. This initiative is the OFFS—the Ownership-Free File System. On any computer file system, every file is owned by somebody. So anything you upload to the internet, somebody owns that, it traces back to somebody. So if you have a system where everything is visible, and there's no ownership of anything, then by definition, that's the end of copyright. Anything that gets put up into that system is irreversible. You can't remove it, you can't trace it, you don't know where it came from, and everyone can see it. So they're building this system. And this system, once it emerges, it'll grow. And it'll absorb data. Anyone will be able to access it, and people will start dumping tons of shit into it, and everything on it will be accessible to everyone, and completely untraceable. So again, the sociopolitical implications of such a facility are huge.

So Carlo Formenti may be wrong about how long the window of opportunity is going to be open. As long as the geeks are not under the control of the corporations, who knows what could happen. What I do know is that intellectual property is a central pillar of the knowledge economy, and if it is no longer possible to control and sell access to knowledge, then a lot of things about the capitalist economy are going to change. The elimination of the middleman in distribution systems could be just the beginning.

WE TALK ABOUT the information economy, but manufacturing is still a key element of the economy, as is resource extraction. For alternative lines in manufacturing, the place to look is Argentina, where it is generally agreed that a neo-liberal approach, including a sell-off of key elements of the economy to foreign owners, led to an economic collapse at the beginning of the twenty-first century. Instead of accepting that their factories were closing, workers decided to take over the factories and run them collectively.

Firstly, their action challenged the idea that owners or shareholders should be able to unilaterally decide to close down a factory, sometimes throwing thousands of people out of work and destroying entire communities. Secondly, workers really do know how to run the factory, and they proved it in Argentina, creating an entire movement of self-managed workplaces. The new government under Néstor Kirchner integrated this approach into the policy of the government to a degree by making the existing occupations legal, though the government does not encourage this as a solution because of pressure from the industrial elite. But the Argentine workers showed it could be done. In the restructuring of the global economy that is taking place in reaction to the economic crisis, governments should make rules for the conduct of transnational corporations so that they are required to take into account the interests of workers and communities as well as the interests of their stockholders and CEOs. It is a testament to the extremism of neo-liberalism that even such a modest suggestion seems radical in the current context. Barack Obama has made a small step by promising to use powers of taxation to penalize companies that ship jobs offshore and reward companies that keep them in the United States.

The importance of autonomy and participation in decision-making for the workers has been accepted by some progressive corporations, but there are limits within the capitalist structure. Since the central modus operandi is private ownership, competitiveness, and therefore secrecy, democratic decision-making by workers is of necessity limited to their particular areas of work. The farther up in the hierarchy, the less democratic the decision-making. The potential of an economic system in which workers truly run their own workplaces has never really been tested. Under what we call socialism, it was the state bureaucrats who ran the factories, and they were just as removed as owners and managers in a private system. Increasing experiments in worker and user control, decentralization, co-operation rather than competition, and democratic process can potentially transform our existing economic system. The experiments are already under way.

Equally as important, however, is the democratization of the state, and for that we have to take a look at the political system, which, after all, is very closely aligned with the economic system.

14

AND WHAT ABOUT POLITICAL POWER?
Is the Party Over?

OVER THE YEARS I have had to acknowledge that political parties seem to be just about the most intractable organizations around. I have been trying to convince the New Democratic Party to change since the 1980s, using various methods. Frankly, it was easier to win legal abortion in Canada against the power of the church, the police, the courts, and the government than to get this rather weak third party to change in any fundamental way. The pressure on political parties to conform to the existing political system is so great that they seem incapable of behaving in a way that is accountable, transparent, democratic, and effective. It is no wonder that so few people want anything to do with them.

My generation of activists expanded the notion of politics, arriving at an understanding that social movements, such as the women's and environmental movements, far from being special interest groups or interlopers in the political system—as they have been labelled by right-wing politicians—have actually been the most important forces for change in our political system. Ever since the early twentieth century, trade unions participated in electoral politics through a close, often institutional, alliance, with labour parties, such as the NDP in Canada. But the movements that emerged in the 1960s maintained a greater autonomy from political parties, pressuring the parties from the outside or making alliances with activists inside the party to make change. Today, many activists believe that it is movements alone that will make the changes we need, and that political parties are anachronisms of a previous age that cannot adapt to the new politics of this one. However, my experience tells me that unless we change power at the top while we are building power from the bottom, the change will only be partial. I am frankly not sure whether this means retaining political parties as we know them. In any case, I think we need to learn how power can be exercised at a government level in a manner that is dramatically different than that used today.

It's not going to be easy. We need to find ways of working simultaneously or through a collaborative division of labour to ensure the combination produces more powerful and more creative forces for change than has proved possible through focusing only on, for example, building electoral parties, organizing labour militancy, or becoming immersed in social movements. Perhaps the Obama campaign provided some example of what this new kind of political organizing looks like: reaching out beyond our usual networks, organizing through communities (geographic and online), welcoming new leadership through sharing resources and training, and making political organizing fun again by re-establishing that sense of community—*Ubuntu*—that makes people feel powerful. Community organizing, which the Republicans tried to make a dirty word in the presidential campaign, has actually re-emerged as the most effective political strategy.

The efforts I have been involved with, starting with the Campaign for an Activist Party in 1988, and ending with the New Politics Initiative in 2002, attempted to persuade a social democratic party that its future lay in an alliance not only with the labour movement but also with all the various social movements for change that had emerged and were emerging.

The Workers' Party (PT) in Brazil, which was discussed previously as the initiator of the participatory budget, is a different kind of party.

Emerging from dictatorship in 1985, the PT was founded as a unitary party of the Left, incorporating everyone from social democrats to Trotskyists. With a charismatic, popular, working-class leader in Lula da Silva, the party has managed to stay together, despite significant differences of strategy, especially since Lula's election in 2002.

In both South Africa and in Brazil, what looked like revolutionary parties were elected and then in many ways failed to achieve the transformations their supporters were looking for. Most importantly, neither the ANC nor the PT have significantly changed the economic system, although in both cases these parties, under the pressure of social and trade union movements, have delivered improvements, however minimal, in the daily lives of millions of poor people, reforms that in the case of Brazil underpin Lula's continuing popularity. Their failure to significantly challenge both national and international defenders of the economic status quo is closely related to their failure to use their considerable democratic mandate to democratize the state institutions that have historically protected these economic interests. Both parties presumed that the election of a new kind of leader would create the change they sought. A lesson from both experiences points to the resilience and concerted capacity of the hidden powers of the state apparatus, ultimately overpowering and deradicalizing the democratic impetus of these potentially transformative parties.

At the 2003 World Social Forum in Porto Alegre, Brazil, which took place just as Lula was coming to power, an extraordinary panel discussion on that issue took place. José Genoino, president of the PT, and Willy Madisha, president of COSATU (the union federation in South Africa), explained two sides of taking state power in a fascinating dialogue on political parties and social movements. Genoino told the crowd: "The challenge of the Left is to be an affirmative alternative to authoritarian exclusion, commodification of life, and objectification of people." He continued that the priorities of the PT were democracy as a fundamental value and the struggle for rights. "We walk on two feet," he explained. "One foot is the democratization of the state and the other the building of strong, autonomous social movements."

Madisha drew his lessons from the quick and heartbreaking slide to the right of the ANC in South Africa. "When the ANC was elected, we thought the road ahead would be easy. The ANC went from being a liberation movement to a traditional party that is only interested in winning elections in such a short time.... It is simplistic to blame the ANC leaders, since a similar fate has met almost every left-wing government that has won power." He warned the PT that the real fight begins once the new government takes over.

I was struck by how closely these lessons were to the conclusions many of us drew from the experience of the Bob Rae government in Ontario. In 1990, the New Democratic Party took power in Ontario on a platform of change. Within months, the party backed down from its promise of public automobile insurance, the most popular part of its platform, because of pressure from the industry. It went downhill from there, and, despite some good policies, the government was an incredible disappointment to the activists who had worked so hard to elect it.

If the ANC could not resist the pressure to follow the dictates of global capitalism, who could? In fact, despite the promise of the PT president, the Brazil's Workers' Party and its working-class president, Lula, have also been a disappointment to those who supported them.

A more in-depth explanation of what happens to a party in power is revealed in an interview by Hilary Wainwright with Marco Aurelio Garcia, a major leader of the PT and currently Lula's foreign policy advisor. In it, he explains that, as in South Africa, the most talented people in the party went to work for the government—meaning that the party did not have the capacity to make constructive criticism of the government. Then conservative economic policies, which began as a transitional method to stabilize the economy, became more central to government policy. He explains that balancing the budget, reducing inflation, and lessening vulnerability are important to stabilizing the economy, but:

> People didn't vote for Lula to do this. People voted for Lula because they wanted major social transformation. So the party should have found a way of carrying out this long-term structural change while also promoting some short-term changes of the kind that society was asking for. But it did not do this, so it lost its character and its credibility and became separated from the social movements. This did not happen because it became bureaucratic; on the contrary, it became bureaucratic because of the separation from the social movements.*

This is demonstrated, Garcia points out, by the fact that in two years, the Lula government spent four times more on land reform than the previous government did in eight years, because there was pressure from the powerful landless movement, which remained independent from the government. On the other hand, there was little pressure on bringing down interest rates, and therefore little action. His view is that the party should play a major role in keeping the government's feet to the fire, but instead the party focuses too much on keeping the government in power and not enough on pushing it do to the right thing once it is there. He says the majority of the party agrees with his criticisms of the government, and this creates a malaise. Again, we might look to the Obama campaign for the massive grassroots network it created, a network rooted in the community that is looking to the new leadership for change and can be mobilized to push for that change or push against those trying to stop it. Combining social movements with this kind of grassroots political network might be the kind of accountability and support network that progressive leadership needs to actually make change.

Of course, the denunciations we often hear from some elements of the international Left do not give the PT credit for the work they have

---

*Interview by Hilary Wainwright with PT in *In the Eye of the Storm: Left-Wing Activists Discuss the Political Crisis in Brazil*, eds. Hilary Wainwright and Sue Brantford (TNI: 2006) available as PDF at www.tni.org.

done, including creating a hundred thousand jobs a month and transferring income to eight million poor families through a kind of family allowance. But the point is that although these are important reforms, they do not lead to a transformation of society, which is what people expected from the PT. Once again the ideas on which the party is founded don't seem to work very well once it is in government—given the demands of governing in a capitalist context.

Again, the similarities with the NDP government in Ontario from 1990 to 1995 are interesting. Most of us in the social movements felt that the NDP had simply caved in to pressure from industry and media and, by the end of their reign, had so forgotten what they stood for that they imposed a social contract on the public sector, which was such an act of arrogance and betrayal that it still affects the trade union movement in Ontario.

The view from inside the government was, of course, different. Frances Lankin, one of the most senior cabinet ministers in the Rae government, talked to me about these lessons in an interview:

> One of the things I felt after our government ended and I saw so many of the gains lost, was the question of how we work in government with outside movements. I feel we failed to make the conditions for sustained change. I think we acted with a Cadillac wish list of the things we wanted to get done. Instead, you have to create the conditions for change.
>
> We said, "Change the law and the attitudes will follow," but you need more time for the attitudes to change. Had we approached government and relations with movements in a way as to bring people together and see where change was possible and public opinion could support the change being made, instead of using the existing dynamic, we might not have lost in the end.
>
> I don't feel any bitterness at all, unlike some of my colleagues and people in the movement. To this day, they blame everything that's bad today on the Rae government. There's been no real

work to bring people together and learn lessons about how to do
things right the next time.

I think Lankin hit the nail on the head. The coming to power of a
progressive government is just the beginning of change. There is no
quick way to take over a state that is organized to serve the interests
of capital and turn it around to serve the interests of the majority of
working people. Understanding that a political party needs the
movements to change public opinion and mobilize public support, as
well as to keep the party on track with its vision, is absolutely key, but
it's not the only problem.

IN 2002, using some of the ideas from the PT and some of the lessons
we learned from the NDP experience in Ontario, I got together with
Jim Stanford, who is the chief economist for the Canadian Auto
Workers, and we came up with the idea of the New Politics Initiative
(NPI). We noted that the New Democratic Party was not attracting
the youth of the anti-globalization movement, so we pulled together
a group that was half old-time left-wing activists and intellectuals
and half newly minted activists from the anti-globalization
movement. Stanford and I proposed a manifesto for a new party that
would be, in deference to the anti-authoritarian politics of the new
movement, signed by grassroots activists in addition to well-known
leaders.

The young activists said "No" to the manifesto, because the process
was too top-down, but suggested we put out the manifesto as a discussion paper on the internet and ask for comments and signatories.
Since we had the support of CAW president Buzz Hargrove and NDP
MPs Svend Robinson and Libby Davies, our discussion paper hit the
front page of *The Globe and Mail.*

Within days of the posting, we were engulfed in a maelstrom of
public debate as well as a difficult private process of trying to integrate
the Old Left culture with the emerging New Left culture. The NPI

argued that a new party be a unitary party of the Left, bringing together the NDP and the Green Party as well as movement activists, and base itself on a partnership with social movements and with a commitment to participatory democracy. Many in the NDP, including current leader Jack Layton, easily took up the politics of partnership with the social movements that in the 1980s had been such a hard sell, but there was less general understanding about what participatory democracy would mean in a party. Even though I had just written a book on the topic, in retrospect, I don't think we had much of an idea ourselves. Nonetheless, NPI argued that the NDP had to open itself to the new forces of the anti-globalization movement by initiating the formation of a new party.

Writing for www.rabble.ca after the NPI made its debut at the 2002 NDP convention, I said,

> What became clear over the course of the NDP convention, where we brought a resolution calling for the formation of a new party, was that the NPI is really about transforming left-wing politics by bringing together the best traditions of old left with the radical democracy of the new left.
>
> As Canadian Auto Workers economist Jim Stanford told a caucus meeting after the defeat of the NPI resolution on Saturday, "If anyone had told me that a young woman would be marching around the floor of an NDP convention wearing nothing but an NPI banner, distributing buttons, I would have told them they were dreaming in technicolour."
>
> It wasn't just the spirit on the floor of the convention that revealed the changes; it was also the extraordinary forum that the NPI held on Friday night of the convention. In an uplifting meeting, a wide diversity of people from youth to a couple who had been at the founding convention of the CCF [the Co-operative Commonwealth Federation, party of Tommy Douglas and precursor to the NDP] in 1932 talked about why they supported the NPI.

On the edge of feeling a little like a revival meeting, what was really different about this meeting was that people were sharing their experiences rather than arguing their political points. While the women's movement has for years been using the techniques of sharing experiences to build a common politic, the political left had never before embraced this kind of discussion. Almost everyone had a voice here. You didn't have to have fully formed political views to speak, and the most unexpected people got standing ovations.

Even physically the meeting drew together the old ways and the new. Some people lined up at the mike and others spoke from their seats at a roving mike. To a person, every participant, even hardened old activists like myself, felt inspired by the experience.

There is some difficulty in intervening in a convention based on old top-down politics with a new, open, participatory politic. So the NPI made mistakes. They could have been better organized on the floor. Some people who should have been able to speak couldn't. They weren't able to counter the spin about NPI being a hard turn to the left. Yet, instead of recriminations, everyone openly admitted the weaknesses and moved on.

The NPI was able to bring a bit of the spirit of the anti-globalization movement onto the floor of the NDP convention, chants, costumes, and face paint included. More than that, in a profoundly cautious political party, 40 percent voted for a radical proposal to initiate a new party. Indeed the impact may have been strong enough to open the NDP to formally including a political opposition for the first time in its history.

The other side of the activity of the NPI is to challenge the anti-globalization movement and other social movements to understand not only the importance of electoral politics but also the value of the NDP itself. This convention showed clearly that the NDP is really a party of working people. On the flight back, I sat next to an older woman who after three days of intense convention had to wake up at 5:30 a.m. to go to work at her plant. She and thousands like her see the NDP as the party that best represents their interests.

The contempt of many on the left for the NDP misunderstands the profound working-class nature of the party and its importance to the political life of thousands of working people who see no other institution in society speaking for them. The NDP may rarely do justice to this important role, but no other force on the left, except the trade unions, can claim this kind of mass representation at all.

On the left internationally, two currents are emerging. On the one side, social democratic parties in England and most of Europe are moving to the right and embracing the so-called "third way," meaning corporate globalization with a slightly more human face.

The other current is emerging through the anti-corporate-globalization movement and some socialist parties in Latin America. This current strongly opposes corporate globalization and sees radical democracy, engaging citizens at every level of government, as the way to counter corporate power.

So the work of the NPI is just beginning. The caucus at convention decided to build local NPI chapters and continue to bring the NDP and grassroots activists closer together.

As someone who has given up on the NDP more than once in my long political career, I feel a greater sense of optimism today that a new kind of political party that brings together most of the forces fighting for social justice is a real possibility.

It's a little depressing to read these words today, but important to assess them. What really happened was that Jack Layton used the rhetoric of the NPI for his run for leadership, and he was supported by NPI leaders such as Svend Robinson and Libby Davies. As most NPI activists were NDP members, they got caught up in this election campaign and the NPI dissolved.

I had noticed that every reform group inside the NDP that I had worked with over the years would collapse after whatever electoral contest it was working on, so I proposed that the NPI have a life both inside and outside the NDP. It didn't matter. When the leadership race came, nothing else mattered. Since the NPI was divided on Layton's leadership, it decided not to take a position or run its own leadership candidate, and so it became irrelevant to the internal life of the party and withered away.

Jack Layton has since turned the NDP into more of a professionally driven party than it has ever been. Instead of participatory democracy in the party, what we have is informal social networking. Layton does this himself as a form of damage control every time the party makes a move in a direction that activists don't like. The party considered it a victory when it won eight more seats in the 2006 election won by the Bush-loving Conservative Party of Stephen Harper, infuriating a lot of social movement activists. In the 2008 election, the party recognized the error of its ways and turned its fire on Harper, thus improving its presence in Parliament and somewhat healing its relationship with social movement activists.

I was right that what was most important about the NPI was its attempt to change the culture of the NDP. This wasn't even a conscious decision; it was just what happened when MP Libby Davies made the suggestion that, instead of the usual attacks against the party leadership, we ask the assembled people at the NPI caucus why they were there. This gave power to the young people to try to transform the polarized atmosphere on the convention floor.

It was the process of the NPI that had the power, not so much its political proposals. At the end of the convention, delegates came up to me with tears in their eyes. "Don't leave the party, Judy. We really agree with you, but we just don't want to take the risk of starting a new party."

In retrospect, the NPI was too little, too soon. It has taken a decade or more even to begin to ask the right questions about how to transform political power. Events in Brazil and South Africa, as well as the experiences of Venezuela and Bolivia and the Obama campaign in the U.S., have given us a lot of information about what works and what doesn't. And the experiences of two decades of organizing under neo-liberalism gives us more of a vision of what a participatory democracy might really look like.

In Quebec in February 2006, activists from several social movements and small left-wing political groups did found a new party of the Left called Québec Solidaire. It was co-chaired by Françoise Davide, the most visible leader of the women's movement there. Unlike in English Canada where there had been a decline of activism since the mid-1990s, in Quebec, the women's, anti-war, student, and labour movements had been mobilizing successfully right up until 2005, when there was a successful student strike to keep down fees. Nevertheless, Davide, among others, felt a political party was needed to really change things. The sovereigntist Parti Québécois (PQ) includes both left and right forces in its ranks united by a desire for Quebec independence from Canada. Left-wing forces in the PQ accused Québec Solidaire of splitting the left-wing vote. While the party has tried, in many of the ways we have been discussing, to do things differently, they have not managed to break through a marginal electoral presence, despite their rather high-profile leader. While I am less and less inclined to put energy into a political party these days, I am still persuaded that some form of party is necessary to challenge power, and that electoral politics remain the site of politics for the vast majority of people. In the Global South, elections have begun to take on more and more meaning, with country after country rebelling against stolen and phony elections.

The crisis of representative democracy, where masses of people have turned away from voting, is starting to turn around in several countries, most particularly in Spain, France, and now in the United States—although in 2008, Canada saw the lowest voter turnout in the country. The system of representative democracy is in crisis, but even a small step in another direction, such as Barack Obama's "Yes we can" campaign, can draw masses of people back into believing that change is possible through elections.

The Green Party in Germany is probably the best example of a political party in the advanced capitalist countries that tried to do things differently. The Green Party emerged in 1979 from the social movements in Germany and set out to transform politics in a number of ways, including democratizing the party process, achieving gender parity, and building a counter-power through alliance with the social movements.

A thorough balance sheet of the aims of the German Greens set against their outcomes has been developed by Frieder Otto Wolfe, a founding member of that party. The Greens attempted to use consensus as a method of decision-making. While they acknowledged the need for eventual majority decision, the method of consensus was a way of ensuring the views of everyone involved would be heard.

Political decision-making in our society is almost always a choice among polarized options, with most people simply choosing sides. A consensus process allows for a much fuller and more representative exploration of ideas and experience. If part of the transformation we seek is to overcome the domination of one group over another, consensus methods of decision-making are necessary. The Greens used them quite successfully in some ways, achieving such unusual alliances as those between rural peasants and urban queer groups in opposition to nuclear armaments. But, according to Wolfe, polarization is such a central feature of our political system that consensus, even within a party with shared principles and a program, became impossible to achieve.

Gender parity was a principle that was maintained by the party, but it did not turn out to be as transformative as the original party founders had hoped. What is interesting about the balance sheet of the Green Party is that it does not so much show the party "selling out"—as movement activists are only too willing to believe—but rather demonstrates a fundamental incompatibility between the politics of transformation and the politics of winning elections. So perhaps it is only in a situation of societal transformation that a party can also transform itself.

One of the most interesting electoral experiences happened recently in Spain, where a right-wing government's attempts to pin the Madrid subway bombings on ETA (a nationalist group in the Basque country) stimulated a massive response from a network of grassroots organizations that basically threw the government out of office.

In a poll three days before the election in March 2004, the right-wing Popular Party had a majority. On March 11, thirteen bombs exploded on three suburban trains. Two hundred people were killed and fourteen hundred injured. Activists worried that if it were re-elected, the government would use the bombing as an excuse to repress all radical opposition—as they saw happen in the United States after September 11. The next day the government called a demonstration against terrorism that brought seven million people out into the streets. But instead of supporting the government, the protestors bore banners reading "Who did it? We want to know." The ETA denied responsibility, but the government kept insisting.

That day, the networks that had mobilized against the war in Iraq issued a call for *cacerolazos*, or pot-banging demonstrations, for Saturday, March 13, under the slogans "The dead are ours. The wars are yours!," "PP [Popular Party] murders," "Franco's sons," "No to government disinformation." The *cacerolazos* were built almost entirely through cell-phone messaging. For every text message received, ten or twenty were sent out. These went beyond the usual activist communications to their families, workplaces, and places of study. One of the activists, Mayo Fuster Morell, reported in the online *Mute Magazine*: "Everywhere the bleep of SMS messages announced the latest news that spread from mouth to mouth through the crowd.... No flags, parties. Leaders, organizers, or orders. Participation is horizontal, spontaneous, and massive. A video is aired in which a group close to Al Qaeda claims responsibility for the attack, but none of the official media reports it."

Realizing it was in trouble, the government tried to get the Electoral Council to delay the election, claiming that the demonstrations were illegally organized by the Socialist Party. The Electoral Council refused, and the result was a massive turnout in the election and the defeat of the Popular Party. "They now know," wrote Mayo, "that, in forty-eight hours, a people can overturn any government."

Young people with little interest in electing the Socialist Party just decided that it was critically important to defeat the PP and took advantage of a highly mobilized population and a terrible error on the part of the government to defeat them. A large number of youth also mobilized in France during the last election, although they did not manage to defeat the Right. And, of course, an even greater number of young people are mobilizing through the Obama campaign in the U.S. elections. In all these cases, the method of participation in the election campaign is quite different than we have seen before—a different way of doing politics.

At the beginning of the last election in Canada, Jack Layton and Stephen Harper refused to accept the participation of Green Party leader Elizabeth May in the televised leaders' debate, even though her party was running about 10 percent in the polls and, through recruiting a sitting independent, had a Member of Parliament. What followed was no less than a national cross-partisan uprising, demanding that she be included. Layton backed down after it became clear the issue was not going away, and then Harper backed down, and May was included. This kind of citizen activism, which is greatly facilitated by the Web, may in fact be a new way to force changes on political parties. In the Canadian election, climate change groups posted sophisticated websites suggesting strategic voting (for the progressive party most likely to win) in swing ridings. It is difficult to say if this had a major impact on the vote, but it was a major part of discussion during the elections. There was also a groundswell of support for some kind of coalition among centre-left and left-wing parties to stop a very right-wing Conservative government. If the New Politics Initiative had succeeded and the Greens and NDP had merged, there might have been an electoral breakthrough for the Left in an election in which the Liberals were particularly weak and the majority of the electorate was opposed to the ruling Conservatives. In Canada's undemocratic first past the post system, the Conservatives won a substantial minority even though more than two-thirds of the electorate voted against them.

IN BOLIVIA, the state is very weak because decades of opposition by social movements have succeeded in bringing down government after government. It was this dead end that convinced the indigenous movements that they needed their own political instrument. In some ways it is easier for the MAS (Movement Towards Socialism, led by Evo Morales) to make dramatic changes, but still those changes are being stymied, either by pre-existing laws or by the opposition of the Right.

Created as a political instrument of the social movements, the MAS is not a political party like the others. Candidates are selected in mass assemblies of all those involved in indigenous social organizations. Anyone who is active in one of these social organizations is automatically a member of the MAS. There is tremendous polarization, both in the Congress and the Constituent Assembly, because the changes being proposed involve nothing less than re-founding the country on a new—in Evo Morales's words—"anti-neo-liberal, anti-colonial basis." So the minority that benefits from the status quo is fighting like hell to keep their power, which makes consensus-building exceedingly hard outside the MAS itself. Nevertheless, Morales has been attempting to use these methods to find compromise and to solve some seemingly unmanageable problems.

While it is hard to imagine a political situation like the one in Bolivia developing in an advanced capitalist country, we can learn some lessons from this experience and from that of Venezuela. The first is that change will not happen only from taking state power. Power is something that has to be built. As Hilary Wainwright says in an article on rethinking political parties:* "In general terms one can say that the goal must move from winning the power to govern for the people paternalistically to being a struggle in collaboration with organized citizens to change political institutions from sources of domination to resources for transformation."

One example of how this could happen is a citizen's group called the Guelph Civic League in the small Ontario city of Guelph that tapped into just this approach before the last municipal election. Instead of taking the usual citizens' watchdog role, they decided to ask their neighbours what they valued in their city. Starting with a survey of ten thousand citizens, they developed a list of five values that the people of Guelph supported. They then circulated those values in brochures, saying, "This is what your neighbours think." In the summer leading up to the election, they hired a handful of students to go door-to-door discussing those values. They found people who were willing to run on these values, and let their neighbours know who they were. These candidates won nine out of ten seats on the city council, and they increased voter turnout from 30 percent to 50 percent. It was a simple switch. Instead of telling voters what the candidate thought, it asked voters what they thought and then found candidates who reflected that thinking. Today, the Civic League continues its work by reporting back to voters about how their representatives have supported the values that were adopted. In addition, they are working with other municipal activists to share ideas and develop new strategies for engaging residents in civic government at the municipal level. There are no political parties in Ontario operating at the municipal level, which means citizen groups can relate more directly with politicians, thus avoiding the organizational structure of the party.

As we discussed in Chapter 8, Barack Obama is involving individuals in his campaign in an unprecedented, decentralized, networked

---

*Hilary Wainwright, "Parties and Movements," *Red Pepper* (February 2008).

manner. There is already discussion about how to make sure that Obama is accountable to them. It will be up to the myriad of social movements in the United States to keep up the pressure on Obama, perhaps accessing this network to construct the kind of inclusive, democratic, and compassionate society he is talking about in the campaign.

Using the extraordinarily democratic moment of the primary campaign to mobilize millions of people, Obama actually used the impact of these new voters to pressure the party brass to support him, defeating Hillary Clinton in one of the most dramatic examples of grassroots democracy we have seen in electoral politics. It is precisely this kind of dynamic that Lula's foreign affairs advisor Marco Aurelio Garcia is talking about. For a party to stay true to its vision and resist the numerous pressures imposed on it by the electoral system and capital, it needs pressure from outside that system. For years, I thought that social movements could provide that pressure, and certainly, where they are strong enough—as with the landless movement (MST) in Brazil or the women's movement at certain points in Canadian politics—that works, but can we structure a participatory system that keeps that pressure on all the time?

Spontaneous online discussions throughout the Canadian election had an impact on the media and the politicians, and while it is hard to argue that these discussions shaped the campaign, they certainly influenced it. On the other hand, the focus on the leader has never been greater and the inability of electoral politics to solve anything has never been clearer. The Wall Street collapse fell in the middle of the Canadian and U.S. elections. If elections worked as the democratic moment they should be, there would have been a thoroughgoing and deep discussion of the alternative solutions to the crisis. Instead, in Canada the major discussion was about whether the government should react to the crisis at all, and in the United States, there was more focus on Joe the Plumber, a voter who was critical of Obama's tax policy, than there was on alternative visions for solving the economic crisis.

The gap between horizontal networked politics and the North American election campaigns of 2008 seems like a chasm. Yet the Obama campaign continued to use networking to mobilize new voters, and there seemed to be more online citizen organizing in Canada than ever before. In a nationally televised speech before the U.S. election, Obama promised to involve Americans in their democracy again. Of course, he has already done that not only through unprecedented voter turnout but through the masses of people engaged in the election itself. How he will sustain that once he is elected remains to be seen.

THE PHILOSOPHY BEHIND networked politics suggests that the very idea of representation is problematic. Once again I turn to the discussions at the networked politics seminar in Berlin in 2007. At the end of the three-day seminar we tried to summarize what was discussed. Some of the key questions were how parties that aspire to use a horizontal logic can engage with institutions based on a representative one. We noted that representatives are almost always absorbed by the institution to which they are elected or appointed, and rarely continue to be accountable to those who elected them. Ideas that were floated included sharing the role of representative so that no one person accumulates personal power. One example of this is the role of the Zapatistas' Marcos. Because he is masked and therefore anonymous, different people can play the role of Marcos. It is hard to imagine how this tactic could work in the media-driven politics of the Global North, but the idea of rotating representatives or using people who are not professional politicians to represent their communities for a shorter period of time, as in the participatory budget, might work. The problem here is the need for expertise to deal with the institutions of power effectively. It is a difficult problem that requires a lot more practice and study.

Another tough question we discussed was how social movements interconnect with institutions of power without being absorbed or co-opted by them. One strategy, as discussed earlier, is to create alternative self-governing structures next to the hierarchical representative ones and, over time, the more effective, more democratic methods of governance will win out. Ideally, it should work, but in practice power reproduces itself, and it is rare for any institution or even organization to change its culture without a major battle or a collapse.

A more realistic approach was suggested in the final report to the Berlin group:

> Another way of thinking about it is related to a viral logic, to an idea of exploding this radical distinction between us and them. Then the question is how can this logic of horizontal networking migrate into the logic of state institutions themselves? This is a fundamental but unexplored question which points away from the either/or of the past: either protesting against the state or making demands on it; either taking over the state or creating an alternative. For example, what would a political party look like if it wasn't based on a hierarchical list of candidates, or a hierarchical electoral mechanism?

We have more questions than answers when it comes to political parties, but certainly some of the new ways of organizing at the community and social-movement levels that are discussed in this book can give us some creative ideas about how this might happen. Who would have predicted the more than 100 percent increase in voter turnout in the 2008 U.S. primaries? Who would have thought that a campaign could raise more money in small donations online than from all the powerful political action committees that run U.S. politics? We make the road by walking, and the road to political power that will benefit the majority of people is, like every other journey, begun with the first steps.

All of the elements of the movements we have been looking at in these pages will be necessary to transform the current political system. Like every other progressive social change in history, it starts with ordinary people longing for change, then coming together to imagine it and work for it, and, in working for it, learning with honesty and courage from the experiences—including the defeats and difficulties—of those who have done the same. You may say that I'm a dreamer, but as you have read in these pages, I am far from the only one.

EPILOGUE

Rosa Parks sat so Martin Luther King could walk. Martin Luther King walked so Barack Obama could run. Barack Obama is running so that we can all fly.

—JAY-Z, IN AN INTERVIEW WITH *THE INDEPENDENT*

IT IS THE DAY AFTER the night before, and Barack Obama is president-elect of the United States. Not since the attack on the Twin Towers and the assassinations of the Kennedys and Martin Luther King has there been such a dramatic outpouring of emotion, but this time it's about something positive and global. Not only has an African American been elected president, fulfilling an impossible dream, but he is a leader who is defining a new kind of politics and inviting ordinary Americans to get involved in their own democracy. After thanking the thousands of volunteers who worked for and contributed to the campaign, Obama outlined the challenge clearly in his speech:

> I know you didn't do this just to win an election, and I know you didn't do it for me. You did it because you understand the enormity of the task that lies ahead. For even as we celebrate

260

tonight, we know the challenges that tomorrow will bring are the greatest of our lifetime—two wars, a planet in peril, the worst financial crisis in a century.

This afternoon I went to a student demonstration at Queen's Park in Toronto, to demand a drop in school fees. When I got there, thousands of students were sitting on the road, blocking traffic with tremendous enthusiasm. It was the biggest demonstration I had seen there in a long time, and I couldn't help feeling that Obama's election gave these young people new hope for change.

At a time when the American Empire is severely weakened by a corrupt and hated administration, a financial crisis of historic proportions, and unpopular military adventures, a leadership has emerged to rescue the American dream. Obama began his speech:

> If there is anyone out there who still doubts that America is a place where all things are possible, who still wonders if the dream of our founders is alive in our time, who still questions the power of our democracy, tonight is your answer.
>
> It's the answer told by lines that stretched around schools and churches in numbers this nation has never seen by people who waited three hours and four hours, many for the very first time in their lives, because they believed that this time must be different, that their voice could be that difference ...
>
> Tonight we proved once more that the true strength of our nation comes not from the might of our arms or the scale of our wealth but from the enduring power of our ideals: democracy, liberty, opportunity, and unyielding hope.

The new president will face a very different world from the one it appeared he would inherit when he started his run for office. His staff is already trying to dampen expectations.

This would be the time for Barack Obama to propose a new New Deal for Americans, based on his plan for the greening of America and the needs of the people who have been left behind by this Wall Street–driven paper economy. This would be the time for him to break with the corrupt bailout deal offered to Bush's friends on Wall Street, which will practically bankrupt the government and nationalize some of the failing banks, so the American people benefit from the bailout rather than the Wall Street villians whose greed caused the crisis. This would be the time for him to help forge a more equal union of nations at the global level to ensure that whatever solutions are found to the economic meltdown benefit both the Global South and the most vulnerable in the Global North. Instead, so far Obama is cautiously supporting the bailout package, which is simply propping up a failing system.

As Obama himself has said many times, it is in times of crisis that change is possible. But now he will be inside the framework of the American state. His politics are not radical, but even the modest changes he proposed during the election are already under attack by the machinery of the status quo. From the flood of joyous emails I am receiving from activists across the United States, I am sure they will not sit by and wait for him to do the right thing.

At this point, it is impossible to know what will happen. The United States cannot sustain its military dominance of the world without economic dominance. That economic dominance is being challenged today not only by the Wall Street–led crisis but by the rising economic power of China, the rising political power of Latin America, and the continued resistance of the people of the Middle East to occupation. One thing is for sure, the era of neo-liberalism and market fundamentalism is over—as is the time of the world's only superpower.

The economic crisis has eclipsed the climate crisis. During the time of the U.S. election, there has been little discussion of solutions to climate change. But if the new U.S. government does not move quickly and constructively to reduce carbon emissions, the impact of climate chaos to come will be even greater than the economic collapse. We are in a period of monumental and historic change.

AT THE SAME TIME, another crisis is unfolding almost entirely below the media gaze. In Bolivia, the right wing, with apparent U.S. support, has tried to organize a coup. Mobilizations of indigenous peasant organizations around the country stopped them, but not without loss of life. In Pando, seventeen unarmed peasants were slaughtered by right-wing thugs. What's promising is that the Union of South American Nations (UNASUR) unanimously supported democracy in Bolivia and the presidency of Evo Morales, making it clear to the United States that an intervention would not be tolerated. The MAS so far continues to handle the coup through mobilization instead of violence, maintaining its values even in the face of terrible violence. In many ways, Bolivia offers hope for humanity, holding on to its ideas for change even under extreme pressure. As the United States threatens to pull its trade, Bolivia turns to Venezuela, Iran, and Brazil to make up for the loss.

IN THE UNITED STATES, it's the time for the social movements, some of whom you have read about in these pages, to move onto centre stage. In a period of crisis, organized forces can have a major impact. The uprising of the American people on the Left and the Right against this spurious deal to bail out Wall Street was an important moment, however brief, to expose an economic and political system that has mostly benefited the very richest at the expense of the poor and the middle class—but exposing the system is not enough. Now is the time to put forward new solutions.

THE NEXT FEW YEARS will no doubt be tumultuous. These pages provide ideas for how to navigate the troubled waters of economic and political crisis to build alternative visions of a better world. Ideas are important, but even more important is the base-building of so many people you have read about in these pages. If we are to build a better world—a world in which wealth is shared so that no one goes hungry, a world in which humans understand their role as caretakers of Mother Earth not its destroyers, a world in which many worlds fit, a world in which everyone is valued and can contribute, a world that inspires people to do their best—we have to take a leap from where we are today.

The last lines of the Communist Manifesto are "Workers of the world unite. You have nothing to lose but your chains." Most of us living in Canada or the United States have a lot more to lose. And it is the difficulty of choosing to risk losing some of the material comfort or the comfort of anonymity or the comfort of staying safe that stops us from working for change. The stakes are high. We are at a moment in human history where you can make a real difference. Doing nothing is what is most dangerous. Acting will be worth the risk.

If you are already active, then I hope this book has given you new ideas for making your activism more effective, more sustainable, and more fun. If you are not, I hope it has encouraged you to get more active.

Cynicism and despair is not an option if you believe in a more just, more sustainable, world. I hope this book has inspired you to believe that you, too, can make a difference. As anthropologist Margaret Mead once said, "Never doubt that a small group of thoughtful, committed citizens can change the world. Indeed, it is the only thing that ever has."

Get started.

Judy Rebick
November 2008

ACKNOWLEDGMENTS

So MANY PEOPLE helped me think through and write this book, it would be impossible to thank them all. First, thanks go to the many activists you will meet in these pages. Their work and their thinking is the heart of *Transforming Power*. Special thanks go to Hilary Wainwright, who might have been the co-author of this book if we had got it together over distance and busy times. She has been my inspiration, co-thinker, and friend for almost two decades. Another big thank you goes to Velcrow Ripper, whose friendship has greatly expanded my horizons, pointing me in new directions and challenging me to go beyond conventional political thinking. Pierre Beaudet, Monique Simard, and Carlos Torres encouraged and supported me to do more international work and introduced me to the World Social Forum and to numerous activists and thinkers from Latin America, the Middle East, and Europe.

At the proposal stage, deep challenges from my agent, Linda McKnight, and from Penguin editorial director Diane Turbide pushed me to write a much more accessible book. My editors Pat Kennedy and Heather Sangster contributed greatly to making *Transforming Power* more readable and I hope more convincing. What a great privilege it is to work with highly skilled editors.

A number of students helped me with research, including Amelia Facchin, David Smith, and Winnie Wong. And a special thanks to Michelle Langlois, who works as my assistant at Ryerson and has helped me in so many ways. My position at Ryerson has allowed me the freedom and support to travel, research, and write, and for that I thank the Canadian Auto Workers, who endowed the chair I currently hold, and Carla Cassidy, Colin Mooers, Neil Thomlinson, and Akua Benjamin at Ryerson, who so strongly supported my work.

Several people generously provided comments on various drafts, including Corvin Russell, Cathi Bond, Grace-Edward Galabuzi, Susan Harvie, Seth Klein, Adriana Paz, and Sunera Thobani. Their comments and critiques helped to shape the book; although the content is, of course, solely my responsibility.

Finally, my gratitude goes to my brother, Alvin, who has always been and remains my touchstone.

For a continuing Epilogue to which you may contribute, please visit www.transformingpower.ca.

INDEX

267

hooks, bell, 114
horizontal structures, 50, 136–37.
    See also networked politics
horizontalidad, 50
Human Rights Watch, 91
Hurricane Katrina, 31–32. *See also*
    Gulf Coast reconstruction

IBASE, 22, 169
Indian Act, 192
Indigenous Environmental Network
    (IEN), 31, 112, 116–19, 199
indigenous peoples. *See* Aboriginal
    peoples
International Monetary Fund
    (IMF), 8n, 15, 229
internet. *See* open source
    movement; open source system
Iraq: women in, 91–92
Iraqi social movements, 53–54
Islamaphobia, 99–100, 103

Jenkins, Glenn, 165–66, 167,
    174–76, 224
Jobs with Justice, 28, 133–35,
    144–45
Jones, Van, 10, 72, 79–80, 105–6,
    124–25, 126, 127, 128, 166,
    222, 223
Juris, Jeff, 137

Kai, Stanley, 25
KI Six, 191–99
Kimberley-Clark, 121
King, Martin Luther, 10, 69, 218
Kirchner, Néstor, 50
Kitchenuhmaykoosib Inninuwug
    (KI), 191. *See also* KI Six

Klein, Naomi, 90, 206
Kouri, Rosa, 146, 147, 213–14

labour movement: Days of Action
    rolling general strikes, 37–38;
    organizing in the new economy,
    133–36, 133n, 144–45; relation-
    ship with NDP, 38
Labour Party (Britain), 5, 220
Lander, Edgardo, 187
Lankin, Frances, 156, 244–45
Layton, Jack, 246, 248, 249, 253
leadership: assertiveness, 161;
    co-leading, 167; emotional
    connection, 162–65; emotional
    intelligence and, 157–58; and
    listening to others, 160; male
    model of, 154–56; patriarchal,
    157, 158, 161; positional, 159;
    representative, 167
Lebowitz, Michael A., 47
Left Hand of God (Lerner), 70
Lennon, John, 23
Lerner, Michael, 70–73
liberalism, 5n
Life Is Beautiful (film), 202
Loney, James, 208, 209–11, 216
Lorde, Audre, 97
Lovelace, Bob, 191, 195–96

Machado, Antonio, 11n
MacMillan Bloedel, 121
Madisha, Willy, 241–42
Madrid subway bombings, 252
Malik, Abdul-Rehman, 73–74, 99,
    208
Mandela, Nelson, 68
Marcos, Subcomandante, 16–17,
    257

feminism, 85–89, 89n, 95–96,
97; third-wave feminism, 89n,
93
World Bank, 8n, 15
World March of Women, 89
World Mennonite Assembly, 208
World Social Forum (WSF):
anti-Iraq War protest, 18–21;
Caracas forum, 2–4; emotional
connection, 164; Mumbai
forum, 21, 22–24; Nairobi
forum, 24–27, 43; origins,
17–18, 22–23; principles of

horizontality, 137; women's
issues, 26–27, 93
World Trade Organization (WTO),
228
Wright, Beverly, 104
Wright-Parks, Carolann, 160
www.rabble.ca, 1, 182

Young, Christen Linke, 150
youth movement: and alternative
social services, 171

Zapatistas, 16–17